SUNSHIP EARTH

SUNSHIP EARTH

An Acclimatization Program for Outdoor Learning

by
Steve Van Matre

American Camping Association
Martinsville, Indiana

Library of Congress Cataloging in Publication Data

Van Matre, Steve
Sunship Earth

Includes index.
1. Nature study.   2. Outdoor Education.   I. Title.
    QH51.V35   372.3'57   79-26513
        ISBN 0-87603-007-X

Published 1979 by the American Camping Association
Martinsville, Indiana 46151
Printed in the United States of America

TO

Monty and Sue Wells,
whose generous hospitality provided
a warm haven for us at Keego Point
and thus made it all possible.

TABLE OF CONTENTS

ACKNOWLEDGEMENTS

This type of book is seldom written alone. It is a record of the work and ideas of a number of people over a number of years. Four of them were major participants. It is hard to express how important these four people have been in the development of the Acclimatization program and Sunship Earth, especially since they are people who do not seek nor particularly welcome this kind of praise. But without them there would be no Acclimatization program, no books, and no Sunship Earth idea. It's interesting how some people gain the reputation of being leaders in their field. If that honor truly depends upon quality of work, then everyone should know Jim Wells, Bill McKinney, Pat Walkup, and Donn Edwards.

JIM WELLS has been involved in Acclimatization work since he was fourteen. In a sense he grew up with the program, committing large amounts of enthusiasm and energy to it along the way. His special feeling for kids and for what they enjoy comes through on almost every page of this book. Jim understands the importance of structure in learning, the necessity for paying attention to the details, and the need for adding that extra pinch of magic which makes the Acclimatization program so successful. More than anything else, it was Jim's desire to see an ACC outdoor school program developed that led to Sunship Earth. If it can be said of any one person that the Acclimatization program has been built upon his efforts and nurtured by his character, then that person would have to be Jim Wells.

BILL McKINNEY joined the Acclimatization group in 1974 specifically to work on the Sunship Study Station idea. It was a lucky break, for his creative abilities would find their way into every aspect of our work and leave an indelible impression upon Sunship Earth. Although Bill's contributions can be found throughout the book, some of his best efforts went into capturing and recording the action on the Concept Paths and in the Interpretive Encounters. Along with Jim Wells, Bill piloted most of the activities for the Sunship Earth program. Using taped recordings of the actual concept activities with the kids, he was able to add that important "you are there" ingredient to the descriptions found on these pages. Without his effort much of the writing here would have remained rather dry; the kids' responses bring it to life. Bill McKinney's ideas and insights have been a priceless addition to the Sunship Earth materials. His creative efforts will enrich the learning experiences of thousands of young people who participate in these activities.

PAT WALKUP has once again played a vital role in the planning and recording of one of our projects. As the only professional writer in the group, she has helped explain Acclimatization almost since its beginning. Pat has a "magic button" on her typewriter which we frequently call upon to capture the essence of the ACC idea. Frankly, we often find it difficult to transfer to paper the feelings at the center of our work. Pat can gaze off through the barriers of time and place to recapture the feel of a moment now past. Read the "Day in the Marsh" section in *Acclimatization* or the "Nightwatchers" Immersing Experience included here to discover her unmistakable touch. Pat has a gift for creating and expressing fresh ideas and common feelings, a gift which she has shared with all of us.

DONN EDWARDS has been our in-house craftsman from the start. We owe him a great deal. He has struggled to keep us creative in our thinking, clear in our explanations and sensible in our descriptions. It's very helpful to have someone to talk over ideas with—to sit on the rocks, to walk on the beach, to watch the sunset, to listen to what's on your mind, to ponder and to probe with you. Donn is a good listener and a clearheaded observer. It's also very important to have someone analyze your work who understands what you are trying to say. Donn not only understands, he feels it himself. If we wander from our goal, he brings us back. If we get bogged down in disagreement, he remains calm and goes for a walk. Fortunately, Donn likes to walk.

If you set out in search of our Sunship Study Station, you will not find it. The ideas and activities in this book were piloted in a number of places over a number of years. We are particularly indebted though to the Washington County Intermediate Education District of Portland, Oregon, which allowed us to use one of their outdoor schools for piloting much of the Sunship Earth program. Jim Gorter, district environmental education coordinator, supported our efforts even when faced with such strange requisitions as those calling for four old sinks or four hundred new "passports"! Both Jim and assistant director Bob Mann deserve a special thanks from all those who use the Sunship Earth program in the future.

One of the district's outdoor school staff members who joined us in Oregon was Seth Tibbott. We will always carry around a mental picture of Seth wrapped up in an old beach towel, waiting for his clothes to dry after hitchhiking out to the coast in the rain to spend the week working with us. He contributed immeasurably to our work over the years, and he will hold a special place in our recollections of those days.

I would also like to convey my appreciation to the following people who were involved in our Oregon pilot program. They will all be able to show you an idea somewhere in these pages on which they worked during one of those sessions.

Kirk Hoessle*	John Clarke*	Steve Richardson*
Helen Magruder	Sally Wakefield*	Bill Weiler*
Doug Alleccia	Katy Richardson	Willy Noll
Sue Murphy	Molly Siddoway	Cyndi Cashman*
Helene Quarton*	Kim Fine	Iver Love
Jon Lee	Lynn Koller*	Sue Plaisance
Debbie Henry	Bill Hunt	Kitty Davis

The development of the Sunship Earth program was supported from the beginning by Acclimatization Experiences Institute, its associates, friends, and sponsors. In particular, we are indebted to the following members (plus those designated above), whose efforts, ideas, support, and encouragement have brought you Sunship Earth.

*Eddie Soloway	*Bruce Elkin	*Dave Siegenthaler
*Bill Reynolds	*Scott Schrage	*Paul Stetzer
*Alan Crook	*Mike Mayer	*Oliver Gillespie
*Karen Gartland	*Dave Goudy	*Dick Bozung
*John Doty	*Sue Harris	*Miriam Butterfield
*Carol Wood	*Ellis Bacon	*Dave Todd
*Sheryl Stephan	*Brenda Koprowski	*Ray Zimmerman
*Bill Duncan	*Mel Berghuis	*Gerry MacMillan
*Chris Meyer	*Stan Anderson	*Hilde Swenson
*Helene Phelps	*Dick Roberts	*Bill Weller

In working with as much material as we have over the past several years, it is possible, perhaps inevitable, that we have encountered an idea, remembering it later as our own. I apologize if I have forgotten to give credit where it has been due. On the other hand, since we have been working with these activities for so long, in so many places, you may well have run across one of our ideas and believed that it came from someone else. In the extensive sharing common to our field, both situations are likely to occur. I can only hope that I have not erred in my recollections of the people involved.

Finally, I must express my personal thanks to those students who have come to work with me in environmental education and interpretation at George Williams College. Their contagious enthusiasm on one hand, combined with their practical realism on the other, have kept me joyfully searching for better answers—and that is a gift too priceless to be overlooked.

PROLOGUE

You have arrived with seventy-five kids for a week in an outdoor setting to undertake something called environmental education. What do you do?

Here are the specially designed activities that will help the kids learn about energy flow, the cycles of basic materials, the diversity of life, natural communities, interaction among living things and their surroundings, change, and adaptation. And they are fun, for the kids and for you.

Sunship Earth is a complete five-day program for helping kids to understand how their world functions—through seeing, smelling, tasting, touching, and hearing—and to like what they understand.

The program is both the concepts—the water cycle or plant succession, and the feelings—how a handful of soil looks close-up, or what a forest sounds like at dawn.

It is everything from "shrinking" to get a bug's-eye view of the world to being a long-rooted plant in a drought year, from carrying leaky buckets that represent energy flow to becoming fireflies whose dance is part of the fascinating world of night.

Most of all, it is learning about how this very special planet, our "sunship," operates, and how we can both enjoy the ride and help keep the ship going on behalf of all of the passengers.

INTRODUCTION

Remember when you were a kid visiting a candy store? Think back upon all those jars full of rich colors and strange shapes and mysterious-looking textures, each one just begging to be sampled. Can you recall changing your mind about your selection? Trying to make a decision when faced with such an array of choices can be a perplexing experience. The number of possibilities seems to overwhelm you. Sometimes there are just too many variables to sort through, too many factors to weigh and consider: which one, what kind, how many?

The field of environmental education today is that candy store from our past. It is crowded, in a bewildering way, with an ever-growing number of choices. It's no wonder that some people appear to get lost in the process. Faced with much material and little direction, they end up with a bag filled with different kinds of candy instead of a carefully thought out program.

In 1973, our Acclimatization group began toying with the idea of creating a special outdoor program for elementary schools, one that would be based upon the purposes and principles of *Acclimatization* and *Acclimatizing*. We began by examining stacks of environmental education units and poring over dozens of new projects. It turned out to be a rewarding, yet exasperating, task; we found an abundance of material but a paucity of real programs.

As we discovered, environmental education has gained wide acceptance, and the best evidence for its new status can be found in the number of programs and the amount of literature which now compete for our attention. Every conference has its "candy counter" of materials, and like kids with handfuls of pennies we are encouraged to take a little of this, a bit of that, simply because there's so much available. (At the big conferences, they even give you a shopping bag for collecting all the goodies!) As a result, many environmental education programs seem to be paper sacks filled with whatever caught someone's eye, a potpourri which changes after each new trip to the store. These programs seldom focus on any particular goal, yet they always seem to be justified by the undefinable nature of environmental education itself.

This reliance upon sampling a bit of everything in sight is not hard to understand. After all, each year brings a staggering accumulation of new material to our desks, with exciting ideas and innovative activities scattered throughout like educational jelly beans just waiting to be discovered. There are untold thousands of mimeographed sheets, hundreds of brightly-colored folders, dozens of plasticized boxes, and sprinkled on top of it all, scores of government-sponsored curriculum guides, which seem to appear out of nowhere.

Collected in one place, this profusion of new material dazzles even the old-timers. There are projects which depend upon data-gathering activities, projects which emphasize activities for analyzing peer group interactions, and projects which focus on activities for field trips and classrooms and camps. In short, there are projects with something for everyone, or just about everyone. Upon close examination, however, we found it difficult to determine what many of them were really designed to accomplish.

Environmental education has undergone its own identity crisis. We are being inundated with vague, unfocused materials—not real programs, but countless small projects. Some of these new materials seem to have too many goals, while others appear to be a series of lessons in need of a goal. The objectives of many of them are either too broad, or they are hidden in a tangle of verbiage. Some of the new activities are actually familiar projects attached to lengthy explanations which steer them toward a new goal. Others seem to be designed for miniature adults, turning kids into instant city planners and resource managers and pollution control experts.

In the end, none of the material we examined had quite the orientation we were seeking. There were a lot of pieces, including some good ones, but none of them were as comprehensive in dealing with the functioning of life as we had hoped to find. So we decided to back up and start over, to construct our own picture of an effective environmental education program. As if we were working on a complicated puzzle, we elected to put the frame together first.

What sort of frame or goals did we have in mind? First, like a surveyor, we wanted to cast a point of reference for each of our learners—to convey something about their place in the universe. We hoped to establish this sense of place forever in their understandings, or perhaps more accurately in their *feelings*, for we wanted it to become embedded inside them, where it would be a continued source of awareness about who and where they were. Second, like a friendly wizard, we wanted to convey to them a feeling for life's wondrous mysteries—the awesome, yet joyous, systems in which they are bound up with every other living thing on earth. And we hoped that this recognition of miraculous interrelationship would become a mental touchstone against which they could forever check their actions. After much frustrated searching which served to strengthen our awareness of the problems (not the least of which would be our own addition to the deluge of paper products), our Acclimatization team decided to create another model for outdoor programming.

We had our hearts set on a program oriented toward a broad understanding of the functioning of all life on this planet, one that would have some special ingredients: an emphasis on both the concepts and the senses, and a large measure of magic. This program would provide an overall view of man's place in space and what that means for each of us. Frankly, in the beginning it appeared that our ideal program might never exist, for we soon faced a number of difficult decisions.

How much should we do in the city?

While much environmental education can and should take place in the city, we decided that for our program it would be necessary to get away from that setting. For those of us who live in cities, the source of food, the importance of soil, and the cyclical nature of fresh water have become textbook concepts which seem to have little direct impact upon our daily lives. You need only ask a group of young urbanites where food comes from to discover the degree of the city dweller's isolation. Many of us have lost sight of—and thus have lost the understandings of and feelings for—the natural processes upon which we ultimately depend.

Cities tend to overwhelm their residents, to dominate their perceptual fields and thus lead them to believe that cities do, in reality, dominate the unseen processes which support them. The immensity and seeming permanence of our cities tends to instill such a distorted perception. The danger is that those of us who live in cities may begin to see squares of asphalt and concrete as the reality of life and view green contours and fresh streams as ancient shadows, without substance or meaning, without value to our future.

You may be able to see the operation of life's systems in a school building, on a playground, or among the streets of a neighborhood, but it is difficult to get a sense of their working interrelationships in that way. The accumulated bits and pieces discovered in such places often fail to convey the whole picture. Perhaps the workings of natural systems can best be comprehended where they can be seen undisguised—in a natural setting, a place relatively untrammelled by man. In such a place you are brought down to earth in the best sense of that phrase. In such a place you can catch a glimpse of a brightly-colored bird roller coasting among the branches of the trees and realize some of the grandeur of life, taste its freedom, and sense that there is much more to the world than man. For our purposes in this undertaking, then, we decided that there was no good substitute for an experience in an outdoor setting.

How much emphasis should we place upon testing and measuring skills?

When the time came to determine what learning methods we would employ in our program, we decided to emphasize conceptual and sensory activities rather than test kits and data sheets. The task as we viewed it was not to study the minutiae of life, but to grasp the big picture. We wanted to aid in the understanding of ecology while at the same time enhancing personal feeling for the natural world. Because the paraphernalia of scientific inquiry are easy to obtain (perhaps too easy, given the general proclivity for latching onto all the latest gadgetry), there is a danger that we will confuse goals with vehicles. Quantifying, measuring, and analyzing represent a fairly sophisticated level of conceptual ability. We wanted to place our emphasis on actively demonstrating for the kids how the concepts and principles operate. This does not mean that we never use investigatory tools, but that we use them only after initially helping our learners grasp the concepts, and then only as an additional application of those understandings.

Frankly, we also feared entrapment by the idea that things are only real if they can be measured. Many of life's most rewarding, enriching, and heartfelt experiences can barely be put into words, let alone placed on a scale. If we relied too much upon the usual processes of collecting and testing, what would happen to our goals of instilling a sense of wonder, a sense of place, and a reverence for life? If we failed to develop appreciations in our haste to convey understandings, if we overemphasized analytical skills at the expense of deep, natural experiences, what would we gain—people who could take life apart, but cared nothing for keeping it together? We didn't want to run the risk of destroying an innate enthusiasm and curiosity about life by restricting ourselves to a narrow, shortsighted use of rather unlifelike tools. We believed that our tools should fit our tasks.

And what about that all-important ingredient: a sense of magic? We believed that learning should be as rich and exciting and varied as life itself. Our idea of a model included ample amounts of fun. We wanted our learners to get excited about the world we share—not to view it as something they were forced to learn about, but as something they could not wait to figure out. We wanted them to grab on, to exclaim and laugh and whisper and feel good about what they were learning, and thus to feel good about this planet and its magnificent systems of life, including themselves. We believed that magic and motivation were constant companions in good learning. We still do.

How much should we rely upon eco-action projects?

We decided that eco-action projects should be the effect, not the cause of our work. In other words, we would build into our model definite plans for the transfer of the learning to actual home and school settings, instead of using such activities as our starting point. In this way, our eco-action projects would become the practical application of the learning experience, reflecting the success of the program at a personal level for each youngster. In short, we were convinced that a positive, long-term respect for life's systems, a continuing commitment to live in harmony with the earth, would arise out of a matrix of good feelings and sound understandings about life on this planet. From this combination of emotional response and conceptual grasp, we expected the development of a pattern of thoughtful action which would persist for our learners throughout life.

What should we do about correlating our program with the school curriculum?

The general feeling has been that it is better to incorporate environmental education into the present educational structure than to tack it on as merely another adjunct of an overburdened school curriculum. Most educators maintain that by its very nature environmental education should be taught as part of everything else. The advocates of this approach take the position that environmental teachings should permeate all lessons, that they should be a regular part of all subjects, a not-so-subtle message repeated over and over. And, naturally, this increasing tendency toward incorporation is encouraging.

However, experience indicates that humanists can usually be expected to teach about interactions among people, that those with a bent for science are likely to couch much of their material in scientific terms, and that coaches are largely concerned with physical development. How then can those who are not environmentalists teach environmentally? In theory, preparing everyone to include environmental education in their daily plans is possible; in practice, this preparation becomes such a huge undertaking as to make the goal seem almost out of reach.

There is another danger in the integrated approach. Go to the dictionary today in search of a definition for ecology and you may find two explanations. For some etymologists, ecology is no longer merely the study of the relationships of organisms with their surroundings; it has become a branch of sociology as well. This new emphasis on ecology as a study of human interaction helps to explain the origins of some of the school-centered environmental projects, which seem to emphasize the patterns and dependencies in the lives of one species; at best, such projects deal only tangentially with the flow of energy and the biogeochemical cycles of life. They confuse sociological interdependence with ecological interdependence.

Since our goal was to develop a program which focused primarily upon how all life functions, a program which would help youngsters see and feel the earth as a not-so-vast interrelated system of energy and materials, we decided to create an educational program which took place in a different setting, but one that would *contribute* to the regular curriculum of the school. In addition, if we incorporated in-service training for teachers as an essential feature, we could help the teachers prepare for those contributions themselves. Thus the students would be getting the benefits of a specially-designed program, and the teachers would be able to learn right along with their students. Both teachers and students could then extend their understandings into the classroom setting upon their return.

All of these questions took far longer to work through than this overview might indicate. However, once we had answered them, we set out to create a complete outdoor program. If you'll take the time, we think you will find Sunship Earth to be an exciting and enjoyable adventure for learners and leaders alike. In fact, we hope that you will create your own Sunship Study Station.

The Sunship Earth program is like a multi-colored, partitioned box full of carefully selected and ordered activities. It's not a catchall like the box in the desk drawer, filled with random memorabilia from past conferences. Nor is it an empty container decorated with surface platitudes which dazzle the eye and conceal the emptiness. It has its own inner structure.

We believe that Sunship Earth is a larger idea than its separate pieces would individually suggest. Instead of trying to fashion a program out of an assortment of unrelated activities, we began with a conception and selected the pieces we needed in order to realize it, and we know that there will never be an end to our search for more perfect pieces. Although the contents of the program may change somewhat according to the learners, leaders, and location, its purpose and structure should remain the same.

Above all else, then, a Sunship Earth program must aim for knowledge in both the head and the heart. It must proclaim clearly and joyously:

Hey, we're on a sunship!
How does it work and feel?
We're both its passengers and its crew.
What does this mean for you?

S.V.M.
Boulder Jct., Wisconsin
August 1978

I would look at the earth's horizon and see the
earth's atmosphere. It is very beautiful. It is blue
and white and gold and orange. And it is so thin
and fragile. That atmosphere is all that keeps
earth habitable, but it's no thicker than the skin
on an orange—no, thinner than that, like the skin
on an apple. There's no way to explain how clearly
you can see the fragility of the earth. You have to
have been there.

Gerry Carr
Skylab 4

THE IDEA

Sunship Earth

Operating Principles

Acclimatization

Senses

Concepts

Mechanics

Solitude

Magic

Ecological

The Story of Life: EC—DC—IC—A

Energy Flow

Cycles

Diversity

Community

Interrelationships

Change

Adaptation

Learning

Concepts

Gimmicks and Props

Building Concepts: IAA Learning Model

Guidelines

Chapter One

SUNSHIP EARTH

Right now, while reading these words, you, along with the earth and all its other passengers, are moving rapidly through space. You are simultaneously spinning with the planet on its axis, rotating around a medium-sized star, turning slowly over and over in a spiral galaxy, and speeding through some obscure corner of the universe. You are on a voyage with no measurable end and no definite beginning. In fact, orbiting at over 65,000 m.p.h., you're lucky to be able to keep this page in focus!

This planet called Earth, this whirling globe we share, travels through realms of uncharted darkness, attached to one source of life-giving energy—its own sun. In reality, all of us ride on a "sunship," a small rock caught perfectly in the gravitational pull of a nearby nuclear inferno. We journey with the sun, tied by invisible but unbreakable threads to our source of light, heat, and energy.

Sunlight is the fuel of all life on earth. It powers our sunship. And despite all of our technology, we cannot yet understand how a tiny, green disc in the leaf of a plant manages to capture the sun's rays. In a microsecond, too fast for our detection, the sun's energy is plucked from the sky to begin its path from plant to animal to animal. This process remains one of the great mysteries. Yet the plant doesn't stop there. In capturing that ray of sunlight, the plant not only creates a particle of sugar, but also gives off in the process a bit of oxygen, which animals must breathe in order to combine it once again with the plant's sugar and release the sunlight-energy it contains. For us, this is the greatest magic act of all. In one split second we have gained both our food and the oxygen we need to burn that food in our own chemical processes.

Who are we? Like all other forms of life on earth, we are sparks

2

of organized energy. In a sense, we are bottled sunshine! Our largest organ is our skin, a strong membrane encapsulating about fifteen gallons of the liquid of life. Each of us uses the sunlight-energy stored by plants, breathes the oxygen released by plants, absorbs the nutrients which plants draw from the soil. In short, like all animals, we are predators, depending upon plants for both our sustenance and our ability to make use of it. And many of us prey to some degree upon other animals who originally consumed the plants for us. For the length of our life, then, we are destined to be fellow travelers on the most magnificent trip of them all, the journey of Sunship Earth, but our dependencies far outweigh our contributions to this voyage. Sunlight, air, water, soil, and plants—man's brief existence depends on these.

Pause to consider that for millions of years no form of life here knew of the journey it was taking, although every plant and animal that has ever lived upon the earth, from the microscopic protozoa of the soil to the largest creature of the sea, has been a "passenger" on this fantastic trip among the stars. What an inestimable thrill it is to be aware of this journey, to feel and see ourselves as passengers, to have a glimpse of the grandeur of life. All our other concerns must seem pale and trivial in comparison with this immense realization. In the infinity and eternity of space, amid the birth and death of countless suns, our planet is only a small, softly-covered sphere that exists for a twinkling, an individual life only a mere glistening on its surface. On the universal stage we are a mere speck, upstaged by the brilliance of a thousand stars more luminous than our own. Ours is a minor action taking place in the corner of a small scene, in an act without a number, in a play that can only be imagined. But right here and now that little drama takes on major significance.

Put another way, we are not the pilots of Sunship Earth; we are not in control. We are temporary passengers, and can only make the best of a short stay. We are both young and old only once. In the end, our tissues will become the tissues of other plants and animals, other passengers, for the earth's limited supply of the materials of life must be used carefully over and over.

As human beings, however, we are passengers who have by chance become crew members as well. And although our omnipotence is a myth, our omniscience a delusion, we have reached a stage at which our abilities, or lack of them, imperil all life on earth. What makes our situation so sad, so poignantly tragic, is that we know the damage we do. Of all the passengers, among all the teeming life of the earth, we alone know the significance of our actions. Ironically, we are apparently the only form of life which can jeopardize the voyage for all the others.

Should someone inquire of us if we would allow our fellow passengers to tear holes in a life raft we shared, or if we would willingly board a craft piloted by someone who didn't know how to fly, we would probably think the questioner slightly mad in both instances. Yet fully aware now of the interlocking relationship of life's systems, and cognizant of our own limitations in fully understanding how all life functions, we have undertaken both of these supposedly unthinkable actions. This "sunship," its health and well-being, should be our foremost concern, for with knowledge comes responsibility. We are gifted with an awareness which demands that we observe astutely and act wisely. We must become ever alert to the rhythms of the earth. We must become attuned to its natural harmony and flow, and our constant watchword must be *caution, caution.*

Unfortunately, caught up as we have been in our minor play in this little corner of the galaxy, we have misread our scripts. We have unthinkingly let ourselves become entrapped by the small daily concerns of living, the proximity of which makes them appear more urgent. The task before all of us, then, is to re-learn our earthbound lines and polish our recently discovered roles as passengers and crew members of Sunship Earth. There is no other choice. Our generation and all those who succeed us must learn anew that every action we take will be played out against this backdrop of who and where we are.

On the other hand, our responsibilities should not weigh so heavily upon us that we cannot enjoy the journey we are on. Let us rejoice in both our travel and our role in the journey, for in a way, we too are the substance of stars. We can stand on a clear night and look up at other stars in awe, feel the spinning of our planet in the wind, hear the soft rustlings of life around us, smell the richness of the land and taste its moisture, and, best of all, sense our eternal relationship with Sunship Earth.

Chapter Two

OPERATING PRINCIPLES

Where We're Coming From

ACCLIMATIZATION (uh-CLI-ma-tiz-A-shun)— (1) To feel at home with the natural world. (2) to be aware of the ecological processes which govern life and to understand one's role as a part of those processes. (3) To increase both sensory awareness and conceptual understanding of the natural world.

As an educational program,
ACCLIMATIZATION is . . .

a program which helps people of all ages build a sense of relationship—through both feelings and understanding—with the natural world.

The Acclimatization program grew up in the sixties at a boys' camp in northern Wisconsin. Its growth was influenced by numerous insights gleaned from the areas of education and communication, fertilized by the awakening environmental awareness of the times, and favored by the play of sunlight on water, the rich greens and browns and the captivating sounds and smells of a northwoods forest.

The Acclimatization program was created partially out of frustration with the usual identifying-collecting-dissecting-testing approaches to nature. It was molded by people who were excited about kids and learning and life itself, who liked to laugh, but who took their work seriously, who wanted to open up new doors of perception for their learners. These people knew they were

5

embarking on a new journey, but had none of the trappings of status or tradition to weigh them down. A buoyancy, a lightness of spirit, carried them along.

The Acclimatization program began with a simple goal: to turn kids on to the natural world, to help them love it, not for its labels and fables and fears, but for its feelings. ACC (as the kids always called it) was not meant to change the world, nor permeate all education, nor solve the environmental crises at hand. It set out to affect the feelings of a few kids, to convey a bit of understanding about how life works and a bit of sharpened perception which would allow them to make those understandings more concrete. Although many programs today fairly cry out for more sense-heightening activities, ACC is concerned with *both* the senses and the concepts. It helps youngsters to recognize natural communities as their preeminent home, to re-accustom themselves to the natural heritage we all share.

Acclimatization is a program filled with wonder and contact and joyous laughter, with whispers punctuated by "come see!, feel this!, smell it, shh . . . listen, WOW!" The excitement is contagious. Once you have caught it you cannot help but convey it to others. It is the excitement of holding the world close—of feeling a kinship with all living things. Acclimatization promotes understanding, but an understanding that eventually transcends knowing.

Acclimatization has four major components: sharpening SENSES, building CONCEPTS, providing opportunities for SOLITUDE, and emphasizing the importance of the MECHANICS of learning. In the end, these four elements are held together with a special glue—the glue of MAGIC in living and learning with joy.

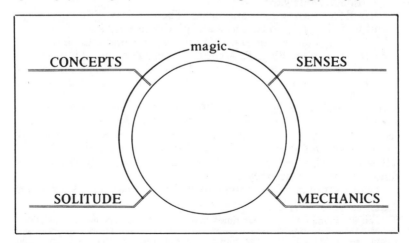

Senses

From the beginning Acclimatization has included numerous sensory activities. Many kids approach the out-of-doors today as if encapsulated in plastic bubbles, cut off from contact with much of

life by a set of admonitions:
   Don't get dirty!
   Don't put things in your mouth!
   Don't get wet!
   Keep your clothes clean!
   Don't stare.
   Whisper, don't shout.
   Don't daydream, pay attention, sit still.
   Don't get too close—it'll bite!
   Don't touch it—it's slimy, gooey, mucky.
   Watch out for bugs, spiders, snakes, poison ivy!
   (*and things that go BUMP in the night*).
In short, life for many youngsters is something to look at, not touch.* Acclimatization is designed to change this situation. Our aim is to help young people interact more directly with the fascinating array of living things around them and to appreciate nature for what it represents—that tightly-woven fabric which supports them and to which they, in turn, contribute. At the same time, we want to help them understand that every action they take has a direct impact upon those natural systems.

Concepts
   For many young people today, their concepts about life embody pragmatic warnings about the places and things around them, ideas which have been cultivated by example since early childhood:
   NICE places are places which you have to sweep up, rake up, pick up, and clean up. They are places which you mow, trim, prune, or pave. They are okay places to play, like the school-grounds or your yard.
   BAD places have weeds and pests. They are overgrown, messy, and usually dangerous. They are places to stay away from.
   NICE things are warm and soft and let you mistreat them.
   BAD things bite, sting, scratch, and peck. They are things which you squash, kill, or back away from. (Bad things cannot be brought into your house unless you are using them for a school project.)
Many of these concepts about life, its elements and functions, have been formed for kids by commercial advertisements which insist on using words in misleading ways, and by parents and leaders who do not understand the extent to which our language reflects our view of the world—in other words, by the whole cultural milieu in which they live.
   A few examples of the extent to which our language shapes our

---

*It is an unfortunate irony of our times that many of the very institutions which should be counteracting such views—parks, preserves and nature centers—have become so concerned about the number of their visitors that they are often unconsciously perpetuating people's separation from the natural world around them. A formidable legion of signs—**stay on the trail, don't pick, keep off, don't run, don't touch**—have become commonplace solutions for handling today's visitors.

youngsters' view of the natural world points up the seriousness of the problem. For many young people today:

SUNLIGHT is important for having picnics, going to the pool, and playing in the yard. It also has some vague connection with photo . . . something or other and that green stuff in leaves.

ENERGY is something you run out of, and you get it back by resting or by building power plants.

CYCLES are Hondas or Harleys.

COMMUNITIES are places where people live.

ECOLOGY means that you pick up litter and go on paper drives.

As a program, Acclimatization has overcome these MIS-conceptions about what the world is like. We begin by reversing the usual areas of emphasis.

Traditional education differentiates conceptual learning and generalizes sensory awareness. Youngsters are encouraged to view the world as an infinite set of boxes—there are always smaller boxes inside the box before them. They study the world by studying smaller and smaller boxes. In short, they gain knowledge by adding to their stock of facts day by day. The senses, however, are lumped together in one homogenized mass. Kids are encouraged to believe that they should not trust their own perception and thus should do little to sharpen their senses. They are told to be objective, disregard emotions and feelings, and experiment to find the truth. Even when they "take a look" at a problem, they rarely *see* anything; they merely talk it to death in the classroom.

In ACC we reverse this approach. We differentiate in our sensory awareness and generalize in our conceptual understanding. We strive to strengthen individual senses, but opt for the big picture in understanding life.* The minutiae of life's workings are not of foremost importance for us; our goal is not pulling apart the insides of the frog, but understanding the frog inside the pond and the pond inside the water cycle.

Traditional Education Model	Concepts differentiated (focus on smaller and smaller bits of material)	Senses undifferentiated (emphasize thinking more than perceiving)
Acclimatization Model	undifferentiated (emphasize the big picture)	differentiated (focus on sharpening individual senses)

---

*This does not mean that in the Sunsip Earth program we think the "small picture" of life is unimportant, but only that such study should be self-motivated and should follow the individual's grasp of the big picture. In fact, as you will discover, we provide opportunities for investigating the small picture.

Mechanics

In traditional education, going outdoors to learn usually means going on a field trip—roughly equated with playtime, or with going on a hike (something like a forced march). Most of the field trips are of the "follow-me-gather-round" variety. Occasionally that means filling out worksheets, but most of the time it means listening to the leader talk about what the leader knows something about, while ignoring everything else. In the end, it usually means identifying an object, then collecting a sample to take back and cut up in the lab.

In ACC, going outdoors has always received the same careful attention to planning and detail that is usually found in the more thorough classroom curriculum guides. Our emphasis is upon achieving full participation, gaining enthusiasm, and taking some of the randomness out of learning experiences. By constantly refining the mechanics of our activities, we can achieve these goals.

Solitude

Just as they have preconceptions about "nice animals" and ingrained inhibitions about using their senses, youngsters have been given a negative impression of solitude. Solitude has become a synonym for punishment, boredom, escape:

Kids are told, *"Go to your room! You're grounded! You can't go alone* (or be left alone), *Listen to the leader—don't talk!"*

Solitude frequently means sitting in class in silence (but not daydreaming), escaping a bad situation or running off, being lonely or rejected.

It is not having a transistor radio or stereo or your own TV.

It is imposed after failure in a game, or when the parent or leader is mad, or when you don't have anything to do.

People who like it are strange, usually not "well-adjusted."

Loud things are for getting attention: bells, whistles, and shouts. Whispers are for secret things: talking in class, planning an escape, and breaking the rules.

In Acclimatization we encourage daily periods of solitude, in places where one can be in direct contact with the basic elements of life: light, air, water, and soil.

Solitude enhances the acquisition of such non-verbal skills as waiting, watching, and receiving. It sharpens awareness and refreshes our sense of harmony with the world around us. It helps us sort out what is happening to us, or gives us time just to "be."

Magic

What is this magic in living and learning that we believe is so important? Words can never convey the real scope of this idea. It is an undefinable quality which holds the various components of Acclimatization together, and then transforms them into something which is more than the sum of the parts.

It is exhilarating joy.

It is simple fun.

It is excitement, enthusiasm, and eagerness.

It is a pinch of fantasy and a pound of adventure.

It is usually part of an emotional rather than an analytical response.

It's an "Oh, WOW!" perhaps followed by an "Aha!"

It is frequently shared.

It is something tied up with caring, with someone doing something for someone else.

It is often part of a feeling of flowing with things—not being pushed, but pulled, by the event, the happening.

It is intense involvement: a loss of self-consciousness and time-structuring.

It is delight in the moment.

In the end, magic is all of the above, and none of the above. Fortunately, it is best known by itself, not the words that describe it. It is felt rather than explained.

In ACC, magic is the all-important ingredient. It's what makes our learning activities captivating for kids and leaders alike. After all of our efforts at designing sensory and conceptual learning experiences, at examining the smallest detail of the mechanics involved, if we cannot weave some bright threads of magic through the activity, we toss it out. Learning and magic should be constant companions in the adventure of living.

Since its beginning fifteen years ago, Acclimatization has become one of the most widely used programs in the general field of environmental interpretation and education. Although we never anticipated that it would be picked up by so many different groups, we have been pleased by its wide appeal and acceptance. Today, there are Acclimatization programs for people from all walks of life, taking place in all kinds of settings. It has been adopted and used by hundreds of schools, nature centers, parks, camps, social agencies, church groups, and similar organizations as an integral part of their work. *Sunship Earth* is the first of a projected series of Acclimatization programs designed for special groups.

TOUCHSTONES OF ACCLIMATIZATION

Principles

People learn best when they feel what they are learning.

An understanding of basic ecological concepts is too important to leave to the vagaries of chance or circumstance.

People of all ages respond better to sharing than to showing.

The best learning experiences start where the learner is, not where the leader is, and the experience, not the leader, is the best teacher.

In a good learning experience the medium should be the magic: the magic of discovery and wonder and joy.

There are wide worlds of perception and emotion that language cannot begin to describe, nor words measure.

Experiencing solitude enhances the nonverbal skills of waiting, watching, and receiving.

Daily contact with the elements of life refreshes our sense of being and renews our certainty of becoming.

Premises

The human species is neither the omnipotent conqueror nor the omniscient steward of the natural world.

Mankind's most important natural resources are not the material things, but the natural communities of life from which those things are taken.

Heightened feelings combined with increased understandings form the matrix out of which positive environmental action arises.

A key facet of healthy growth is the understanding that self-awareness is increased through natural awareness.

Living *in* a more natural environment should be undertaken primarily for the opportunity to better live *with* it—for the harmony and joy it brings.

Because of the interrelatedness of all life, our focus should be upon activities which promote harmony instead of those which encourage a sense of power.

What We're Trying to Convey   OPERATING PRINCIPLES—
                                                                 ECOLOGICAL

Considerable attention has been given in the past several years
to the ecological concepts considered appropriate for each grade
level. A few programs have come up with an all-purpose set of
concepts applicable to all grades; most have opted for a disjointed
set of activities without a coherent context, thereby escaping the
problem. In addition, different programs have based their work on
different numbers of concepts. Obviously, no one has a secret
formula for determining a set of ecological concepts with which
everyone will agree. The study of how life works is too broad for
such exactness. Our initial efforts produced an appalling list of
slightly less than one hundred possibilities! We used the following
criteria in trying to realign our original notions about what was
important:

Do more with less.
(Keep it simple, thus usable.)

Deal with the big picture of how life works.
(Don't get bogged down in the minutiae.)

Focus on the basic functions of the sunship.
(Don't spill over into other areas.)

Provide some sort of cohesiveness.
(Keep it on target.)

Frankly, it took several years to cut our list of concepts down to
manageable proportions. During that time three primary questions
kept reappearing in our discussions: *how does all life on this planet
function, who lives here,* and *how do living things work together?*
We called them the "Big Picture" questions. Later, we added
another: *where are we?* Like the writer who completes the final
chapter of his work only to discover that he should have started
there, we decided to take as our central theme *our place in space.*
Once we had adopted the idea of "Sunship Earth," the supporting
concepts fell in place rather easily. Today, we are working with
seven major concepts: ENERGY FLOW, CYCLES, DIVERSITY,
COMMUNITY, INTERRELATIONSHIPS, CHANGE, and ADAP-
TATION.

The "Story of Life" at the end of this section is designed to
convey the essence of each of the seven ecological concepts which
form the core of our Sunship Earth program. Exact definitions of
these concepts are difficult to find. Environmental education is a
field of study which lacks concise, agreed-upon definitions of its
terminology. Sometimes it resembles one of those situations where we
know what we're talking about only as long as we are talking with
someone who has had a similar set of experiences, but once we try to
explain our ideas to a newcomer, we are hard-pressed to find the right
words.

No attempt at placing these concepts in a particular order can be completely successful either because natural systems do not operate in a fashion which lend themselves to man's models. Moreover, we have had to simplify our descriptions for elementary school kids,* specifically for the fifth and sixth graders we had chosen as our target learners. However, we have come up with the following diagram to help youngsters visualize the way in which these concepts fit together. It is a tool for reinforcing the point that energy for life flows from the sun. Sunlight powers the cycling of materials in the air, water, and soil, and causes the movement from diversity to community to interrelationships to change to adaptation to diversity to community to interrelationships, and so forth and so on. Finally, a simple mnemonic device, EC-DC-IC-A, is paired with the diagram as our study station slogan. It is a formula which helps the learners retain the various concepts, while the diagram provides a visual pattern.

---

*In one of his novels Aldous Huxley wrote about the dangers of eloquent oratory. He suggested that by their very nature all public speakers are liars, since one cannot simplify without leaving something out. No doubt the same point could be made about much of our educational effort. We are in a dilemma. In order to convey essential ideas in a way that aids comprehension and prevents boredom one must simplify, but in doing so the risks of distortion increase. Thus, we have elected to speak here of plants instead of "chlorophyll-producing" plants as the processors of sunlight; we ignore chemosynthetic bacteria and those strange clams which apparently contain their own chlorophyll, and we treat homeostasis and the genetic pool indirectly at best. Such examples are not meant to cover all of our omissions, and you will probably find your own favorites, but they point to the kinds of problems we were concerned with. Conveying the essential information on how life functions is a difficult task. We hope that you will not only be patient with us, but help us in our struggle.

EC-DC-IC-A
The Story of Life

E

C-AIR

C-WATER

C-SOIL

Interrelationships—Change—Adaptation—Diversity—Community

The Story of Life: EC-DC-IC-A

**E
ENERGY FLOW**

Sunlight energy is transferred in decreasing amounts from those growing things which can capture it (plants—food producers) to those which cannot (animals—food consumers) to those which obtain it from the dying of others (certain plants and animals—food decomposers) . . .

**C
CYCLES**

As these producers, consumers, and decomposers grow and die, they are using life's essential chemicals or nutrients, taking these nutrients from and returning them to their reservoirs in the earth's air, soil, and waters over and over again . . .

**D
DIVERSITY**

These essential chemicals or nutrients and the sunlight energy available have varied greatly in both amount and quality in many places and times, permitting a great number of different plants and animals to share the earth . . .

**C
COMMUNITY**

Groups of different plants and animals are thus found living together on the earth in areas where the amount and quality of both the sunlight energy and these essential chemicals or nutrients best meet their individual needs . . .

**I
INTERRE—
LATIONSHIPS**

In meeting their needs all these plants and animals are constantly interacting with one another and with their surroundings in different ways . . .

**C
CHANGE**

Because they are in the process of both acting upon their surroundings and being acted upon, all plants and animals and the places where they live are in the process of becoming something else . . .

**A
ADAPTATION**

In the overall story of life, some plants and animals end up with new and successful ways of meeting their needs by solving the problems brought about by the altering of these conditions where they live.

ENERGY FLOW

Sunlight energy is transferred in decreasing amounts from those growing things which can capture it (plants—food producers) to those which cannot (animals—food consumers) to those which obtain it from the dying of others (certain plants and animals—food decomposers) . . .

Sunship Earth is solar-powered. Sunlight supports all plants and animals in the film of life covering the earth. It flows through space in a great stream to bathe the surface of this planet each day. It is taken from the sky first by the plants, then flows along different paths or *food chains* as it is used by the animals.

The sunlight captured by green plants is used first to split carbon dioxide into *carbon* and oxygen, and water into *hydrogen* and oxygen. Next it is used to fuse the carbon, hydrogen, and oxygen into a *carbo-hydrate* or particle of sugar. The excess oxygen given off by the plants as a by-product of this process supports the animals of the earth.

The animal uses this oxygen when it eats a plant to break down those *carbo-hydrates* it is consuming. Only in this way can animals make use of the sunlight energy first captured by the plants. The arrangement is an efficient one, because what happens in the cells of the plant is just the opposite of what happens in the cells of the animal. The plant takes in carbon dioxide, water, and energy and produces sugars and oxygen. The animal takes in those sugars and oxygen and produces carbon dioxide, water, and energy. Respiration in animals is like a negative image of photosynthesis in plants.

However, and it is a big "however," a large proportion of that sunlight energy released in the animal is converted to motion and heat as the animal goes about its daily life. Thus the *flow* of sunlight energy is diminished. At the top of the food chains, other animals eat the plant-eating animals in order to get the sunlight energy they need. In this process even more of the sunlight energy is lost in the body heat of the animals it passes through.

Nonetheless, it is a very practical system. Some plants and animals or decomposers obtain their sunlight energy by breaking down the bodies or wastes of other members of the food chains. As the flow of energy dwindles, smaller and smaller organisms utilize the last trickle of sunlight in the soils and seas of the earth. And always there is a loss of useable energy in each transfer.

CYCLES

As these producers, consumers and decomposers grow and die, they are using life's essential chemicals or nutrients, taking these nutrients from and returning them to their reservoirs in the earth's air, soil, and waters over and over again . . .

Hydrogen, carbon, oxygen, nitrogen, phosphorous, and sulfur are the basic building materials of all life. Because there is a limited amount of these materials available on the earth, they must be used over and over again by all living things. They are taken from their reservoirs in the air, soil, and waters of the earth to move through the food chains and webs of life, before returning to their reservoirs in the wastes and decay of all plants and animals. Only through this cycling of building materials is life able to continue on the earth.

This intermixing of parts of the earth's air, water, and soil produces the substances of which all living things are composed. The fundamental process is the same for a hand or a leaf. In fact, the only essential difference between a molecule of the hemoglobin in your blood and a molecule of the chlorophyll in a green leaf is that the first has a bit of iron for its center and the second a bit of magnesium. This means that the basic structure of the substance which plays such a vital role in capturing sunlight differs by only a single atom from that substance which carries the oxygen needed by your cells for releasing that sunlight energy in you.

Plants and animals grow by drawing directly or indirectly upon these great reservoirs of building materials and using the sun's energy to combine the materials to form the tissues of their bodies. When they die, those tissues are broken down and the materials are released for other living things to use. In this way the basic building materials of life pass through complex cycles, all powered by energy from the sun.

DIVERSITY

These essential chemicals or nutrients and the sunlight energy available have varied greatly in both amount and quality in many places and times, permitting a great number of different plants and animals to share the earth . . .

Sunlight and the building materials needed by living things are present in differing amounts and qualities in different places; the number and types of plants and animals found in an area are influenced by the availability of sunlight and these basic materials. When the stream of light from the sun and the building materials moving in and out of the earth's reservoirs vary in amount or intensity, the resulting conditions for life vary greatly over the surface of the planet. These continually changing mixtures of energy and materials support a great variety of living things upon the earth.

Imagine the earth as a ball traveling through space, covered with a film of air, water, and soil, warmed and energized by the sun. Each plant and animal exists in that film as a complex living bubble of energy and materials; each is the beneficiary of a unique combination of sunlight, air, water, and soil. The variety of these "living bubbles" in the film covering the earth presents an astonishing kaleidoscope of shape and color. From sycamores and jellyfish and giraffes to alligators and bamboo and kangaroos, to violets and beetles and eagles, this film is a panoply of the stuff of life.

This variety results in an overall endurance. It assures that something can take advantage of almost any change in the surrounding conditions. It seems to guarantee that life will continue: where some living things are unfit, others are prepared. The stability, and thus continuity, of life in an area appears to be a function of the rate of the energy flow, the rate of the chemical or nutrient cycling, and the diversity of species and interconnecting food chains present there.

COMMUNITY

Groups of different plants and animals are thus found living together on the earth in areas where the amount and quality of both the sunlight energy and these essential chemicals or nutrients best meet their individual needs . . .

Communities are mixed groups of plants and animals occupying a specific area of the surface of the earth. Each community is a pool of those "living bubbles" in the earth's film, grouped together in that place because it is there that they can best meet their needs of life.

Size is not the determining factor for what is to be called a community. It can be as small as a rotting log or a puddle of water, as large as a forest or a lake. The boundaries of the larger communities are determined by the shape of the land and the particular mixture of sunlight energy and building materials available.

Within a larger community, a complex arrangement governs the daily lives of its members. The actual place where something lives in a community, the place where it meets its needs of life, is called its home or *habitat*. For some animals, this is a very small area; for others, it is a very large one. A few animals, usually the predators at the top of the various food chains, cross the boundaries of many communities in order to fulfill their needs. The role or job in the community performed by any group of the same kind of plants or animals is called its *niche*. Different kinds of plants and animals cannot occupy precisely the same niche in a community, at least not for long. One group will force the other out. Together, the habitat and niche of an individual plant or animal spells out its address and profession within its community.

INTERRELATIONSHIPS

In meeting their needs all these plants and animals are constantly interacting with one another and with their surroundings in different ways . . .

All plants and animals interact with other things in their surroundings. Communities are inter-connected and inter-related groups; they are dynamic associations of living things. Within each community life percolates through its pool by day and by night. Its members grow and die, rest and reproduce, absorb and release. Each living thing affects all the others in its pool and so, in turn, must be affected by them. They are all tied together, bonded by their needs.

The ways in which the members of a community are related to one another and to their surroundings are based upon the kinds of interactions which they have with their neighbors: sometimes they are *cooperating* (although usually unintentionally); often they are *competing* for the same things; invariably they are *depending* on them for some portion of their needs.

The more diverse the community, the more varied are these interactions. And an increase in the diversity of these interactions improves the chances that a dynamic balance of life will be maintained in an area. The complex community as a whole is more tolerant of extremes in its surroundings and more resistant to the impact of outside forces.

Finally, since all plants and animals are connected by the flow of energy and the cycling of chemical nutrients, not only are the members of each community interconnected, but each community is also connected to all the others on earth.

CHANGE

Because they are in the process of both acting upon their surroundings and being acted upon, all plants and animals and the places where they live are becoming something else . . .

Everything on the earth is in the process of changing—the living and the dead, the animate and the inanimate. All plants and animals are slowly building themselves up, then breaking down. This ebb and flow in the pools of living things, which all plants and animals bring about and, in turn, are affected by, characterizes the dynamics of life on earth.

Without knowing it, the plants and animals of one kind of community are often preparing the way for other kinds of plants and animals and a new community to replace them. Through their interrelationships with each other and with their surroundings, they are creating the conditions necessary for something else to succeed where they now live. In a way, their success assures their demise. The surroundings act upon them; they act on each other; they act upon their surroundings.

Moreover, as the earth whirls through space, the same natural forces which sustain its life also change its features. Glaciers and volcanoes and earthquakes rend and mold the surface of the land. Wind, water, fire, and ice splinter and sear and scour its contours. In time mountains erode to plains, and deserts sink beneath seas. As with living things, so with the earth itself: everything becomes something else.

ADAPTATION

In the overall story of life some plants and animals end up with new and successful ways of solving the problems brought about by the altering of these conditions where they live.

Some plants and animals arrive at new ways of meeting changes in the flow of energy and the cycles of life's building materials. They are better prepared to respond to new demands because they happen to have special ways (structures or behaviors) which allow them to continue to be successful in a particular role. Since they are the ones that survive to reproduce others like them, over time their new structures or behaviors become commonplace. The diversity of a community's interrelationships provides a type of "biological reservoir" for the demands brought about by changes in the conditions of life.

In a sense this process decides the future of life on earth, for how well specific kinds of plants or animals fit their niche and how well they can meet the changes which take place in their habitats will determine their success. Each organism interacting with others in its community is a unique organism. And there is no way of knowing which ones may carry with them the key for adjusting to the problems which lie ahead. In the long run, because of their vastly different characteristics, some kinds of plants and animals will end up with different solutions for similar problems, while others end up with similar solutions but for different problems.

A stream of sunlight fuels the earth,
Circulating reservoirs of building
 materials sustain its passengers.

A complex film of "living bubbles"
 separates it from the void of space

Grouped together in percolating pools
 of life, those plants and animals
 that survive the ebb and flow of change

Assure that the earth will remain
 a "living planet"
 on its journey among the stars.

How We're Going About It   OPERATING PRINCIPLES
                                                      LEARNING

By way of introduction to our method of learning, it should be pointed out that the Sunship Earth program is for those who can join their students in a great adventure—in reaching out to the world around them, touching it, and saying, "Hey, there's a lot here that I've missed." People learn when they are excited. And people learn best and retain longest what they feel good about learning. In Acclimatization programs our emphasis will always be upon adding the magic necessary for making the learning experiences vivid, encouraging a whole body response, and balancing seriousness with fun and good feelings.

Sometimes we are asked why we do not include more science and less magic in our work. In such conversations we have found that science usually refers to more naming and testing, a rather narrow view of the scientific method. Science is the systematic approach to gaining knowledge and reaching conclusions. One can be systematic without emphasizing names and tests. Nor does adding magic mean subtracting order. Concept formation can be both scientific and magical.

What Are Concepts?

Although it may often appear to be a popular bit of jargon scattered across a page of a manuscript or sprinkled willy-nilly through an educator's speech, the term *concept* does have a useful place in our vocabulary. Concepts are general notions about things. They are mental constructs which serve to classify or categorize everything with which we come into contact. Concepts can be as simple as "rock" or "person," as large as "universe" or "nation." In any size, however, they are tools for thinking.

Concepts are not static frames. They change. New data will cause them to grow; a lack of data will cause them to wither. Some concepts have more staying power than others. These are the very abstract or very concrete ones. Once formed they are broad enough to encompass much new data, or simple enough to be almost unaffected. Most concepts are so changeable that they cannot absorb too much data without drastically altering their form.

Concepts and concept statements (principles) are the brain's way of making sense out of the world. They are an ordering of phenomena; they are our way of explaining the world around us. If you are sitting in a chair while reading these lines (and chairs come in a variety of sizes, shapes, and materials), then your concept of "chair" should be fairly concrete. You are using a chair; you have a lot of contact with one. But if at this moment you are not using a chair, in fact, if you cannot even see one, then "chair" is an abstraction for you. It exists only in your mind. For most people, most concepts fall somewhere along a continuum from the concrete to the abstract depending upon their individual circumstances. Our task at the Sunship Study Station is to make some abstract concepts more concrete for our learners.

When a small child unfamiliar with cows points to one in a field and calls it a dog, we should not be too surprised (nor too confident that a verbal correction will prove successful). At a distance, cows appear to be four-legged creatures about the size and shape of a dog. But just one firsthand, concrete experience with a cow will give that child a whole new concept to work with in the future.

Another way to keep track of all this is to picture concepts as folders in the brain's filing system. They are the mental receptacles for the stimuli which we receive. And abrupt rearrangements are not the prerogative of kids alone. Hardly a day goes by that each of us does not suddenly grasp a different perspective on an old concept—a previously formed receptacle which new data suddenly changes. Enlightenment is a good term for many such concept-altering experiences. They are "aha!" responses to new data which matches up just right with one or more of our concept "folders," enhancing the rest of the material already there.

Since concepts govern our perception of the world, it follows that we can change our perception by changing the structure or variety or relationships of our concepts. Behavior follows perception; thus, we can change the way our learners act by changing the way they perceive the world. Because learning is easier when we have well-developed concepts to use in organizing new stimuli (materials), developing basic ecological concepts about the world will aid our learners both in making sense out of the future, and in deciding what that future will hold.

Why Do We Use so Many Gimmicks and Props?

For some people the idea of using props is anathema to the whole idea of education out-of-doors; that is, if an activity can conceivably be conducted indoors, then it should not be included in an outdoors program. Others argue that while the activity may be satisfactory, we should not use "un-natural" props to conduct it.

Basic ecological concepts tend to be abstract because they are so large. Grasping the overall functioning of the water cycle by looking at raindrops, or streams, or clouds is difficult. What is needed is something that will tie all of these elements together, to make the whole concept concrete. Although the resulting activity may be one which could be utilized indoors, that does not mean that the activity should be confined there. Our activities take place where both the operation and implications of the concepts can be immediately seen, where the student can immediately *apply* the understanding in a natural setting. The context and surroundings in which these activities take place are highly important, because grasping the overall functioning of the water cycle *without* looking at a raindrop, stream, or cloud is also difficult.

Our reason for using props is based upon our beliefs about the nature of learning. We believe that examining a long list of examples of the concepts in operation (or parts of them) will not necessarily produce a good understanding of the overall concepts. Too often, the discovery method has been used as a defense by those who would rather talk about things than expend the time and energy necessary to create exciting learning activities. The discounting of the gestalt principle of closure (upon which the real discovery method is based) at the very point where it is most important—in providing the structure which is necessary for learning to take place—is unfortunate. On the other hand, our approach of discovering *applications* of the concept, once it is formed, gives the student a framework within which to work. The application process provides the necessary closure.

So we start with an activity which focuses on the essential idea of the concept, or part of it; then we proceed to find examples in our immediate surroundings. Once the participant has a conceptual frame with which to work, new data (examples) can fit into that frame, enriching and reinforcing the basic understanding. Yes, we begin with props and gimmicks which help us demonstrate the working of the concept, but these are used in an overall program, one which blends activity and example.

We also believe that we should justify taking kids to the out-of-doors by focusing on the larger goal, not just listing skills which they will acquire. After all, one could also learn how to measure pH in the classroom. In fact, that's where we place it. We believe that it is better to work on such a skill in the classroom, and apply it as a concept-building tool later, than it is to try to develop the skill and the concept at the same time.

How Do We Go About Building Concepts?

Our IAA learning model has three components: *Informing, Assimilating, Applying.** Since three of the mornings at the Sunship Study Station are devoted to concept activities, these components can best be understood in that setting. Here's how they work. A group of five or six youngsters arrives at one of fifteen separate concept stations. They begin by receiving specific information about one of the seven concepts emphasized in the program. In this instance, the information is found in their "passports" and takes the form of a key concept statement and a paragraph elaborating upon that statement. In addition, a wooden prop box at each station has the name of the concept printed on its side, and the key concept statement on its lid. For reinforcement the leader asks someone in the group to read the explanation for the concept at each stop.*

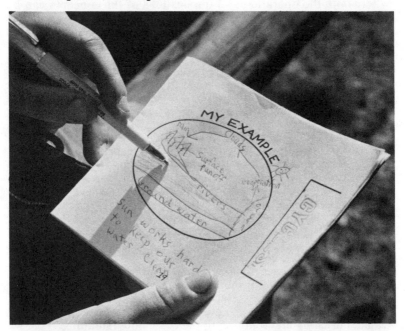

*Thanks to Dr. William Hill for his work on this model.

*Each afternoon during Quiet Time the teacher asks several students to share with the group something from one of their completed concept stations. And before coming to the Sunship Study Station, the teacher conducted a classroom activity on the nature of concepts in general—what they are and how they work. The passport material itself is augmented by additional information conveyed through dining hall displays on each of the natural communities, and displays on each of the concepts are set up in our discovery room, the Outlook Inn.

Once the participants have taken in the information at the station—reading, listening, seeing—the next step involves them in an activity which will aid in the assimilation of the concept idea. To assimilate means to absorb and incorporate, to digest. Each of our stations is based upon an activity which will aid the learners in *assimilating* one concept understanding. Learning means doing something with information received. It is not a passive but an active process. One must engage the information, act upon it, do something with it. We've told our learners how the concept works; now we want them to act it out, to become physically involved in a demonstration of the information received, to perform actions which will aid them in comprehending and retaining the concept idea.

Once the learners have been through the assimilating experience, have taken in and processed the information, we want them to use their understandings. Each entry in the passport is followed by a task which calls for applying the concept idea. In this case, *applying* means that they will locate examples of the concept in their immediate, natural setting. Once found, these examples are recorded in their passports. In this way, they do something with their information. They use it immediately. It's not something to store away for regurgitating later. Their understanding is reinforced. They find their own illustrations.

To cap this sequence, we use rubber stamps of the concept word. We reinforce the idea in the youngster's passport by stamping the name of the concept on the page completed.

After receiving their stamps, everyone is asked to rejoin the group in order to share their examples and thus to see other examples brought in by their peers. The example which the group feels to be the best is marked off for the others who will follow. A sighting scope (a piece of plumber's pipe stamped with the concept) is left behind pointing out the group's application of the concept. The group members can, in turn, peer through other scopes left behind by the groups who preceded them.

As you can see, at the Sunship Study Station we are drawing upon both Skinnerian and Brunerian learning theory. We are concerned with both immediate terminal behaviors and long-range perception (while trying to integrate the cognitive and the affective in the process—Huxley, Brown, et. al.). In addition, by working with fifth and sixth graders, we are reaching kids just at that stage in Piaget's hierarchy when they are intellectually ready to deal with abstract ideas. While not meant to be an exact and all-inclusive representation, the following chart should help clarify the instructional theory behind our approach.

SUNSHIP STUDY STATION   INSTRUCTIONAL
THEORY

SKINNER (programmed or stimulus-response learning)

+focus on terminal behaviors
(the application portion of the IAA model)

+emphasis upon positive, frequent reinforcement
(the leader's comments in conducting the activity,
the youngster's feeling of accomplishment in solving
the problem or performing the task, and the passport
stamps awarded)

+organization of material in small, specific units
(the overall plan of the program)

+prompt feedback
(the primary responsibility of the crew counselor)

+elimination of the likelihood of wrong answers
(the emphasis placed on active doing, not passive
answering)

+stress upon designing learning activities
(the responsibility for learning is shared with the
leader)

+elimination of the adverse nature of questioning
(questions used which facilitate the flow of the
activity instead of testing the learner)

BRUNER (discovery or field theory learning)

+focus on reorganizing perceptions
(the overall theme of the program)

+emphasis upon structure
(the attention to details and the stress on reaching
closure)

+assurance of active participation
(the emphasis upon mechanics)

+creation of a relaxed atmosphere about learning
(the absence of testing and the presence of ''magic'')

+attention to the provocative nature of tasks
(the challenge of concept-building activities)

+permission of mistakes
(the group problem-solving approach)

+stimulation of awareness
(the primary goal of the program)

+emphasis on the importance of attitudes
(the constant concern about how students *feel* about
what they are learning)

Is Our Learning Model Used Just for the Concept Paths?

Our IAA learning model is not limited to use at the concept
activity stations. It is used throughout the entire program. The
chart below shows the various elements of the program and where
each falls in terms of our IAA model.

Informing	Assimilating	Applying
Passport Applications	Concept Paths	Passport Tasks
Advanced Organizers	Magic Spots	Sunship Meeting
Welcome Aboard	Touch the Earth	"Model Planets"
Passport Statements	Discovery Parties	Passengers' Guide
Dining Hall Displays	Immersing Experiences	Logs
Cabin Materials	"Border Dispute"	
Outlook Inn	Quiet Time	
Evening Stories		
Closing Ceremony		

If you analyze the program elements assigned to each part of the
IAA model in terms of the hours given to each activity (both at the
study station and back at school), the inverse relationship between
the number of activities in each part and the number of hours
involved becomes clear. There are more activities at the informing
level than at the applying level of the model, but more hours are
spent on the applying activities.

What Guidelines Do We Follow in Conducting These Activities?

Acclimatization leaders have been working with kids in the
out-of-doors for over fifteen years. During that time we have
learned a great deal ourselves, about motivating learners, setting
goals, assuring participation, and holding attention. The following
guidelines represent a distillation of insights about the learning
process taken from many small experiences repeated again and
again over a long period of time. They apply equally to almost
everything we do.

Start Where Your Learners Are, Not Where You Are.

Wherever possible we use analogies that connect with what our learners already understand. We eliminate as many of the complicated terms as possible. We try to keep it simple.

The analogies we use may not be suitable for other groups. We have tried to design activities which would be appropriate for a range of students from differing backgrounds, and we have tested them in a variety of settings with mixed groups. However, all leaders must figure out where their learners are and begin at that level—not at the level of our kids, but *their* kids!

Avoid Using Identifications as Your Goal.

Naming is not nature. Those who would have us see the world as an endless list of names have condemned us to a rather shallow existence. In figuring out the order of the world we must not believe that it becomes what we have named it. The world exists; it spins through space regardless of our attempts to unlock its secrets.

The problem is that once we name something we frequently tend to stop thinking about it. It becomes more often something taken for granted than a special something to cherish. Naming can also limit our perception in the opposite way. In walking down a path we tend to focus upon what we can name; we pass over those things whose names we have not committed to our memory bank. In short, we often tend to stop thinking about what we can name and miss seeing what we cannot name!

Today, it is also widely believed that if you know a person or a thing, you will want to know its name, for with a name it becomes a special something that you can love and respect and not harm. However, if we can only love and revere what we can name, then we will remain forever limited. Individual people have individual names, but trees and birds and flowers and such do not. We can never know the names of all the people on the earth, nor even all the *kinds* of plants and animals.

In Acclimatization we do not focus on identification. It's not because we think names are unimportant, but because we think they are not the most important objectives of environmental education. We do not want an endless parade of names to get in the way of what we are trying to accomplish.

Talk Only When You Have Given the Group Something to Focus On.

In Acclimatization we have always been afraid of that compelling tendency to talk too much, to rattle on and on in too much detail, to convey all we know, to stroke ourselves by listening to our own erudition. This guideline forces us to be more specific in what we are trying to accomplish. Our emphasis is placed upon active participation in learning—not on information, but on what our learners do with information.

Pull Rather than Push Your Learners.

We don't intend to force kids into learning. We plan to entice them. If we have to push them into participating in an activity, then the activity is failing; it is crying out to be replaced or reworked.

In education, it's easier to pull than push. Even our colloquial expressions convey that idea: to be "pushy" is to be overly aggressive, to "pull for" is to cheer on, to "pull off" is to accomplish something. So we try to pull our learners along (in the sense of attracting them), not push them (in the sense of pressing or coercing them).

Pay Careful Attention to the Details.

It's too easy these days to decide to do less, when more is needed. In ACC we believe that if we care, our learners will care. We show our concern by considering the smallest details of the learning experience, by adding those extra efforts which proclaim: "Hey, these people care—look what they did to get ready for this; they take it seriously; this means something to them."

Use Questions to Facilitate the Flow of the Activity.

Once again, what we are after is action, not passive listening. We want to escape the old game of twenty questions where the leader tries to get the learners to come up with his or her one-word answer. (Usually for a question that the learners did not ask in the first place.) We want to eliminate the atmosphere that identifies the leader as a teacher-tester, and substitute for it the feeling that the leader is a learner-helper. We do not want to threaten, to pose, to probe.

Particularly at first, it is vital that we ask our questions of the entire group. That is, we state our questions without focusing on anyone (just toss them out), and pause for an action-response. We do not imply that we expect an answer. We imply that what we want is action. If we ask how something looks upside down, we are likely to get more doing than verbalizing.

Even better perhaps, we can ask the questions of ourselves. We are part of the group. Our questions will not be judgmental if we include ourselves in the asking, if we say, "I wonder how it feels," instead of, "How does it feel?" Once such an open atmosphere has been created, our learners will rapidly begin to open up themselves. After all, this is not "school," it is an adventure.

Frankly, this guideline is difficult to follow. It means that we have to consistently ask ourselves, "Where is this question taking me?" or, more importantly, "Where is it taking my group?" It means eliminating a lot of questions that don't seem to go anywhere. It places the responsibility for the learning on the activity we have designed, not quizzing techniques for *bringing out* the understandings. If the activity is good, it should convey the understanding itself. We should not have to pump our learners endlessly to make sure that the activity does its job.

In the end, we should remember that holding attention is better accomplished by a task than by a question. We try to make our questions an integral part of our tasks.

THE MODEL

Welcome Aboard

Sunship Study Station

The Literary Analogy

The Living Analogy

The Week in Review

The ACC Vehicles

Acclimatization Walks

Concept Paths

Immersing Experiences

Discovery Parties

Interpretive Encounters

The Staff and Setting

Crew Counselors

Station Leaders

Assistant Station Leaders

Classroom Teachers

Timetables

Chapter Three

"WELCOME ABOARD"

Entering the building, the students find themselves in a dimly lit eight-sided room. Cardboard partitions form the walls, and a parachute suspended from the roof of the building drapes over them to form the ceiling of this room.

The students are seated on benches, facing away from the door through which they entered. On both sides of them the walls are labeled EC-DC-IC-A . . . OPERATING PRINCIPLES governing the existence of all passengers. Those to the left read: "The sun is the source of energy for all living things"; "The building materials of life must be used over and over"; "Plants and animals live together in areas that meet their special needs"; and on the right: "Everything is becoming something else"; "To survive, everything must fit how and where it lives"; "Differences in living things provide for the success of all life."

In front of the students are three panels. The center panel is a landscape mural, under which appears the caption, "All living things interact with other things in their surroundings." The panels on both sides of the mural contain large white windows; one is labeled "SPACE," the other "TIME."

As they come in and sit down, the students hear music—a slightly eerie melody that fills the room with anticipation. When all are seated, the music dies and the lights go out, except for one small ray that calls their attention to an object in the room they hadn't noticed before. A sphere, hanging from the ceiling, has been painted to resemble the photographs of earth as seen from space. The ray of light slowly fades.

In the window to the right of the mural, a hidden projector beams the opening frame of the film, "Cosmic Zoom," accompanied by a stirring piece of music.)

The picture is of a young boy and his dog in a rowboat. The view enlarges as the camera backs up; the boy and boat become smaller as the entire lake is brought into view. As the camera lifts higher and higher, the scene begins to include more of the countryside and nearby city. From the vantage point first of a jet airliner, then of a rocket moving farther and farther away, we see the North American continent and then the entire planet with a background of limitless space.

But the camera movement continues. Out, and farther out, it backs away from that boy, rowing on the lake on a summer afternoon. The planet, the solar system, the galaxy, the Milky Way recede in the distance. Then other galaxies come into view, countless galaxies, until we get a sense of the vast expanse of the universe.

The camera hovers in space, then begins to zoom back, past other galaxies and into our own, through the solar system back to Earth. It drops back rapidly, again finding the lake on which the boy is rowing.

(The film stops, plunging the room into darkness again, except for a single soft beam of light. This beam attracts attention to the center panel, directly ahead, where there is a drawing of a native American chieftain, a mountain, a forest, and, in the distance, a planet. From behind the panel comes a deep resonant voice.)

"Welcome.

"I hope you're enjoying your trip today. It's hard even to imagine, but at this very moment, we are traveling at an incredible speed. This ship, which we call Earth, is rotating to the east—that's to your right—at a speed of over one thousand miles an hour. At the same time, it is orbiting a medium-size star, the sun, at over sixty-five thousand miles per hour. Meanwhile, this solar system is whirling through the Milky Way galaxy and the galaxy is zipping through space, all at astounding speeds. I hope you're having a good ride.

"You have just seen a view of this ship as it exists in the universe. We called it a 'sunship' because, as you will learn, it is powered by the energy of the sun. Of the passengers on the sunship, only a few, the astronauts and cosmonauts, have ever actually seen the earth from space. But thanks to this magic window, we have been taken to the edge of the universe to see where we really live.

"This sunship has been traveling on its journey for billions of years, even before there were any passengers to speak of. It has been on automatic pilot all this time, and things have been going well until lately. In the last one hundred and fifty years or so, the human passengers in particular have begun interfering with some of the mechanisms. The ride has been getting a little rough, and some of our fellow passengers have been complaining. Even a hundred years ago, there were people who feared that the mechanisms were being tampered with and that the sunship could be destroyed.

"One of those was a native American named Chief Seattle, who lived in the 1850s. That was before your time, over a hundred years ago, but this room has another magic window through which you can hear the chief as he gave his warning. This former passenger of the sunship had never heard of spaceships or satellites, but he understood how life on this planet works."

(*The room falls quiet and the light goes off, again leaving only a tiny spot of brightness on the globe suspended overhead. To the left, the screen of the time window is filled with color as scenes from a portion of the film "Home" appear and the voice of Chief Seattle permeates the room*).

"You must teach your children that the ground beneath their feet is the ashes of our grandfathers. So that they will respect the land, tell your children that the earth is rich with the lives of our kin. Teach your children what we have taught our children—that the earth is our mother. Whatever befalls the earth, befalls the sons of the earth. If men spit upon the ground, they spit upon themselves.

"This we know. The earth does not belong to man; man belongs to the earth. This we know. All things are connected like the blood which unites one family. All things are connected.

"Whatever befalls the earth befalls the sons of the earth. Man did not weave the web of life; he is merely a strand in it. Whatever he does to the web, he does to himself . . . "

(*As the film fades, both the spotlight on the globe and then, a few seconds later, the light on the mural are brought up again.*)

"Perhaps now you understand why you are here this week. You will be involved in many activities, and your purpose in all of them is to gain the feelings and understandings that Chief Seattle was talking about. The key to the story of life on earth is contained in the letters you see on the side walls: EC-DC-IC-A. Take a close look at them. During your stay here you will learn the meaning behind the letters in that formula. You are to learn how the sunship operates so that you can act on that understanding before it is too late.

"You should remember, however, that even now there are humans tampering with the automatic pilot. This is your final warning: learn to respect this planet and its workings before you destroy it."

(The lights suddenly disappear, leaving the room dark and silent for about ten seconds. Then the small spot illuminates the earth model above their heads. As the leader walks to the front of the room, a spotlight comes up on him. He's holding a colorful globe.)

"Perhaps Chief Seattle understood so much because he lived closer to nature. We have lost touch with nature and no longer realize how amazing the systems of life are here. You know, if I had a planet just like earth, only the size of this globe, and you could see clouds and plants and oceans and animals moving around on its surface, people would come from all over the world to marvel at it. But the point is, we're already on such a planet! It's just because we're so small that the earth seems so huge. In space, it's smaller even than this, and it's full of things to see and learn . . . and touch."

(Walking through the group to the back of the room, he swings open the doors and lets a stream of sunlight in.)

"Let's go out now and touch the earth. Let's see it with new eyes, smell it with greater appreciation, touch it with more care, taste its many flavors, and hear its special music. And let's carry with us the point of view that all things are fellow passengers on Sunship Earth."

Chapter Four

SUNSHIP STUDY STATION

Hey, we're on a sunship!
How does it work and feel?
We're both its passengers and its crew.
What does this mean for you?

These four lines sum up what the Sunship Earth program is trying to accomplish. We want to acquaint young people with the earth as their place in space, help them get to know it better through firsthand contact, and then convey some basic understandings of how its systems function. In addition, we want to help them see that all people here have a dual role as passenger and crew member, and finally, give each one of them a chance to explore the personal significance behind this new awareness.

In Acclimatization our aim is to help people of all ages build a sense of relationship—in both feelings and understandings—with the natural world. We want to promote a way of viewing the natural world that will encourage a loving, caring interest in it. In this sense, Acclimatization is a product: a behavioral pattern which reflects a deep, inner sense of identification with both living and nonliving things.

All Acclimatization programs are based upon the belief that a fuller mind/body understanding and appreciation of our relationship with the natural world will lead people to take positive environmental action:

1. They will make more ecologically sound decisions in their individual life-styles.
2. They will pursue future (or further) involvement in environmental projects and programs.
3. They will support or participate in data-gathering efforts to aid them in making wiser environmental decisions.

4. They will develop a broader perspective from which to view the day-to-day experiences of their lives.

In the Sunship Earth program we believe this sense of relationship will help the youngsters get started on the process of environmental decision-making for themselves.

In short, we are trying to instill a consciousness in the learners about what and where they are, a lifelong frame of reference about the earth and its systems. They are crew members on the sunship because unlike other passengers they can know where they are and grasp the significance of that knowledge. We want them to understand that every action has an effect, and at the same time to feel the relatively small overall role that human beings play in the processes of life. For even though · they are important crew members in terms of life here, they are nonetheless subject to the same natural processes as the most humble protozoan.

The Literary Analogy

Comparisons between the planet earth and a spaceship are only about as old as the first glimpse man had of his home planet from the broad and humbling perspective of space itself. Since the first pictures were returned from the moon, the analogy of "Spaceship Earth" has been an effective explanatory device. It has been used by many ecologists in their desperate attempt to help people understand the earth's vital and fragile life-support systems.

We draw on the spaceship earth analogy, but make two useful variations. First of all, we refer to the planet as "Sunship Earth" to emphasize the importance of the sun as the life-giving energy source and to de-emphasize the subconscious comparison to man-made space ships, a comparison which tends to elevate man once again above the natural systems of the earth. The concept of the sun as the primary source of energy, the view of other fuels as stored sunlight, and the exhaustible nature of these stored supplies were major conceptual objectives we had in mind in developing this program. Secondly, and this distinction is crucial, our program goes beyond the usual textbook analogy and uses the Sunship Earth model to design an unusual kind of educational experience. The kids don't just learn about the similarity of earth to a sunship, they live it. They are not at school. They are not at camp. They are at a Sunship Study Station. Their mission is to increase feelings and understandings. It is an important mission.

The Living Analogy

People who go on a journey usually get an orientation before departing. At least, they usually find out something about the area for which they are heading, pick up a map to use in planning the route they will follow, and check out the functioning of the vehicle they will use to get there. Yet on our journey through space, most of us appear supremely confident that everything will be satisfactory even though we don't know where we're going, have only the vaguest idea of our route, and seem determined to treat

the vehicle with a haughty disdain. Obviously, we are in desperate need of a reorientation to the earth and its systems before traveling much farther on our journey aboard this relatively small planet.

"Sunship Earth," then, is the theme that permeates everything we do in our outdoor program. It gives continuity to our approach, and provides a good analogy as well. It reunites two of the often dichotomized elements of the outdoor school: curriculum and residence. The former generally carries the full weight of any educational objectives; the latter involves all of the day-to-day necessities of living quarters, meals, and recreation.

It has been our experience that people, especially youngsters, learn the patterns they live. So the inclusion of eating, sleeping, and playing as part of the complete learning program is important. Or, more appropriately, making the most of the opportunities for learning that these hours of time can offer is important. In the cabins, at meals, at campfires, and on rainy days, the Sunship Study Station is still a learning center. "Crew" members live in cabins as passengers on the sunship, with daily reminders of what that means. Even at meals, there is a focus on the sunship analogy. The food we eat, the air we breathe, our living quarters, and our playing fields are all part of the sunship and its natural communities of life. That awareness permeates the routines.

So Sunship Earth is not concerned with just the portion of the day labeled "school" or "class" time on the schedule. It is a model for the entire experience, beginning before the kids arrive and lasting beyond their departure from our small study station.

What follows is a brief summary of the overall program, The Week in Review, descriptions of the Acclimatization vehicles, and a description of the support services and the physical layout necessary for operating a Sunship Study Station. The Timetables at the end of this chapter present one way of putting the program together for a five-day resident experience. There are other shorter, even nonresident, possibilities.

The Week in Review

MONDAY

Three classroom groups arrive about mid-morning. They are welcomed by staff members, who board the buses at the main gate to explain what's coming up as they ride in. Wearing wooden discs inscribed with their first names, the staff's goal is to create a solid and unified, yet warm and friendly, first impression.

From the parking area, everyone heads for the COMMUNITY MEETING. At this first session (attended by all staff, *including* the cooks and maintenance people), the week's tone is set: this is a community of people working together on an important retraining mission. After brief introductions of the staff and the classroom teachers, the three classes are divided into mixed crews, meet their crew counselors, receive their own wooden name discs, and depart. All activity during this part of the morning is directed toward giving the new residents a chance to take stock of their surroundings (staff, cabins, dining hall, nurse's station, Outlook Inn, paths and trails, plants and animals, etc.).

Following lunch each class meets with its own teacher for QUIET TIME. This is a period set aside each day for the teachers to help the kids share discoveries about their fellow passengers and themselves. Traditional education has suggested that intellectual knowledge can sometimes be acquired in an emotional vacuum. It is possible to know, and yet still not understand or have any feelings about the subject. During the Quiet Time, the teacher's role might be that of an active listener, an unaware alien from another planet, or a facilitator for a values building exercise, but it is never that of a lecturer or interrogator. The Quiet Time provides both a change of pace and a chance to see the sunship concepts in a different light. It is a relaxed time for learners and leaders alike.

In the early afternoon all crews assemble outside the Rec Hall for the WELCOME ABOARD presentation. This is a multimedia demonstration which sets the stage for the week ahead. It is a briefing for the journey through space that the kids have been traveling on for years. Through simulation they see how small the planet is from an outerspace perspective. And as passengers on this planet, they are given an important task for the week. Their mission is to find out how Sunship Earth operates and how its human passengers can avoid tampering with its automatic systems.

TOUCH THE EARTH, which follows this presentation, is a special ACC WALK that focuses on the concluding ideas in

Welcome Aboard—

Let's go out now and touch the earth.
Let's see it with new eyes, smell it with greater
appreciation, touch it with more care, taste its
many flavors, and hear its special music.

After these initial get-acquainted-with-your-planet's-life activities, the youngsters receive a personal LOG to use throughout the
week for recording discoveries about themselves and the life
around them. To introduce the use of the Log, the crews take off
with their counselors for an area where each person will locate a
MAGIC SPOT, a place to sit alone and be touched by the rhythms
of life. It is a chance to find and "adopt" a small spot in the natural
world. It is a time just to let things be, to draw or write if
something comes to mind, but primarily to sit and absorb. The
Logs contain special suggestions for helping the crew members
utilize this important part of each day.

Monday afternoon winds up with some TIME OUT activities.
Some of the kids usually head for the OUTLOOK INN to join one of
the "expeditions" being offered; others may have their heart set
on trying to move the earthball across the playing field, and a few
are often content with just poking around for a while. This is a time
for everyone to get away from the thinking and the impact of it all
and just have some fun.

Each evening at the Sunship Study Station finds everyone
involved in some type of WORKSHOP: groups may be learning
how to bake bread, remove unwanted plants from the garden
patch, weave napkins for the dining hall, design a puppet show for
the campfire, or learn a specialized skill, while helping with the
overall care of the Study Station facility. All workshops focus on
activities which will contribute to the good of the community. And
most of them emphasize simple ways of making do and having fun.

Afterwards, a CAMPFIRE brings everyone together at the place
where their first day began, the site of the Community Meeting. It
is an appropriate place, for our campfires are also a type of
community event themselves. There are the traditional
activities—songs and skits and stories—but an appropriate song
here might be the "Circle Game," while one of the crews might
perform a skit on why the heron has long legs, and a station leader
might tell a story about the amazing mammal that flies.

Monday ends with the kids in bed listening to a quiet EVENING
STORY read to them by their counselors.

TUESDAY

The first activity of the day requires everyone's presence in the
Rec Hall. It is the long-awaited presentation of the Sunship Study
Station PASSPORTS. A formal arrangement of special counters,
including clerks with visor caps, signifies the seriousness of the event.
Everyone shows up with the special pouches made in school two weeks
before.

Three CONCEPT PATHS take up the bulk of Tuesday, Wednesday, and Thursday mornings. Five crews and their counselors, plus one station leader, report to each path. Before they split up to go to their respective stations, the crews receive a brief description of what lies ahead from the station leader who is coordinating their path for the day. The activities on the Concept Paths demonstrate the functioning of the seven concepts represented by the EC-DC-IC-A formula.

Individual Passports play a recurring role as the "passengers" travel from station to station. First, they help introduce the concept idea with a key concept or transfer statement, followed by an explanatory paragraph. Then, at the end of each station's activity, there is time for the crew members to enter their own examples of the concept in action, to find an application of the concept idea in the natural world around them. Finally, their Passports are stamped with the name of the concept to indicate that they have traveled another step on their journey toward understanding the sunship.

After lunch and Quiet Time, most of the kids go to the DISCOVERY PARTY (the remainder are involved in special projects at the Outlook Inn or are pursuing a special interest of their own). The Discovery Parties are less structured than our other activities, more open to impulse, and more specific in encouraging the kids to explore, to poke around, and to find interesting things on their own. They are light in tone yet center on a serious task. The first one of the week is called "Lost Letters" and involves rediscovering the lost meaning of the word "discovery."

A mid-afternoon snack provides a short break before everyone regroups for the first IMMERSING EXPERIENCE. These are activities designed to break down the sensory barriers between people and the natural world. They are multisensory and strive to change the vantage point of the participant, thereby encouraging a fresh view of what may have already been familiar. Today's Immersing Experience turns each kid into a ranger in his or her own "Micro-Park."

Magic Spots, Time Out activities, Workshops, the Campfire, and an Evening Story complete the program for another day of sunship exploring.

WEDNESDAY

Wednesday begins with a rotation of the groups to another of the three Concept Paths, followed by Magic Spots later in the morning and new activities in the same categories as those of Tuesday afternoon (i.e., Quiet Time, a Discovery Party, an Immersing Experience, and Time Out). However, after the evening Workshops, there are small Crew Campfires for each cabin group, followed by a special nighttime Immersing Experience called "Nightwatchers."

THURSDAY

The Concept Paths and Magic Spots once again take up the morning, but after Quiet Time in the afternoon, there is an all-community INTERPRETIVE ENCOUNTER. Designed to focus on a single concept, in this case the concept of community, the Interpretive Encounter requires a larger block of time for more in-depth work. This one is a "Border Dispute," a re-enactment of an ancient quarrel between the "Elves" and "Trolls" who once inhabited a remote area of the Sunship Study Station.

The remainder of Thursday afternoon includes another new Immersing Experience and the Time Out activities. The evening program is the same as on Monday and Tuesday: Workshops, Campfire, and Evening Story.

The regular Campfire on Thursday is followed by a special presentation about the place of each of the concepts in the EC-DC-IC-A formula and about their interrelationships. The warm atmosphere of the last night in camp creates an ideal setting for tying together the concepts with which the crews have worked all week. Called JOURNEY HOME, the ceremony takes place at a separate site and involves an Indian story about some young people who had a similar set of adventures long ago. It summarizes the story of life and presents all the youngsters with a personal symbol of their new awareness.

FRIDAY

After packing up, everyone heads for an open field on Friday morning to take part in a special Interpretive Encounter, "Model Planets." Applying their newly acquired understandings of the EC-DC-IC-A formula, small groups attempt to design the systems of life for a model planet. The best ideas end up being transferred to the only planet capable of sustaining life in this sample solar system, the third planet from the sun, but there is a surprise ending.

The SUNSHIP MEETING provides an opportunity for the kids to begin to act on the insights and understandings they have gained all week and just summarized in the Model Planets experience. It has the excitement of a political convention, with all the trappings—banners, signs, delegations, and speeches. Each group presents to the assembled passengers its nominations for bad environmental habits and its recommendations for constructive solutions. At the end, the teachers literally take the ball in accepting the PASSENGERS' GUIDE, a papier-mache globe full of ideas for transferring the kids' new awareness and understanding back to their school and home settings. The kids have come up with many of the ideas themselves during the morning; others have been provided by the teachers and staff during the week. We hope that the insights the students have gained about their planet will have an effect on their actions in the future, both in their own lives and in the lives of those with whom they come in contact. This tool makes it easier for the classroom teacher to carry on the sunship idea, even after the group leaves the study station.

Friday ends with a return to the special sunship room where the activities for the week began. The emphasis this time is on "Beginnings Not Ends." The special effects, the mysterious voice, the lights fading and coming on—all convey the feeling that the students are, indeed, passengers on an incredible journey through space, and that they are *important* passengers because they have gained understanding and, along with it, a new sensitivity to and feeling of responsibility for all life.

The ACC Vehicles

These are the categories of activities that we have developed in our Acclimatization work. Each of them is designed to contribute in some way to our goal of helping people of all ages build a sense of relationship with the natural world. The activities within each category meet a particular set of criteria to ensure that they actually do contribute to the objectives for which they were designed. What follows is an analysis of each of the major vehicles beginning with the ACC Walks, according to the specific activities developed for the Sunship Earth program. I have also listed the criteria which these activities were designed to meet.

ACC WALKS

"Touch the Earth"   (Monday afternoon)

Acclimatization Walks:

+focus upon fresh, innovative ways of experiencing the richness of nature
+include brief, structured activities
+emphasize introducing the natural world in a non-identifying, non-discussing, nonthreatening way
+utilize built-in methods for assuring both full participation and a smooth flow from one activity to the next
+involve sensing, sharing, and empathizing activities
+require the leader to set the overall tone, then conduct each activity

One crucial element of the ACC program is the effort to reawaken people to the sensory experiences of the environment, restoring to those whose senses have been directed primarily toward the visual messages of reading and television-watching the sounds, textures, smells, and tastes of their environment. We reintroduce them to the infinite variety of natural surfaces present on our sunship. Sensory rediscovery aids both visual and non-visual perception; it is the direct accumulation of data that is so important to the learning process. So the "Welcome Aboard" simulation which begins our Sunship Study Station program is followed by "Touch the Earth," a special kind of "ACC Walk" designed to handle seventy-five youngsters, and aimed at re-awakening individual senses and sharpening perception for the experiences in the week ahead.

CONCEPT PATHS

"A Path"   (Tuesday, Wednesday,
"B Path"   and Thursday
"C Path"   mornings)

Concept Paths:

+focus upon assimilating and applying to the natural world a series of ecological concepts
+include established concept-building activity stations
+emphasize employing short, simple, and concrete tasks
+utilize special tools for presenting, reinforcing, and transferring information
+involve activities which encourage natural observation and examination between stations
+require the leader to guide the group through a series of experiences

On Tuesday, Wednesday, and Thursday mornings, the youngsters are involved in one of three different "Concept Paths." Each path consists of a series of five stations with a separate concept activity at each station. Together, these paths are at the heart of our learning program. Crews of five kids and a leader rotate during the morning from station to station on each path. The stations themselves are stops along the path where the activity of the crew, not the talk of the leader, conveys the concept. Activities along the three paths are designed to convey the seven main concepts: Energy Flow, Cycles, Diversity, Community, Interrelationships, Change, and Adaptation. An activity on one concept path may convey one part of the concept, such as the concept of food chains as part of the larger concept of energy flow, while another station another day will focus on the way food energy is lost as it is converted to heat. A "key concept statement" reinforces the action at each station and helps assure transfer for those concept-learning activities which have different components on different days.

IMMERSING EXPERIENCES

"Micro-Parks"
"Earth Studios"
"Curious Heron Walk"
"Nightwatchers"

(Tuesday, Wednesday and Thursday afternoons, plus Wednesday evening)

Immersing Experiences:

+ focus upon expanding individual feelings for the natural world
+ include a procedure which assures a sensory barrier-breaking experience
+ emphasize making the familiar unfamiliar by changing the participant's perspective
+ utilize a theme which promotes direct contact with a piece of land and its life
+ involve opportunities for individual sharing and self-expression
+ require the leader to coordinate individual or small group efforts

Immersing means getting wet all over, and that's what these activities are, sometimes literally but always figuratively speaking. Total sensory involvement with the natural world is the goal of four of our activities (one each on Monday, Tuesday, and Wednesday afternoons and one on Wednesday evening). "Immersing Experiences" are activities for plunging in, getting close, using all one's senses and becoming completely caught up in the experience. They are designed primarily to change the participants' perspective, to get them in touch with the land and its life in ways which guarantee participation and contact.

DISCOVERY PARTIES

"Lost Letters"   (Tuesday and
"Artists and Scientists"   Wednesday afternoon)

Discovery Parties:

+ focus upon building a sense of wonder and place
+ include tasks for encouraging personal exploration and making
  individual "finds"
+ emphasize making firsthand contact with natural places and
  things
+ utilize the participants in deciding moment to moment where to
  go and what to do within a specific undertaking
+ involve opportunities for leaders to share both wonder and
  knowledge
+ require the leader to set the stage, then respond more than
  initiate

Freewheeling and fun, the "Discovery Parties" are afternoon
activities that encourage crew members to discover for themselves
the marvelous things that live on our sunship. They are light in
tone and, in a sense, they are excuses to poke around, explore, and
share. There is just enough structure to hold a group together,
enough freedom to allow for individual discoveries. The discovery
vehicle is similar to a natural history walk or talk in that the leader
provides appropriate comments, but different in that the participants
find the objects and the leader *responds*.

INTERPRETIVE ENCOUNTERS

"Border Dispute"   (Thursday afternoon
"Model Planets"   and Friday morning)

Interpretive Encounters:

+ focus upon developing a deeper understanding of a single
  ecological concept
+ include activities which flow in small steps from the concrete to
  the abstract
+ emphasize incorporating peer-to-peer interactions in the
  learning process
+ utilize a problem-solving story line
+ involve longer, ongoing roles for the participants
+ require the leader to set up and direct the overall activity

The in-depth development of a single concept is what the
"Interpretive Encounters" are designed to accomplish. There is
more time to develop the concept from something the youngsters
can see and touch to something they can understand. Still, the
focus is on what the kids do, not what the leader says. Even though

one encounter may have several activities, similar in nature to those performed at the concept paths, they all tie in to one theme and all relate to the same concept.

The Staff and Setting

The Sunship Study Station model presented here was set up for three classroom groups, or approximately seventy-five youngsters. It requires a program staff of fifteen crew counselors (high school or college students), four station leaders (usually college graduates) and three assistants, plus three classroom teachers (who accompany their classes). The following breakdown presents an encapsulated view of the responsibilities for each group. A plus(+) or minus(-) by each activity indicates whether the staff member plays a major or minor role in the activity.

Crew Counselors are responsible for leading all of the small group activities and working with the kids in their daily living routines.

+Orientation
+ACC Walk—"Touch the Earth"
+Magic Spots
+Morning Cabin Time
+Concept Paths
+Immersing Experiences
+Interpretive Encounters
+Evening Story
+Crew Campfires

-Time Out activities
-Workshops
-Sunship Meeting
-Passengers' Guide

Station Leaders are responsible for coordinating the entire program. Because there are three classroom groups, several of the activities take place in three locations (Concept Paths, Immersing Experiences, ACC Walk), and one station leader works with the crews and their counselors in each area.

+Community Meeting
+Welcome Aboard
+Concept Paths
+Immersing Experiences
+Interpretive Encounters
+Passengers' Guide
+Closing Ceremony

-Magic Spots
-Discovery Parties
-Workshops
-Sunship Meeting
-Time Out activities

One of the station leaders works directly with the teachers. He conducts an in-service day for them several months before they bring their class to the study station in order to introduce the program and to help them prepare for their involvement. He visits their classroom two weeks before their arrival to present the "Passport Applications" to the kids. During the week the teachers spend at the Sunship Study Station, he works with them in planning their activities and in designing additional lessons to use upon their return.

Assistant Station Leaders are responsible for handling the special presentations and facilities, evening activities, and the daily living routines.

+Arrival   -Welcome Aboard
+Mealtime activities   -Sunship Meeting
+Time Out
+Passport Presentations
+Discovery Parties
+Outlook Inn
+Workshops
+Campfires
+Departure

Classroom Teachers are responsible for conducting those activities which focus upon their own classroom group and designing those activities which will be utilized back at school.

+Quiet Time   -Evening Story
+Time Out   -Sunship Meeting
+Discovery Parties
+Workshops
+Passengers' Guide
+Sunship Monitor

Obviously, such a complex program requires a good supportive staff in addition to those listed above. We believe that the manager, secretary, nurse, cooks, and maintenance people must be incorporated as an integral, truly vital part of the program.

The model we have presented here takes place in a resident center. However, Sunship Earth programs could be organized at a day-use facility. The only real criterion for a setting, resident or nonresident, is that it be located where there are some fairly wild, "unmanicured" areas to use in conducting the Concept Paths and other activities. Naturally, the type and availability of buildings, and the use and condition of the land will make a difference. However, in this respect a lot can be done with a little. Success depends more upon the staff than the site.

This model is also set up to operate for the better part of five days. If you have a shorter period of time available, then you will need to reorganize the activities, balancing sensory and conceptual activities in order to achieve the same effect that we have here. As with any program, the overall impact of Sunship Earth may be lost if it is spread out over too long a period of time or squeezed into one that is too short or diluted with other activities.

When you adopt the Sunship Earth idea, we hope that you are accepting the goals of the program as well. Those goals are more important than the trappings that surround them. If you have other objectives, they may not fit easily into the context of this program, and we would hope that you would analyze your objectives carefully and proceed accordingly. If the Sunship Earth program can accommodate other needs which you have, without destroying its integrity, that's tremendous. But beware, for so often in education we tend to extract the essential elements of a program, replace them with a potpourri of unrelated activities, and then stand back later, scratch our heads, and wonder why the program didn't work as well as promised.

As a gestalt therapist once put it, sometimes we get so wrapped up in the sizzle, we never get to the steak. Naturally, we would rather see Sunship Earth offered as an adjunct or an option, than see its highlights sprinkled like spice over a melange of other activities. However you proceed, we wish you luck. If we can be of assistance, please call upon us.

SUNSHIP STUDY STATION TIMETABLES

	MONDAY	TUESDAY	WEDNESDAY	THURSDAY	FRIDAY
7:00 a.m.		Morning Wake-up	Morning Wake-up	Morning Wake-up	Morning Wake-up
7:30 a.m.		Breakfast	Breakfast	Magic Spots	Breakfast
8:00 a.m.		Cabin Time	Cabin Time		Pack-up
8:15 a.m.				Breakfast	
8:30 a.m.		Passport Presentations			Mocel Planets
8:45 a.m.			Concept Path B: "Declaration of Interdependence"	Cabin Time	
9:00 a.m.		Concept Path A:		Concept Path C:	
9:15 a.m.		"Cradles to Coffins"		"Missing Passenger Hunt"	
9:30 a.m.			"Cliff Hangers"		Mag c Spots
9:45 a.m.		"On the Street Where You Live"			
10:00 a.m.	Arrival				
10:15 a.m.	Community Meeting	"Guess Who's Coming to Dinner"	"Food Factory"	"Tools and Tasks"	
10:30 a.m.			"Sun's Bucket Brigade"	"Chain Gang"	Sunship Meeting
10:45 a.m.	Orientation	"Mr. Sun's Restaurant"			
11:00 a.m.			"Root Sellers"	"Soil Sinks"	
11:15 a.m.		"Peanut Patch"			
11:30 a.m.			Magic Spots	"Best Deal on Earth"	Pass=nger's Guide
12:00 Noon	Lunch	Lunch	Lunch	Lunch	Lunch

Time					
1:00 p.m.	Quiet Time				
1:30 p.m.		Quiet Time	Quiet Time	Quiet Time	Closing Ceremony: "Beginning and Ends"
1:45 p.m.	Welcome Aboard	Discovery Party:			Departure
2:15 p.m.	ACC Walk: "Touch the Earth"	"Lost Letters"	Discovery Party: "Artists and Scientists"	Interpretive Encounter: "Border Dispute"	
2:45 p.m.		Snack			
3:00 p.m.		Immersing Experience:			
3:15 p.m.			Snack	Snack	
3:30 p.m.		"Micro-Parks"	Immersing Experience:	Immersing Experience:	
3:45 p.m.	Magic Spots		"Curious Heron Walk"	"Earth Studios"	
4:00 p.m.		Magic Spots			
4:30 p.m.	Time Out	Time Out	Time Out	Time Out	
6:00 p.m.	Dinner	Dinner	Dinner	Dinner	
7:15 p.m.	Workshops	Workshops	Workshops	Workshops	
8:15 p.m.			Crew Campfires		
8:30 p.m.	Campfire	Campfire	Immersing Experience:	Campfire	
8:45 p.m.					
9:00 p.m.			"Nightwatchers"	Ceremony: "Journey Home"	
9:15 p.m.					
9:30 p.m.	Evening Story	Evening Story			
9:45 p.m.			Evening Story	Evening Story	
10:00 p.m.					

THE PREPARATIONS

Passport Applications

Teacher Planning

Personal Preparation

Classroom Preparation

Leadership Roles

Lesson Development

Curriculum Development

Course Goals

Concepts

Concept Components

Instructional Objectives

Learning Experiences

Learning Outcomes

Chapter Five

PASSPORT APPLICATIONS

"Right here. It's a weird thought, but this little dot in the picture is pretty close to where our solar system is in the Milky Way galaxy," explains Bill, during his visit to the class that will be arriving in two weeks at the Sunship Study Station.

"Just think of it. At this very minute, we're orbiting a bright little point of light, like one of these. Our sun, actually a star, is more than ninety million miles away from us. And we're traveling, this very minute, at a speed of over sixty-five thousand miles per hour, circling the sun once every year. That means that right now we're traveling through space around the sun at a speed over one hundred times faster than the speed of a jet plane!

"We depend on this star that we call our sun for the energy that makes life on this planet possible; so the earth is really like a 'sunship,' receiving its energy from the star it orbits.

"The place where you're going the week after next is called a Sunship Study Station because what you'll be doing is learning more about how our sunship operates."

Going to the chalkboard Bill writes "EC-DC-IC-A" on it in large letters. "Take a good look at this formula. It's the key to your whole week at the Sunship Study Station, In fact, this formula is the story of how life works on this planet. Everyone repeat it once with me . . . Now say it to yourself a couple of times: 'EC-DC-IC-A.'

"When you come back to school after your week with us, you'll know what those letters represent, and you'll be able to share with others that important information."

"Where is this station place?"

"Well, let's take a closer look," Bill answers, pulling out a picture of the earth as seen from space. "This small orange point here shows the location of our Sunship Study Station. We've got it pretty well set up now, and I think you'll like the facilities."

Bill then describes the cabins they'll be living in and adds the reassuring information that meals will be provided. "As human passengers on the sunship, it's very likely that you'll be running into some other animal and plant passengers, too," he tells them.

Fielding questions about what they'll need to bring, Bill passes out lists of the clothing and other articles that are recommended for a stay at the Sunship Study Station. The list includes necessary items such as a pair of old sneakers and a long-sleeved shirt, but also strongly recommends that certain items be left behind. "This list should contain just about everything you could possibly need at the Sunship Study Station. You won't be needing radios, hair dryers, or stereos," Bill emphasizes.

"But speaking of needs, something you'll all have to have is a special passport like this one of mine. It will guarantee your admission to various parts of the study station. Each time you enter certain areas at the station, your passport will be stamped with the official seal of that area. So it's really important that you each have one. Right now, I'd like for each of you to fill out these passport applications."

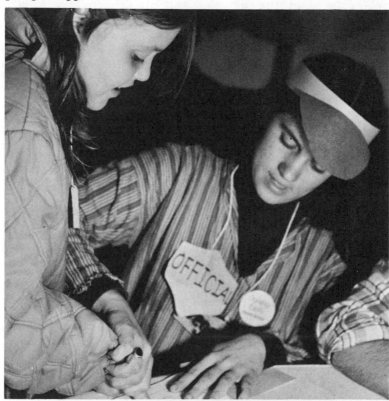

OFFICIAL PASSPORT APPLICATION

Sunship Study Station

WHO ARE YOU?

NAME _____

ADDRESS: .

   Galaxy _____

   Planet _____

   Country _____

   State _____

   County _____

   Town _____

   Street _____

SCHOOL _____

GRADE _____

How many times have you orbited around the sun as a passenger on Sunship Earth? _____

I, _____ ,
would like to learn more about how life on earth works in order to be a better passenger on our Sunship.

I know that my Sunship Study Station passport will admit me to many outdoor learning adventures and help me to discover more about the Sunship I live on. Therefore, I hereby apply for an official Sunship Study Station passport.

_____
Signature

_____
Date

"You'll notice that on the back of the passport application there is some information about some of your other needs," Bill points out. "Take a look at it now because you'll have to figure these problems out before you come to the study station."

WHERE ARE YOU?

The planet earth is really like a spaceship. Right now, it is carrying us around the sun at a speed of over 65,000 m.p.h. That's once every 365 days.

Our nearest star, the sun, is over 90,000,000 miles away. The sun is like the earth's mother ship because it supplies the energy that enables us to live. For this reason we call our home, the earth, a SUNSHIP.

THREE THINGS YOU WILL NEED...

"Welcome to the magical world of the out-of-doors."

So that we don't run short of anything during your stay at the Sunship Study Station, we are trying to figure out how much air, water, and food each passenger will need.

Air—with each breath that you take, you inhale about 1,000,000,000,000,000,000 atoms of air. If you average 12 breaths a minute, you will breathe 17,280 times in one day. How many atoms of air will we need to have on hand for you during your stay at the station (5 days)?

AEI

Water—the average Sunship passenger living in the United States uses 1,600 gallons of water per day for food, washing, and other uses. How much water will we need to meet your water needs for the five days you spend with us?

Food—a large portion of this water will go towards making sure there will be enough food for your stay. For example, it takes about 1,000 gallons of water to produce one quart of milk and about 3,000 gallons of water to produce one pound of meat. If you drink 3 quarts of milk and eat 2 pounds of meat while you are at the Sunship Study Station, how much water will that take?

"As I said, these are very important documents," Bill repeats, holding up his passport, "so each of you should have a place to keep your passport safe and dry. I have this special waterproof pouch for mine, and your teacher has already agreed that it would be a good idea for each of you to make one.

"I'm going to leave this pictures of the Milky Way and the Earth behind so you can get used to the seemingly crazy idea that we're traveling through space.

"See you in a couple of weeks."

Chapter Six

TEACHER PLANNING

Teachers play an important role in our Sunship Study Station model. They do not just accompany their students. Although high school or college students serve as crew counselors, conducting many of the activities each day, the teachers work directly with the station leaders throughout the week. They are an integral part of the staff.

Running a complete five-day Sunship Earth program with teachers alone would be difficult. There is just too much to do. Sunship Earth is a comprehensive program which includes everything the kids do for over four full days. Rather than ask the teachers, who are already caught up in a crowded curriculum, to attempt to plan the activities and construct the equipment necessary for the Sunship Earth program, we have arranged for them to participate in a different fashion.

At the Sunship Study Station the professional staff members or station leaders handle the planning and coordinating of the entire program. In this way the teachers have time to prepare special experiences for the week and design activities for the kids to use in applying their new understandings when they return to school.

Personal Preparation

It is most important that the teachers have rather clear expectations about the Sunship Earth program and what part they will play before they arrive. They need plenty of time to plan and prepare for the experience, time both for their students and for themselves. To facilitate the teachers' preparations we suggest that the following materials be distributed:

+An initial "Briefing Sheet," which they receive six months

prior to their participation in the program. The Briefing Sheet explains the general purpose and content of the program, but requests that the teachers not include the Study Station concepts in their lesson plans nor explain too much about what will happen during the week.

+A Sunship Study Station "Trip Planner" to copy and send home to the parents. These planning sheets explain the who, what, when, where, and, most importantly, the why of Sunship Earth. In addition, they invite the parents to sign up for helping to conduct the Time Out activities and Evening Workshops.

+A "Personal Skills Inventory" form to fill out and return to the Sunship Study Station office. Sent out two months prior to their visit, the inventory asks the teachers to rate themselves on their ability to lead the Evening Workshops and Time Out activities listed, leaving space for suggestions for additional workshops or activities which they feel they could handle. However, we do not include just any activities in the program. Specific criteria (i.e., Principles and Premises of Acclimatization, ACC Guidelines, Sunship Earth objectives, etc.) determine whether other activities are suitable or will interfere with what we are trying to accomplish.

Classroom Preparation

There are several ways in which the kids become involved in the preparations for their week at the Sunship Study Station:

+A special box of materials is sent to the teachers about one month before their departure. In it, there is a list of key words which the students are asked to learn (and practice using). An understanding of these words will provide a simple type of "advance organizer" for the students' thinking. Some of them will help the students link up new pieces of information; others will provide helpful tools for participation in the various activities. However, the teachers are asked *not to teach these words in a Sunship Earth context*. They should play down the idea that these are words the kids will have to *know* at the Sunship Study Station, and emphasize instead that the reward will come in the activities there.

relate	depend	synthetic	carbohydrate
interrelate	interdepend	molecule	decay
compete	cycle	environment	interact
cooperate	energy	precipitation	flow
decompose	oxygen	condensation	carbon
consume	hydrogen	nutrient	pH
bacteria	evaporation	atom	calories
CO_2	H_2O		

In addition, there is a set of materials for helping the kids learn several skills: making soil and water pH tests, using light meters and soil augers, taking air, water, and soil temperatures, etc. Finally, a copy of Allan Eckert's *Wild Season* is included for the teacher to read to the class.

+Three weeks prior to their visit the students are asked to fill out a "Personal Interest Inventory" sheet, which the teacher will forward to the Sunship Study Station office. These sheets will be tallied and used to plan Time Out activities, Discovery Parties, and Evening Workshops for the class.

+A representative of the Sunship Study Station visits the classroom two weeks beforehand to conduct the "Passport Applications" session, to answer questions, and to pass out needs lists and materials for making the Passport pouches.

Leadership Roles

Teachers take on several key leadership roles during the Sunship Earth program (some of them may receive college credit for their work during the week).

+Teachers serve as leaders for the Time Out activities and the Evening Workshops. Contacted beforehand by the station leaders, who have evaluated their responses on the Personal Skills Inventory Sheets, the teachers are asked to prepare to conduct two or three of the recreational activities in the afternoons and two of the workshops in the evenings.

+Teachers are the reporters for the *Sunship Monitor*, the official newspaper of the Study Station. This role gives them an opportunity to view the activities the kids are involved in without being passive observers. As reporters (with press badges and tape recorders), they are able to move around easily, interviewing the kids about activities and observations.

+Teachers meet with their own classes during Quiet Time. The period set aside after lunch each day gives the teachers an opportunity to meet with their classes in a relaxed setting. Some of the activities during this time are based on the materials designed by the teachers during the week.

Lesson Development

One of the primary functions of the classroom teacher during the Sunship Earth program is to prepare for the continued application of learning when the kids return to their schools and homes. To guarantee that the Sunship Study Station is not merely an isolated week of experiences, but rather an integral part of the school year, the teachers spend a portion of their time during the week developing their own lesson plans. In addition, they must prepare for the "Sunship Meeting" on Friday morning, where they will speak in response to their students' presentations and design the classroom tasks (or applications) which will be placed in the "Passengers' Guide" for the class to use when they return.

Sunship Earth should be an opening unit for the class instead of a culminating one. The teacher can follow up with the kids back at school, tying new information in with the concept folder prepared at the study station, reinforcing the concepts with additional activities, and expanding upon the implications of the concepts in their daily lives. If a fifth grade class completes the program at the Sunship Study Station in the late spring, we suggest that the fifth and sixth grade teachers switch classes for a week or arrange between themselves to have the fifth graders report on their experiences to the sixth grade teacher after they return. In this way, the future sixth graders will be able to utilize their "Passengers' Guide" with their teacher in the fall.

Curriculum Development

Each school will necessarily have to undertake its own analysis of how best to integrate the Sunship Earth program into its existing curriculum. However, the following chart, prepared by Jim Wells as a consultant for the Intermediate Education District in Portland, Oregon, may serve as a starting point. Jim's task was to illustrate how the objectives of the concept paths could be fit into traditional educational models. Obviously, this chart excludes some important elements of the program, but it does suggest one possibility for analyzing and presenting the concept building activities in traditional terms. The same type of analysis could be made of the program in terms of building values or developing skills for scientific inquiry and social interaction, or could focus on the multidisciplinary nature of the activities themselves.

COURSE GOAL	The student knows that the sun is the source of energy for all living things.
CONCEPT	**ENERGY FLOW**
CONCEPT COMPONENT	PHOTOSYNTHESIS
INSTRUCTIONAL OBJECTIVE	The student understands that the leaves of green plants are the only thing on earth which can change the sun's light into energy-rich sugars.
LEARNING EXPERIENCE	"FOOD FACTORY"
LEARNING OUTCOME	The student will be able to draw a picture of something that can change the sun's energy into food and label that picture with the structures and materials that are involved in making food.
CONCEPT COMPONENT	FOOD CHAINS
INSTRUCTIONAL OBJECTIVE	The student understands that the sun's energy follows certain paths once it is captured by the green plants.
LEARNING EXPERIENCE	"MR. SUN'S RESTAURANT"
LEARNING OUTCOME	The student will be able to draw a picture of a food chain that has at least three links in it and show in the picture how the sun's energy flows from one link to the next.
CONCEPT COMPONENT	ENERGY LOSS
INSTRUCTIONAL OBJECTIVE	The student understands that as energy moves from the sun to plants and on to animals, much of it is lost.
LEARNING EXPERIENCE	"CHAIN GANG"
LEARNING OUTCOME	The student will be able to draw a picture of or list two living things that are losing energy and show how it happens.
COURSE GOAL	The student knows that the building materials of life must be used over and over.
CONCEPT	**CYCLES**
CONCEPT COMPONENT	AIR CYCLE
INSTRUCTIONAL OBJECTIVE	The student understands that the earth's limited supply of air is used over and over as plants and animals trade oxygen and carbon dioxide with one another.

LEARNING EXPERIENCE	"THE BEST DEAL ON EARTH"
LEARNING OUTCOME	The student will be able to draw a picture of two living things, each taking in and giving off two different components of the air, then label which component is being taken in and which is being given off by each living thing.
CONCEPT COMPONENT	WATER CYCLE
INSTRUCTIONAL OBJECTIVE	The student understands that water on the earth is moved by the heat of the sun through a great cycle, to be used over and over by living things.
LEARNING EXPERIENCE	"SUN'S BUCKET BRIGADE"
LEARNING OUTCOME	The student will be able to draw a picture of the water cycle which includes titles for at least three parts and illustrate the drawing with arrows showing the cycle's movement of water.
CONCEPT COMPONENT	SOIL CYCLE
INSTRUCTIONAL OBJECTIVE	The student understands that the soil provides plants with the nutrients which they need to grow, and that bacteria break down waste matter, returning these nutrients to the soil.
LEARNING EXPERIENCE	"CRADLES TO COFFINS"
LEARNING OUTCOME	The student will be able to draw a picture of something nearby that is taking nutrients out of the soil and something that is putting nutrients back, then label which is which.
COURSE GOAL	The student knows that differences in living things provide for the success of all life.
CONCEPT	**DIVERSITY**
CONCEPT COMPONENT	VARIETY AND SIMILARITY
INSTRUCTIONAL OBJECTIVE	The student understands that no two living things are alike.
LEARNING EXPERIENCE	"ROOT SELLER"
LEARNING OUTCOME	The student will be able to draw a picture showing how at least two different plants in an area are suited to different conditions of life and explain how this difference can help a community.

COURSE GOAL	The student knows that plants and animals live together in areas that meet their special needs.
CONCEPT	**COMMUNITY**
CONCEPT COMPONENT	HABITAT AND NICHE
INSTRUCTIONAL OBJECTIVE	The student understands that plants and animals can only live where the conditions are suited to them, and that each has its place and role in that area.
LEARNING EXPERIENCE	"ON THE STREET WHERE YOU LIVE"
LEARNING OUTCOME	The student will be able to list or draw a picture of four things living together in a natural community and then indicate the job of each living thing.
COURSE GOAL	The student knows that all living things interact with other things in their surroundings.
CONCEPT	**INTERRELATIONSHIPS**
CONCEPT COMPONENT	CO-OPERATION
INSTRUCTIONAL OBJECTIVE	The student understands that some plants and animals are related because they work together to meet their needs.
LEARNING EXPERIENCE	"MISSING PASSENGER HUNT"
LEARNING OUTCOME	The student will be able to draw a picture of or list two living things, working together and helping each other to survive, and to show how they cooperate with each other.
CONCEPT COMPONENT	COMPETITION
INSTRUCTIONAL OBJECTIVE	The student understands that some plants and animals compete for the same sunlight, water, or food.
LEARNING EXPERIENCE	"GUESS WHO'S COMING TO DINNER?"
LEARNING OUTCOME	The student will be able to draw a picture of either two plants or two animals competing for the same thing and indicate what they are competing for.

CONCEPT COMPONENT	DEPENDENCE
INSTRUCTIONAL OBJECTIVE	The student understands that all plants and animals are tied to other plants and animals because they depend on the others for something they need or something they cannot do for themselves.
LEARNING EXPERIENCE	"DECLARATION OF INTERDEPENDENCE"
LEARNING OUTCOME	The student will be able to show how two living things depend on each other.
COURSE GOAL	The student knows that everything is becoming something else.
CONCEPT	**CHANGE**
CONCEPT COMPONENT	ORIGINS AND TIME
INSTRUCTIONAL OBJECTIVE	The student understands that everything on the earth is changing over time, even though those changes are sometimes so slow that we cannot see them.
LEARNING EXPERIENCE	"SOIL SINKS"
LEARNING OUTCOME	The student will be able to describe or draw a picture of a change happening nearby which began a long time ago, and then label the change.
CONCEPT COMPONENT	STAGES
INSTRUCTIONAL OBJECTIVE	The student understands that everything is changing over time and that several stages of change can often be seen at the same moment.
LEARNING EXPERIENCE	"CLIFF HANGERS"
LEARNING OUTCOME	The student will be able to draw a picture of or list a series of changes happening nearby in which the first change is tied to the second, and the second to the third, then label each stage of the change.

COURSE GOAL	The student knows that in order to survive everything must fit how and where it lives.
CONCEPT	**ADAPTATION**
CONCEPT COMPONENT	PROBLEMS
INSTRUCTIONAL OBJECTIVE	The student understands that the shape and behavior of each kind of plant or animal is suited to the kinds of problems it must solve.
LEARNING EXPERIENCE	**"TOOLS AND TASKS"**
LEARNING OUTCOME	The student will be able to draw a picture of two living things that have different adaptations to solve the same problem, and title the picture with the problem.
CONCEPT COMPONENT	SOLUTIONS
INSTRUCTIONAL OBJECTIVE	The student understands that many kinds of plants and animals face the same problems in getting things they need, but often have different ways of solving them.
LEARNING EXPERIENCE	**"PEANUT PATCH"**
LEARNING OUTCOME	The student will be able to draw a picture of an animal or plant that has a special solution to obtain food or protect itself and then briefly describe how that solution works.

THE UNDERSTANDINGS

Concept Paths

Concept Path A

"Cradles to Coffins"

"On the Street Where You Live"

"Guess Who's Coming to Dinner?"

"Mr. Sun's Restaurant"

"Peanut Patch"

Concept Path B

"Declaration of Interdependence"

"Cliff Hangers"

"Food Factory"

"Sun's Bucket Brigade"

"Root Seller"

Concept Path C

"Missing Passenger Hunt"

"Tools and Tasks"

"Chain Gang"

"Soil Sinks"

"The Best Deal On Earth"

Interpretive Encounters

"Border Dispute"

Discovery Parties

"Lost Letters"

"Artists and Scientists"

Chapter Seven

CONCEPT PATHS

Jim and his crew of five youngsters are following a narrow path through the forest, eyes and ears alert for signs of fellow Sunship passengers.

They come upon a wooden box propped against the trunk of a tree just to the left of the trail. Lettered on the side of the box, in bright colors, are the words, "Energy Flow." Soon they will be seated in their places in "Mr. Sun's Restaurant," role playing plants and animals and learning about the different links of a food chain, an important understanding for the first concept in the story of life.

In the course of their three mornings at the Sunship Study Station, the crew members will have fifteen such stops to make as they follow the Concept Paths. They will attend a funeral for a fallen leaf and throw a birthday party for a new plant. They will be detectives, census takers, mice and coyotes, guests at a banquet, algae, grasshoppers, snakes, hawks, squirrels, moss, and grass.

They will use binoculars to scan tree branches, look through magnifying glasses to scrutinize a beetle or a lichen, search for a "missing passenger," ring bells, wear gas masks, put on thumbless gloves, eat peanuts, climb a steep ramp, crawl through a tunnel to the inside of a "leaf," carry water in leaky buckets, stand under umbrellas, and squeeze sponges. They will wash their hands in rich, moist soil and taste clear, cold water from a spring. They will encounter King Snoid and his edicts and meet a Root Seller with his bag of tricks. They will take a ride on the air cycle and visit a time machine. And they will crawl on the ground, gaze at the clouds, and peer into hollow trees. They will shout with excitement, whisper in amazement, and laugh for joy. That's what the activities on the concept paths are like. They use stories, props, role playing, and special tasks and challenges to demonstrate the seven key concepts: energy flow, cycles, diversity, community, interrelationships, change, and adaptation.

Each concept station has a prop box, with cue cards for the leader and equipment for an activity that relates to one of the seven concepts. The activities start with concrete examples and proceed to more abstract ideas. Each is only about twenty minutes long, and there are five stations on each path.

In between stations, the group is alert for "passenger sightings" and "discoveries" for their logs. Walking from the site for one activity to the next, the leaders emphasize general awareness of fellow passengers and their roles on the sunship. This emphasis helps provide a natural flow between stops, as well as offering numerous opportunities for the kids to apply their new concept understandings.

The most important thing about the Concept Paths is that the activities, not the leaders, convey the concepts. The activities are fun, as the kids' reactions on the following pages will demonstrate.

CONCEPT ACTIVITY LOCATION CHART

Concept	Component	Activity	Location
Energy Flow	capture	Food Factory	B-3
	paths	Mr. Sun's Restaurant	A-4
	loss	Chain Gang	C-3
Cycles	air	The Best Deal on Earth	C-5
	water	Sun's Bucket Brigade	B-4
	soil	Cradles to Coffins	A-1
Diversity	variety and similarity	Root Seller	B-5
Community	homes and roles	On the Street Where You Live	A-2
Interrelationships	competing	Guess Who's Coming to Dinner	A-3
	co-operating	Missing Passenger Hunt	C-1
	depending	Declaration of Interde-pendence	B-1
Change	origins and time	Soil Sinks	C-4
	stages	Cliff Hangers	B-2
Adaptation	problems	Tools and Tasks	C-2
	solutions	Peanut Patch	A-5

CONCEPT PATH A

A-1   "CRADLES TO COFFINS"

It is the first morning for the concept paths. Jim has met his group at the beginning of their path for the day. He signals them to be silent and, without talking himself, motions for them to fall in line behind him.

After a brief walk, he begins speaking, somewhat mysteriously.

"We have a very sad job to do first thing today—that's why I haven't said anything yet. But I guess I'd better let you know what you're in for."

"Uh-oh, we have to dig latrines."

"No, Judy, but that really isn't too far off. You already know that this morning you'll be going to five stations—this will be one of them. The first thing we should do is get out our passports. Let's see, who wants to read what it says at the top of page eight?"

"I will."

"O.K., Bobby, go ahead."

"THE BUILDING MATERIALS OF LIFE MUST BE USED OVER AND OVER."

"And what about the paragraph below the box?"

"Our sunship's soil provides plants with the nutrients which they need to grow. The soil would soon be useless if there were no way of getting back these nutrients once they had been taken in by the plants. But there are millions of bacteria in each handful of soil that make these nutrients available to be used again. The bacteria break down waste matter and dead plants and animals to return the nutrients which those things contained back to the soil."

"Thanks. There's one problem though. Before things can be recycled they have to die. In fact, such a thing has happened here, and, unfortunately, I have to take all of you to a very sad spot. So I want everybody to put on a sorrowful face and follow me in respectful silence. No smiling; this is *serious* business."

A few snickers are heard from the rear of the line. Jim turns and in a hurt tone admonishes his procession: "Please, *please*, this spot we are going to is a solemn place; we must have respect."

After a short walk through dense forest, the group emerges in a sunlit clearing. At one end, surrounded by a split rail fence, there is a small graveyard full of tiny wooden tombstones.

"What's this?" asks Dick, with no respect in his voice at all. "A burial ground for elves?"

"Oh, no!" moans Jim. "As a matter of fact, a great many deaths happened right here last fall. All around us, the ground was littered with the victims. See, some of them are still lying around out in the open. These leaves were once living things, and now that they've passed their time, they are just left to lie here."

"So I bet you're going to expect us to give these leaves a burial, right?"

"Ah, Dick, you've got it. I'd like all of you to go out and find one dead leaf which looks special to you and give it a name. Then come

on back and we'll see what happens next. Head out slowly now, not too fast, because this is a serious affair. Slowly slide your feet along the ground and hang your heads in mourning, like this.''

The kids begin to get into the funereal atmosphere. An occasional wail is heard as they all drift back with leaves gingerly held in outstretched hands.

"O.K. Do all the leaves have names? Good! Some of you may have been to a funeral, and if you have you know that we never lay people to rest without saying a few good words about them. So, everybody think of one good thing which your leaf did during its life and we'll prepare for the funeral.

"Ready? We need a couple of volunteers over here, someone to hold the coffin while we place our leaves in it and a gravedigger to dig us a good grave.

"O.K., fine. Now our gravedigger will put his leaf in the casket first so he can go dig the grave while the rest of us finish. Dick, go ahead, tell us your leaf's name and say a nice word about it.''

"Well, this is Mergatroid Q. Leaf, and, uh, I don't know, she gave us a shady spot to sit under."

"Excellent, that's very moving. Judy, what about your departed friend there? It looks like only the skeleton remains.''

"This is old Lady Leafy. She was a very sweet lady and throughout her life, she gave us oxygen."

"Hey, that's great! Can you two go dig us a grave about 6 x 6? Inches, that is. And now let's hear from the rest of you."

"Well, this is Laverne the Fern and she gave food to thousands of stray caterpillars. Goodbye, Laverne, wahhhh."

Bigfoot the Maple and Blechh the Rotten are added in due order and then the group heads over to the completed grave.

"Good job on the grave," Jim says, thanking the gravediggers. "Now, before we lay our deceased to rest, let's enter their names on this tombstone. You can abbreviate if you want, and we'll use only one side."

Someone suggests that R.I.P. should be written at the top.

"No, no, no, I've got a better idea! Let's put D.I.P. on the top. Decompose in Peace."

"Thank you, Johnny. You're very thoughtful.

"All right, now, let's all place our leaves in the grave. You may cry if you must; don't be embarrassed. They're off to leaf heaven, you know. Hey, by the way, where is leaf heaven? I wonder what's going to happen to these leaves now that they're dead?"

"Well, maybe they're going to go up in the sky somewhere."

"Ha, they're going to rot and go back into the soil."

"Oh, yeah, what a way to go."

"Well, are we all ready to bid them adieu? WAIT A MINUTE! Let's hold it just a minute! We're all so sad and this is spring, right? Spring isn't supposed to be a sad time."

"No, spring is a happy time, and we're all sitting here bawling."

"That's true. In fact, spring is a time of new growth. Let's try one more thing before we fill in the grave. Everybody go out and find the source of life and growth. Find a seed and give *IT* a name; then come on back."

They disperse and return, each gingerly holding a tiny seed.

"Now, we should find a good place to plant these seeds. Let's figure out what to look for."

"They'll need a sunny spot."

"Yeah, and they'll need lots of water and good soil."

"Hey, how about putting them in the cemetery? There's lots of fertilizer in there."

"Far out! Put it right over my Laverne's dead body."

"She'll be pushing up daisies."

Jim's overwhelmed. "You mean to say a cemetery can be a garden?"

"Yeah, sure."

"Then a funeral can be a party. *And,* it just so happens that in this surprise package here I have just what we need to turn this funeral into a birthday party!"

Pulling out an assortment of party hats and noisemakers, Jim suggests, "Let's sing 'Happy Birthday' as we plant our seeds in the grave with our dead friends. Now, Judy, slowly fill in the grave for us."

A great chorus fills the air as an imaginary cake is brought in and the candles are blown out. Jim asks, "Shall we fill in the other side of our tombstone with our seeds' names? Wait a minute, do we have a tombstone or a birth certificate?''

"It's both!"

"How about the grave, do we call it a cradle or a coffin?''

"It's a cradleoffin."

"No, it's a coffle."

"I know, it's a crawfin."

"Then the end of our leaves is really like a beginning for our seeds. Since the leaf is being broken down by the bacteria in the soil, its nutrients can be used again by another plant. It's not rotting, just recycling. Remember that first line in your passport: THE BUILDING MATERIALS OF LIFE MUST BE USED OVER AND OVER. In fact, pull our your passports and turn back to the page that has to do with this idea. There's a task there which we need to complete. Take a minute and read that first paragraph again, and then go out and find an example around here of the cycle we've just seen and for which we've sung 'Happy Birthday.' When everybody's finished we'll all come back here and share our ideas, and then I'll stamp everyone's passport for this station.''

A-2   **"ON THE STREET WHERE YOU LIVE"**

On the way to the next station, Jim stops a moment and tells the youngsters more about the passport stamps which correspond to the letters in the EC-DC-IC-A formula. He explains that they will be going to five stations something like the first one every morning for three mornings during their stay. Each station has something to do with one of the concepts represented in the formula. But since there are only seven letters, some of the stations deal with parts of the same concept. Although there are fifteen stations, seven different stamps will cover them all. As they walk along, Jim has the kids stop and look around.

"You know, even though we're going to these five special places each morning, some of the best stuff we'll be seeing and doing doesn't earn a stamp at all. In fact, some of the greatest things we'll experience are the things you and I won't have any idea about before they happen.

"That's why we carry these," he says, indicating his binoculars. "They're to remind us to always keep our eyes open on these 'walking stations' so we can get to know some of the other passengers on the sunship. Tomorrow, you'll have a couple of instant cameras per group and Thursday you'll be carrying a whole bunch of things: nets, magnifying glasses, and some amazing little boxes which make bugs look like the wildest monsters you could ever imagine.

"Whenever we see a passenger during the morning, you can go back to the dining hall later and find a picture of that passenger in our big pile of 'Mug Shots,' and then put its picture on our 'Passengers Mural' for this area. I think this will make a lot more sense after our next station, so let's go. But as we go, let's keep our senses on alert; you never know when something may turn up."

Sure enough, something turns up, but it isn't exactly what the kids had in mind, and it is *planned*. Just as the group rounds the bend leading into a park-like area of the forest with a spectacular view of the valley below, they come upon a large sign. In an area which is clearly set apart from the neighboring natural vegetation, there are myriads of ribbon-bedecked surveyor's stakes. The stakes apparently mark out the courses of planned roads within the housing development which the sign announces:

**COMING SOON TO THIS UNIMPROVED ACREAGE
THE UTMOST IN MODERN HOUSING**

A full service community will soon offer people with adequate resources the opportunity to enjoy these previously **undeveloped** and **unused** recreation sites.

"What in the world is this?" asks a shocked Sally. *"I thought we were still at the Sunship Study Station."*

"We were until right this minute when we rounded the bend. We just rent this land and the guy who owns it has some plans for this 'unused acreage.' Of course, people need a place to live, too, but sometimes we don't do a very good job of finding out what is already going on in a place before we build. We'll be taking a closer look at the situation though. Our next station is right here where we're standing. Let's have a look at the key idea and sunship understanding in our passports before we get going. I think we can get a better idea of what we'll be looking for."

Once the group has gone through the passport entries, the leader pulls out of the prop box an assortment of clipboards and "census taker" badges. He explains that there is one thing the group can do in order to have an influence on this developer's plans. They must go and find out just what is going on in this area already. Who lives here? Where do they live? What do they do? The kids will in effect be census takers trying to glean as much information as possible about the inhabitants and their "jobs" in this community.

Each kid in the group is given, along with an official census taker badge, a clipboard which holds the COMMUNITY TALLY SHEET:

Plant/Animal Description	Job or Role	Home address (check one)		
		Basement	Street Level	High Rise

On the back of the sheet, there is a list of community job descriptions which the group is likely to find in its search:

Aerators: Animals which help keep the soil loose so that water can flow more easily and plants can grow.

Garbage Men: Animals which help the community by removing or breaking down dead materials.

Food Producers: Living things in the community which can take in the sun's energy and turn it into energy forms which other residents can eat.

Soil Builders: Plants which are breaking down rocks into finer pieces which will then become part of the soil.

Transporters: Animals which move things from one part of the community to another part. Seeds often ride with these transporters.

Air Conditioners: Things which make the air breathable for others in the community.

Population Controllers: Animals which help control the numbers of residents in the community so that it doesn't get too crowded.

Fertilizers: Community dwellers who help make the soil a better place to grow by adding wastes or reworking the materials.

The group makes a quick run through the definitions and where these job holders might be found. The leader points out the "Home Address" column, and the kids think of a few examples of plants and animals who might live at the different "levels."

The crew is now approaching readiness. Looking over the area someone notices that some of the surveyor's stakes have signs on them. Closer examination of a nearby sign leads to the discovery that it names the street which has been laid out by the builder. The sign the group is circled around reads "Blue Jay Way." A quick exploration of other signs would disclose more streets named after animals: Squirrel Street, Millipede Mile, Sparrow Circle, Amphibian Avenue, Aphid Alley, Tree Frog Terrace, and even the Mole Transit Authority.

Jim explains, "If you look under the tally sheet on your clipboard, you'll see that there's a map with all the street names on it. Every time we find something and put it on our sheet, we can draw an 'X' at the place on the map where we found the resident."

"X marks the spot."

"X marks the spot. And finally, some of these spots will be especially important, too."

Jim then pulls out a sample of a special sign on a long stake. He uses "Caution: Soil Builder at Work" to illustrate the role of these "warning signs" in the overall plan. Jim explains that he will be placing them wherever there are particularly good demonstrations of community projects in progress and jobs being done. The kids can watch for these spots to help them in completing their census. Other signs to be placed along the streets of the community include:

Caution: Soil plowing in progress.
Caution: Seed transporter crossing.
Caution: Air being conditioned.
Caution: Garbage being disposed of here.
Caution: Food factory in operation.

Finally, Jim will have several blank signs for the unexpected community improvement projects kids are bound to come up with.

Tools in hand, the corps of census takers is off to the field. It's not long before a problem has arisen: what to do with residents who are moonlighting on a second, or third, job. The consensus is that they should definitely be credited for their industrious nature. Many sheets begin to show inhabitants with much to offer to the community. Not one is found without a job—zero unemployment. In fact, new jobs soon surface which weren't covered on the sheet.

Even the mosquito is providing food for some segment of society.

Since the kids all sampled different streets, the tallies are soon in. The group meets to look over the results. The notion that nothing is happening in this area appears rather absurd now. A look at the variety of jobs and at how well they are filled leads the kids to the conclusion that perhaps the future inhabitants of these prime sites could learn a few things from the natives.

Standing in front of the billboard where the group began, Jim sums up the importance of their work: "Now that we've seen how many living things already have homes in this community and have examined the important roles they play, I have a suggestion for this developer." Turning the billboard over he reveals a new, simple advertisement:

> SURE, MORE COMMUNITIES NEED TO BE BUILT
> BUT LOOK BEFORE YOU LEAP
> YOU COULD LEARN A LOT FROM A COMMUNITY
> YOU DIDN'T EVEN SEE.

A-3   "GUESS WHO'S COMING TO DINNER"

After leaving "On the Street Where You Live," Jim's group was having a little trouble following their map to the next station, but nobody was the least bit concerned since their route at the time closely paralleled that of a beautiful orange and black bird. In fact, the kids were so deeply involved in the task of focusing their binoculars that when it finally flew off, they were surprised to find themselves so near their goal, the next station's prop box.

"Guess who's coming to dinner, friends?" Jim asks out of the blue.

"*Grandpa?*"

"No, *you're all* coming to dinner. Except for one of you, that person's going to *be* dinner."

"*What?*"

"*I nominate John.*"

"*No one's going to eat me!*"

"Hold on, take it easy. We've got a little game to play here, but first, as usual, let's have a look at the passports."

The station, "Guess Who's Coming to Dinner," deals with the aspect of competition in interrelationships. The kids are informed that in this area, as in all areas, there is a limited amount of food relative to the number of customers.

"In this case we are dealing with an unusually large number of coyotes who are competing for one mouse. Interestingly enough, the consumers are not discriminating in their tastes, but the mouse is. In fact, this mouse is such a connoisseur of predators that he is going to conduct a panel interview to see just who is most qualified to eat *him*. None but the best, of course."

The group leader is to play the role of mouse for the first round of action. He explains that he realizes that the competition among coyotes is intense and that they must be very hungry. But he would like to hear from each in turn just what it is that makes them better than their competitors and therefore more likely to succeed in catching the mouse and satisfying their own hunger. Throughout the interview the "mouse" stresses comparisons between the competing coyotes, thus reinforcing the notion that the interaction in this case is chiefly between competitors and is caused by their common need for the same meal.

"Well, yes, Dick Coyote. I do recognize your great speed and quickness. But, I must admit that I was very impressed by Judy's statement that she would be able to hide during her attack because she's so well camouflaged by her brown sweater. I'm sure you can both understand my position. Only one of you will be able to eat me, and *I* can afford to be finicky. You two are the competitors, and the winner will be the better all-around hunter. Talk is cheap. Your actions will decide."

Once all coyotes have had a chance to present their case, the rules of the game are explained. The winner of the game—the coyote who gets the mouse—will be in the "enviable" position of mouse for the next round.

In the next round, the mouse occupies a central position in a semi-wooded area. Sporting his mouse ears and tail, he can move in a limited space only, in this case along the top of a fallen log. The game is begun when the mouse counts to twenty-five with his eyes closed while the coyotes take up their opening positions, which should be well hidden and at a safe distance from the mouse. Once the mouse reaches twenty-five, the coyotes may begin sneaking in toward their prey. The attack is not completely straightforward, however. Several bells are placed on trees, fallen logs, shrubs, and in other strategic locations along the perimeter of an imaginary circle around the mouse. These are placed in such a way as to be invisible from the inside of the circle, which includes the mouse. They *are* visible to the coyotes outside the circle, who are busily involved in secretly assaulting the mouse from afar.

The purpose of the bells is to accent the importance of cleverness in competition. The coyotes are instructed that even though their overall goal is to be the first to tag the mouse, none may make this move until one of the bells is rung. Any coyote who is spotted by the mouse before the bell is rung is immediately out of the competition and dies of starvation. However, when the bell is rung, it indicates that the coyotes have caught the mouse's scent and he can no longer get away even if he does spot them.

The average coyote will recognize that it is a distinct advantage to be the first to sneak up to a bell, ring it, and get the jump on his competitors. The above-average coyote will recognize that cleverness is even more important than sneakiness. In fact, the truly successful coyote is the one who sneaks in as close as possible to the mouse, disregarding the bells. When another, less cunning coyote rings the bell, the crafty competitor is then within easy striking distance. Naturally, the directions to the players are structured so as to avoid revealing this variable; it must be discovered.

All of those traits which are beneficial to competitive interaction are then reinforced in panel interviews conducted by each winning coyote-turned-mouse. The rounds are continued until the main factors of cleverness, coloration, quickness, and quietness are all discovered, or until time intervenes with the arrival of the following group.

A-4   "MR. SUN'S RESTAURANT"

Jim's group has found a large snake.

"Wow! This has to be one of the best passengers we've seen all morning. The birds are neat, but you can't get this close to them. He's a big fellow, too. Let's add him to our 'On the Street Where You Live' census."

"He'd be a street level dweller."

"He's a fertilizer for sure."

"So—just about everybody's that. I think he's a population controller, too."

"We'll have a chance a little later to place him in a pattern that's important to his life, something called a 'food chain.' For the moment though, since it's a bit far to Mr. Sun's Restaurant—we have reservations for just a few minutes from now—I think we'd better let this passenger get back to his own job in his own community."

"Yeah. Let him go!"

"There he goes. Wow, he sure can move!"

"Let's have a look at the map so we can move along to our next spot. We have quite a banquet in store, *if* we can find out how to get to the banquet table."

The group leaves the trail and emerges in a small clearing, where they find the box of station materials.

"What's that red and white thing behind the bushes over there?"

"Whoa! Wait a minute. That's a table for the special banquet, but we have to figure out a little something about how banquets work out here in the woods before we can seat ourselves at *that* table. Actually, getting seated at the table is a whole lot trickier than you might think. Somebody read us the key idea from the passport so we can get started."

"THE SUN IS THE SOURCE OF ENERGY FOR ALL LIVING THINGS."

"Once it is captured by green plants, the sun's energy follows certain paths. Some animals must eat the sun-fed plants to get energy for themselves. Other animals must eat these plant-eating animals to get their energy. The path that energy takes from the sun to the plants, then to the animals, is called a food chain."

"So that's what you meant about the snake being in a food chain."

"Sure is, and it's a big hint for the game you're about to play. Here's the way this game works. We're all trying to get into a place called Mr. Sun's Restaurant for a great banquet. But the person who is the head of this banquet is very fussy about who gets in.

"Is that Mr. Sun?"

"No, he feeds everybody. This is somebody, or something, else. What we need to do now is get ourselves in order for the great procession which leads to the banquet hall. It's a bit tricky because we aren't going to be able to say a single word. We have to have a silence befitting the occasion, you know.

"In a minute, I'm going to pass out a bunch of cards, one to each person. Each card will have the name of a plant or animal on it. Our job is to line up in the order that these plants and animals will be entering the banquet. And since they're all in the same food chain, the banquet order will be the order of who eats whom."

That doesn't sound too hard. You mean all we have to do is figure out which animal eats what?"

"Well, so far, but here comes the catch. You won't know which plant or animal *you* are. Since you'll put your card up on your forehead like this, everybody will be able to see it and know who you are, except you." Jim holds the card with one finger against his forehead with the name facing out.

"The trick is to figure out where you belong by reading everyone else's cards and looking for a gap you might fill. When the line is formed, since I'm at the beginning of the chain, I'll say, 'I am the sun and I give my energy to . . . ' whoever or whatever is next in line. That person may still not know what card she has until my announcement. She might just know what other animals were on either side of her in the food chain. Anyway, then she will say, 'I am the_____'—whatever card she has—'and I give my energy, which I got from the sun, to the_____,' whoever is next in line. Do you think we can pull it off?"

"Sounds pretty easy to me."

"That's what they all say. Okay, let's give it a try. Whatever you do, don't look at your own card." Jim fans the cards out like a magician, saying "Pick a card, any card. Once you take your card, your lips are sealed. Remember, we want to line up in the order in which these animals eat each other. When we get it right, these cards will be our tickets to the banquet."

All lips are sealed except for an occasional outbreak of laughter as the participants realize the comical nature of their predicament and experience the frustration of trying to line up their comrades, all of whom seem so unbelievably confused all of a sudden. Because he's the sun, Jim has it easy—he goes right to one spot and signals the rest of the group where the lineup should occur as soon as they've got things figured out.

The kids are finding it pretty tough right from the start. You can just see the wheels of the "grasshopper" silently turning: (*All right, this should be easy. There's the Sun—Jim, he doesn't have to do anything. Then there's Helene, she's grass. She must come next to Jim; grass needs Sun to grow. Now, who's gonna come next to Helene? There's Dick, what's he? Oh geez, he's a frog. What do frogs eat? Not grass, I don't think. What else is there? Bobby's a snake, hmm, snakes eat frogs . . . I think. O.K., one left and that's a hawk. Grass, frog, hawk, and snake. No, grass-frog-snake-hawk. Judy's trying to organize everything as usual. She wants to put me in between the grass and the snake, but wait, what about the frog?*) "What . . . " (*Oh, yeah, got to be quiet. I think I must be some animal that eats grass . . . "*)

The wheels keep turning, only now other people's wheels are starting to turn in the same direction. Judy, the hawk, is still having some trouble: (*Every space seems to be full right up the line. I suppose I might fit between the grasshopper and the frog. No, I bet I eat everybody. Yeah, now they're putting me at the head of the line. I must be the top. Ah, and there goes Jim; he's starting off the announcements.*)

"I am the sun and I shine down on the grass and give it the sunlight energy it needs to grow."

"*I am the grass and I give my energy to the grasshopper after I get it from the sun.*"

(*Ha, I knew I was going to be some little thing like an insect, but I didn't think I was going to be a grasshopper! What do I say? Oh, yeah.*) "*I am the grasshopper and I take the energy which I get from the grass and give it to the frog!*"

"Ribbit! *I am the frog and I take energy which I got from the grasshopper and give it to the snake.*"

"*I am the snake. I take energy from the frog and give it to the hawk.*"

"*Wow, a hawk! I take energy from the snake and I—I guess I don't give it to anybody. Right?*"

"You're the top, Judy. But you still get the energy from me, the sun, way over here at the very beginning of things. *And* everybody all the way up the line is just as important to you, and all of us really."

"*Yeah, don't get too bigheaded up there at the top, hawk.*"

"Well, crew, it looks like we're ready to move into the banquet hall. Let's go on in and you'll be able to see what our next problem looks like." Upon entering the "hall" the crew members find themselves in a small hollow completely surrounded by blackberry bushes. A triangular table stands in the center of the area, covered with a red checked tablecloth. It is four feet wide at the broad end, narrowing to a point eight feet away. It is divided into five sections, the largest at the base and the smallest at the apex. Thirty-five plates in orange, brown, green, blue, and gray cover the table in no apparent order. There are more of some colors than others, although that might not be noticed right away. The colors chosen are the same as those on the cards used in the game just completed.

Jim starts off: "Our job is to set the table properly for this banquet. Since my food chain card or ticket is brown, I'll take my place down here at the small end of the table where there's a brown plate, and then I'll give you a few clues for our seating arrangement at this banquet. This time, I'm at the top of the food chain, and it's up to you to reorganize these plates in an order that makes it possible for me to get the energy I need in more or less the same way we saw in our first food chain. I can't get it straight from Mr. Sun, so I'm counting on you all."

"*How are we supposed to figure out where everything goes when there are so many and they're scattered all over the place?*" asks Dick.

"Hold on. There's a couple of other things you need to know which will help you. First and foremost, the game we just played outside the banquet hall was more important than I let on. Actually, you're all going to be representatives for a bunch of other living things who couldn't make it to this meal. That's why there are so many plates. We must set this table for all the plants and animals in a food chain, even though only a few could make it."

"Where are the rest of them?"

"I think they got lost on the way from the airport."

"No, really."

"Don't really know, Helene. All I know is you folks have to take their place. Now, some of you will be representing more plants or animals than others (and this is a big hint); as you can see, there are more plates at one end of this table than at the other. There's a plate here for each living thing in the chain, and all plants or animals of the same kind have the same color of plates."

"So that means if I have an orange ticket here, there are two animals that I am representing?"

"Exactly, and that's what you need to know in order to figure out where you are in the order of who eats whom in this banquet. My card is brown, so I'm at the top, and I've got only one brown plate. I also happen to be a big and hungry bear. See, it says 'bear' right on the bottom of my plate."

"Hey, let's look at the bottom of our plates!"

"Hold it. We'll check that after we get the order fixed. One last clue. Listen very closely. *Bigger animals have bigger appetites.*"

"So, that's nothing new."

"Aha, yes it is, because it means they have to have more of the smaller things they eat in order to stay alive. And here's my last comment: Fee-Fi-Fo-Fum, I wonder where my meal comes from," bellows Jim.

Judy, who is now the lowest organism on this food chain, has the gray card. She is befuddled by the vast number of gray plates on the table, sixteen in all. *"Wow, I sure have a lot of plates."*

"Bigger animals have bigger appetites," Jim repeats. "Fee-Fi-Fo-Fum, I wonder where my meal comes from."

"I've got green plates, and there's only eight of them. This table gets smaller as it goes up towards Jim, I mean the bear. There sure isn't going to be as much room for plates at his end of the table. Let's start moving plates around and see what happens. Can the rows of plates be in any direction?"

"No," Jim explains, "they've got to go between the lines on the table."

Dick cuts in with a sudden outburst, *"Hold it just a second. There are no yellow plates on this table! I've got no plates to set."*

"Yeah, you know something else, there's only four stools here too, not counting the one that big bear is on. Somebody's not going to get a seat. It must be Dick, since he doesn't have any plates, either."

"Fee-Fi-Fo-Fum, I wonder where my meal comes from."

"Whew, we better get going. He's getting hungrier."

"Listen, the table gets smaller and what did he say, there's more animals at one end of the food chain."

"Yeah, and he's a big animal and he's at the small end of the table. Judy, what happens if you line up your plates at the big end of the table, between those first two lines? How do they fit?"

Judy arranges her many plates, and lo and behold, they fit perfectly in the first section at the wide end of the table.

"Who's got the next most plates?"

"I guess I do; anybody got more than eight? I'll see if they fit in that next area in front of the next stool." They do and Helene sits down.

"So there are sixteen things at the end of the table, then eight . . ."

"Who's got four animals' plates?"

"That must be me, and they fit right here."

"And there's just room for my two plates down here. I must be right next to the big bear. That could be interesting."

"So you've all got places in this food chain and your number of plates or animals gets smaller and smaller as you come down to my end."

"Yeah, except for me. This is a bummer," complains Dick.

"Well, Dick, you never know in this banquet business. I'm still pretty hungry, I may just eat everybody but you. I think it's about time to find out who our mystery guests are, and to see whether they've got themselves organized in another food chain that works. There sure are more at the beginning of the food chain than there are down here, which is the way it should be."

The plates are flipped, and sure enough, the algae is eaten by the water insects, who are eaten by the minnows, who are in turn eaten by the salmon, who is finally eaten by the big bear, Jim.

"Sure are a lot of algae plants in this food chain."

"Right. An insect could not live on just one alga per day—each link in the chain depends on having a greater number of living things to feed upon."

"What about the sun? I thought you said we were trying to get the energy from the sun to you, the bear?"

"Ah, the sun. And since this is Mr. Sun's Restaurant, what a shame! Well, we can't very well have a banquet without Mr. Sun's light. After all, THE SUN IS THE SOURCE OF ENERGY FOR ALL LIVING THINGS. Dick, you've been waiting patiently after being apparently left out, but it's no mistake that your card is yellow. In fact, we're going to ask you to play the most important role in this banquet, Mr. Sun himself. Here's your yellow Mr. Sun chef hat, and here, behind the bushes, is your honored seat. We'll just place this tall chair at the wide end of the table down there opposite me. You're the beginning of this banquet which works all the way down through lots of plants, fewer plant eaters, fewer small plant-eater-eaters, and finally down to one big, hungry plant-eater-eater-eater, namely, . . . me. Let's have a round of applause for Mr. Sun."

A-5   "PEANUT PATCH"

Walking between stations, Jim comments that it has been a great morning for bird-watching. "We sure have seen a lot of neat 'fellow passengers' today."

"Yeah, I sure never thought that all birds looked so different. I always thought a bird was a bird."

"These binocs are dynamite. I'm gonna borrow my dad's when I get back and check things out in the woods behind our house. We never use them for anything besides looking at football games."

"Binoculars are great. Say, remind me at lunch and we'll go through that pile of pictures we have in the dining room and put the pictures of the birds we've seen up on the mural. That mural's going to be mighty full this week, with all the airborne passengers passing through on their way up north. I'll bet we've seen more birds than any earlier group."

"Is there a picture of a deer, too?"

"There sure is, a big buck. You know, though, the most amazing thing is that we haven't seen one squirrel all morning. In fact, I think it's so amazing that I'm going to give all of you a chance to *be* squirrels right now. We've just got time to go to one more station before we head back. This is a good station to do last, too. We've seen a lot of different animals this morning. They're all so different because they've got different ways of meeting their needs. If any of you are hungry, we may help you meet that need real soon. It depends on how well you're adapted."

The group runs through the passport entries on adaptation, puts away the passports, then takes seats on a well-worn log.

"All of you have a look at your thumbs."

"Thumbs?"

"That's right. Nothing special about them, is there? Just ordinary thumbs."

"Yep, ordinary thumbs. They've been there as long as I can remember."

"O.K. Now I have a little task for everyone to do, and as you do it, you have to really pay attention to your thumbs."

Jim now pulls a cloth sack out of the prop box and begins tossing peanuts slowly to each of the kids. "Watch the thumbs, watch those thumbs!"

"They're curling around the peanuts. They're what's grabbing the peanut."

"Good, you all pass the thumb test, so we'll start to make things a bit trickier. Remember I said everybody was going to get a chance to be squirrels this morning? Well, the transformation takes a while, but the first step is going to happen right now."

The "Peanut Patch" activity deals with the variety of adaptations. The adaptations of humans and squirrels in relation to the same problem are compared .

At this point the leader will pull out of the prop box an assortment of gloves, all of which have had their thumbs cut off and sewn shut. The kids will be instructed to put them on backwards with their thumbs pressed across their palms. As they lose the human adaptation of grasping thumbs, they begin their transformation into squirrels.

The leader then throws peanuts to each person just as he did before they lost their thumbs. The importance of the thumb in catching quickly becomes apparent.

The squirrel metamorphosis continues as an invisible "magic mask" is passed out to all the kids. This mask will enable them to make the changeover to squirrels more smoothly without feeling the last bit worried about how they look to the rest of the group. Living proof is offered as the leader dons a mask himself (with great ceremony) and immediately begins hopping around on all fours making suspiciously squirrel-like chipping sounds. The transformation is complete.

Now it's the kids' turn. The leader quickly assembles the group in a circle so a few points can be explained.

"Now listen, folks; we're squirrels, right?"

"Chip, chip, chip."

"Good. Thank you. We spend most of our time gathering food, but we have no thumbs. 'TO SURVIVE, EVERYTHING MUST FIT HOW AND WHERE IT LIVES.' Therefore we must have some *adaptation* which will help us to survive in our food-gathering role. I'm going to scatter out some peanuts here, and whoever among us are the best squirrels with the most squirrel-like adaptations are going to be the most successful nut gatherers. One other thing to remember: squirrels are not only nut gatherers, they are nut eaters. Go—and *no* thumbs."

Buck-toothed kids have never had it so good as the adaptations begin to surface. Various storage possibilities are attempted, but (perhaps through a subtle leader example) cheek pouches are soon a common characteristic of Tuesday morning squirrels.

After the "props" have been consumed, Jim asks Bobby to read from his passport the task which each of them must complete before they can receive their stamps.

"O.K., just a second . . . 'Draw a picture or name an animal or plant around here that has a special solution for getting food or protecting itself. In one line describe how the "special solution" works.'"

"Thanks, Bobby. O.K., group, if you take a look at the top of that page, you'll see that this sunship understanding has something to do with the last item in the EC-DC-IC-A formula. In fact, this understanding is one of the most important parts of the story of life. So it's important that we really know how this idea works. Before you start looking for your examples, you might read over the passport explanation again and think about what we just did. Give a holler if you need some help."

CONCEPT PATHS—
GENERAL GUIDELINES

Passport Presentations

+On Tuesday morning everyone reports to the Rec Hall thirty minutes before the opening of the Concept Paths. A new sign has been placed over the main door: "Passport Office." Inside, other signs are posted on the tables and nearby pillars:

> "Passports are Non-transferrable"
> "Keep Your Passports in a Safe Place"
> "Only Sunship Earth Citizens are Eligible for Passports"
> "Keep Your Passports Protected from Water, Wind, and Loss"

+Three groups of tables are set up and manned by visored clerks (counselors) to process and present the passports.

TABLES

Group One   1. Students give their names to the clerks.
2. Completed "Passport Applications" are pulled from the file and stamped RECEIVED (plus the date).
3. The passports are issued, then the students roll their index fingers on an ink pad and press their prints in a special box on the passports.

Group Two   4. Clerks ask the students to sign their official signature on the passports and write in their teachers' name and the schools they attend.

Group Three 5. Clerks use a corporate embosser to imprint the Sunship seal on the first page of the passports, notarizing them as official documents.

+When all passports have been issued, the three station leaders meet with their respective classes and explain how the passports work. Afterward they lead their groups to the beginning of the first Concept Path.
+Each morning at the beginning of the path a station leader briefly describes the concepts the class will be working on for the day, then divides them up into groups of five and assigns them a crew counselor or guide.
+Props: Tables, ink pads, file boxes, pencils, visor caps, passport office signs, sunship seal embosser, passport applications.

Setting Up the Paths

+Try to arrange your Concept Paths so that each one goes through a different community. (Consider the possibilities for a water-based community, too.) If you are using the paths with a large number of groups over a long period of time, you may want to include clearings surfaced with bark chips for the concept stations. (Be sure to place each station near some good examples of the concept it is dealing with, e.g., a nurse log or stump near "Cradles to Coffins.")

Prop Boxes

+Each station should have its own prop box. The boxes should be durable, weatherproof, and large enough to contain the station's props, pencils, stamp and pad, and cue cards. (You may want to have locks for them.) Stencil or paint on the side of each box the name of the station's key concept and on the lid the key concept statement.

+To make the box stormproof, and thus prevent saturated ink pads and props, the last group of the day should cover it with a piece of heavy-duty canvas.

+Rubber stamps should be secured to the prop boxes. (Insert screw eyes in the handles of each one and attach cords.)

+The prop box should be located near the spot where the station's introduction is given. The box might be mounted on a post or stand, or set on a convenient stump.

Cue Cards

+Prior to guiding groups through the Touch the Earth activities and the Concept Paths, the crew counselors are led through each activity playing the role of the fifth grader, while the station leader plays the role of the counselor. The staff acquires familiarity with the station by this process (learning by doing).

+In addition to such participation, the counselors should become familiar with the "Cue Cards."

+Cue cards are important aids to the crew counselor, who in many situations has a limited amount of time available for training and spends only one week at the study station. Each activity comes with a set of 5" x 7" laminated cards. They provide a step-by-step outline of the activity. A set of cue cards can be used in different ways, depending upon how familiar a counselor is with the functioning of a station. Each set should have the following features:

1. Title Cards. The first card in each set of cue cards gives the crew counselor all of the important information for conducting the activity.

   Station Name: The title of the activity.

   Concept Name: The key concept word.

   Concept Statement: The short sentence that is always associated with the concept. It is used as a verbal signal or transfer statement to help the learner relate activities associated with the same concept that are held at different times and places.

   Concept Component: The particular aspect of the concept with which this station deals.

   Key Words: The terms which should be used during the activity. These words are important in helping the learners understand the relationship between the concept and the actions they are taking.

   Props: The materials necessary for conducting the activity.

   Key Phrases: The short cues which sum up each step of the activity.

   Passport Entry: The page number in the passport which contains the information for the station. This page number follows the first key phrase.

2. Paragraph Descriptions. Each set of cue cards includes a descriptive paragraph of each step in the activity. The counselor can flip through the whole set, scanning each card.
3. Key Lines. Each cue card has a couple of key lines in each paragraph printed in bold letters. Just the main ideas of each step are highlighted in this way and thus serve as quick cues for the counselor.
+The crew counselors, after conducting the activity a couple of times, may only have to glance at the key phrases to keep on track. If they get stuck at one step, they can check the step number by the key phrase and turn to the paragraph that describes that step in more detail.

The following is a sample set of Cue Cards for the first station presented here, "Cradles to Coffins."

CRADLES TO COFFINS

CONCEPT:	Cycles
CONCEPT STATEMENT:	THE BUILDING MATERIALS OF LIFE MUST BE USED OVER AND OVER
CONCEPT COMPONENT:	Soil Cycle
KEY WORDS:	Nutrients, Decay, Bacteria, Soil Cycle
PROPS:	Tombstones, Coffin, Noisemakers and Party Hats, Marking Pen and Trowel.

1. Read Passport information (pg. 10)
2. Review deaths of last fall
3. Go to graveyard
4. Find and name leaves
5. Think up good deed
6. Dig grave
7. Recite good deed
8. Bury leaves
9. Find seeds
10. Change cemetery to garden
11. Begin birthday party
12. Collect props
13. Complete Passport task
14. Share examples
15. Stamp Passports

1. READ PASSPORT INFORMATION about soil cycles on **page ten**.

2. SET THE STAGE FOR THE PROCESSION TO THE GRAVEYARD . . . "Living things must die before they can become recycled. Many deaths happened here just last fall. Follow me in silence and I'll show you this sad spot."

3. Act sorrowful as you GUIDE THE GROUP TO THE GRAVEYARD.

   Talk in a hushed voice and EXPLAIN LAST FALL'S SAD EVENT— thousands of dead leaves fell to the ground. Hold up a leaf as an illustration.

   Suggest to the group that it is only fitting and proper to PAY RESPECTS TO THE DECEASED.

4. Ask each one to FIND ONE SPECIAL LEAF AND THINK UP A NAME FOR IT.

   Set the tone for the funeral—an occasional wail will help.

5. After everyone collects a dead leaf, suggest that they THINK UP ONE GOOD DEED which their leaf did during its lifetime for an eulogy.

6. Appoint the first person to find a leaf to be the GRAVEDIGGER and ask him/her to dig a shallow hole with the trowel.

7. Appoint a kid to be the coffin bearer. If necessary, begin the memorial by recognizing an attribute of your own leaf; for example, "My leaf, Stubby, helped to recycle oxygen into the atmosphere so animals can breathe."

   Then, ASK EACH KID TO SHARE A THOUGHT ABOUT HIS OR HER LEAF and drop it into the coffin box.

8. Again, in a hushed and saddened voice, ask the coffin bearer to take the leaves from the coffin and ceremoniously PLACE THE LEAVES IN THE GRAVE WHILE THE KIDS WRITE THE NAMES of the dead on the tombstone. Use only one side of the "stone" and suggest that they abbreviate if necessary.

   Pass your handkerchief around to mop up the tears and cheer things up a bit, while explaining that the leaves will soon be on their way back to LEAF HEAVEN—that is, they are going to rot and go back into the soil. Explain the role of bacteria as the real morticians of life.

9. Say, "Wait a minute! Spring isn't supposed to be a sad time; spring is a time of growth and life. FIND A SEED AND GIVE IT A NAME." Suggest that seeds can be found almost everywhere, but they'll have to look closely. "Every plant has a way of reproducing itself."

10. Suggest that everyone might want to bury their seeds and ASK WHERE A GOOD SPOT MIGHT BE FOUND.

    Acknowledge those kids who propose that the freshly dug grave would be an ideal spot with all the right conditions. Reinforce the idea by saying, "The cemetery can be a garden for new life."

11. TURN THE FUNERAL INTO A GRAND BIRTHDAY PARTY. Pass out the noisemakers and party hats and sing a chorus of "Happy Birthday" while burying the seeds on top of the dead leaves. Pantomime blowing out the candles on a cake.

12. Collect the noisemakers and hats. Then say, "LET'S WRITE DOWN THE NAMES OF OUR SEEDS ON THE BACK OF THE TOMB-STONES, because in a way every tombstone is like a birth certificate." Gesture to the grave and say, "I wonder if it is a cradle or a coffin?" Conclude with . . . "The end of our leaves is really like a beginning for our seeds."

13. Have everyone COMPLETE THE TASK IN THE PASSPORTS. Help those who are having problems.

14. Ask the kids to SHARE THEIR PASSPORT EXAMPLES with each other.

15. When the kids have shared their ideas with the whole group, stamp THE OFFICIAL CONCEPT STAMP in their passports.

Opening and Closing Stations

+All the props and cue cards should be ready to use upon arriving at a station. The crew counselors should always check to see that everything is in order and that the stage is set for the next group before they leave for the next station.

+The first group leader to use a station should take on the responsibility of opening the station for that day, including posting the signs, setting up the props, etc. The last group leader should close the station for that day, storing away signs and props and checking for prop damage and needed replenishment of supplies (e.g., peanuts for "Peanut Patch," ink for the stamp pads, pencils, etc.).

Reading Passport Entries

+Ask the kids to join you in forming a circle. (Linking arms at the first few stations will help the kids form a real circle.)

+Check the cue cards to find out on which page of the passport the station's entry will be found. Ask the group to pull out their passports and turn to the indicated page number. Select someone to read the entry and suggest that everyone else follow along. (You should be alert for nonreaders in your group. Ask for volunteers.) Finally, ask the group to put away their passports, and then reemphasize the key parts of the entry for the station. (Point out to the group which part of the EC-DC-IC-A formula the station concerns.)

Conducting the Activity

+Repeat the key concept statement yourself during the activity and praise those kids who use it: "O.K.! That's the idea, 'Everything is becoming something else.'"

+*Use every opportunity* for selectively reinforcing the concept idea: "That's right, energy flow means that sunlight is captured first by the plants, then flows into the animals when they eat those plants."

+ Peer group status is important for upper elementary students. It's a good idea to keep your eyes open for some desirable behavior by each student during the morning and express your approval of it.

+ When the activity calls for reaching a conclusion, encourage the group to slow down a bit and think over the alternatives. Discourage them from blurting out the first thing that pops *into* their heads. Premature verbalization may be detrimental. Keep in mind that we did not base our descriptions of the concept activities on the worst day we ever had in conducting them. There were plenty of times when everything did not go as smoothly as in the examples presented here. Don't get discouraged if your first time out proves less than perfect. Review the descriptions and guidelines and go back and re-read the ACC Guidelines in the "Operating Principles" section. (On the other hand, you will often be surprised that it does go just as well as in the narratives.)

+ Be wary of "What is it?" questions. Explain to the kids that an endless list of names will just get in the way. Try responding to such questions with a silent examination of the object itself. Most of the time you will probably discover that the kids were merely curious about something instead of desperate to learn its name.

(The *names* of the stations are not important, either. The idea is to help the kids remember the functioning of the concept, not the name of the station where the activity took place. When referring back to the stations, use the activity/concept as the identifier.)

Recording Examples in Passports

+ Upon completion of the activity at a station, regroup the kids at the prop box and read with them in the passports the task which they must complete. Explain to them that they must go off independently in the nearby area and discover something in the natural world that relates to the task and the sunship concept or concept component that they just learned.

+ Distribute pencils from the prop box and explain that the examples which they select should not be abstract, but things that they can actually see or touch in the natural world around them. If they choose to draw pictures, they must be sure to include captions that will help interpret the drawings. Also, remind them not to use the same example that was used at their immediate station. (For example, one should not use "a squirrel's chisel-like teeth" as an example of adaptation after visiting the "Peanut Patch.")

+ Be alert for those who might need help in discovering an

example. Rephrasing the task or inviting a fellow student to help out is sometimes necessary. (If everyone seems to need help, find an example as a group first, then have them seek out their own examples.)

I After the examples are completed, stamp the official concept stamp in the passports. While stamping each passport, repeat the key concept statement for that station. This further strengthens the relationship between the activity and the key concept and will serve as a cue or signal for transferring the concept understanding to other stations. (For example, if the concept statement for cycles is read at the water cycle station, then read again at the air cycle station, the concept can begin to be understood in more than one context.)

Sighting Scopes

+ These scopes can be made with one-inch white plumber's pipe. Use stick-on letters to apply the name of the concept to the side of a tube, and attach a two-foot length of cord for hanging it.
+ After finishing a station, the crew counselor takes a scope from the prop box supply. The group must set this scope up somewhere along the trail while moving on to the next station. The counselor should challenge his group to find an interesting example in the natural world of the "key concept" they just learned about. The scope should then be set up, focusing on that example. (For instance, one group's scope might be focused on a nurse stump or log after they have completed the "Cradles to Coffins" station.) As a special challenge for following groups, leave a note with a catchy riddle or rhyme that illustrates your find. Subsequent groups walking the trail can then try to figure out the preceding group's example. (Incorrect answers rarely occur, because even though what they see might not be what the preceding group had in mind, they are still applying their new conceptual knowledge to whatever is being viewed.)
+ Sighting Scopes not only provide for additional application of newly acquired understandings, but serve as a useful holding device if a group is still occupying the next station.
+ Later in the morning, instead of having each group leave a scope behind, ask them to find the previous group's scope first, check its sighting, then take it along to use for focusing on their own example.

Getting from One Station to the Next

+ Besides sighting scopes, each trail features other ambulatory activities and devices to aid in natural observation. One class group packs binoculars, another carries bug boxes, magnifying glasses, and sweep nets, and the third has some instant cameras. These are used to focus on spontaneous discoveries along the trail and to provide the group leader with a holding activity in case the next station still has a group. Caution: crew counselors should reward kids for finding interesting discoveries along the trail, but should be warned against launching into mini-lectures or falling prey to "what-is-it?" questions.

+For those groups needing additional directed activity as they move from station to station, the following "challenges" may be used:

Weird Insect Adaptation. The leader distributes sweep nets, magnifying glasses, and bug boxes, and suggests that the group keep a lookout for unusual insects. While out on the path, the kids use their nets to capture a variety of specimens, and then choose the insect which they feel has the weirdest adaptation. Each group brings its candidate to the class meeting at the end of the morning and explains what adaptation makes the insect particularly strange. After the nominations, a vote is held to determine which insect should be put on special display in the Outlook Inn. The winner is checked in at the "Weird Insect Hotel," where it will spend the day on display.

Passenger of the Day. After the station leader distributes binoculars to each group, he explains that they are to be used in a search for all kinds of fellow sunship passengers as the group walks along the path. In addition, he tells the kids that they should keep a sharp lookout for the "Passenger of the Day." He gives them a brief description of this special passenger, and suggests that they use their binoculars for a close-up look. If they sight it while out on the path, they will receive special recognition at the noon meal. Later, all the groups place pictures of the passengers they sighted during the morning on the passengers' murals in the dining hall.

Bug Olympics. Before starting out on the path, the station leader explains to the class group that the "Grand Bug Olympics" will be held at the end of the morning. With the help of magnifying glasses and sweep nets, each group is to find a bug that is adapted to move quickly and smoothly over land.

After a morning's paths are completed, all the groups gather at the Olympic Stadium (a hula-hoop on the ground with a small pennant placed in the center). The station leader clocks each insect, recording the time it takes to move from the center to the edge of the hula-hoop. If the insect takes more than sixty seconds, it becomes disqualified for taking too much time. After each race, the station leader comments on each insect's unique adaptation for locomotion. The group who discovered the insect with the winning time is given a special round of applause at lunch. Naturally, all of the contestants are released after the event.

Group Size Differences

+The ideal group size is five participants; however, most concept stations can accommodate up to seven students. On occasion a group may fall short by one student or become "overpopulated" by a couple of students. Such size variations pose no problem to most learning stations, but in a few cases the group leader will need to fill in as a direct participant, or the extra kids will have to double up with a buddy to play one role between them (In Mr. Sun's Restaurant, for example, where only a limited number of "character cards" are distributed).

CONCEPT PATHS—
GUIDELINES

Cradles to Coffins

PROPS:
Cemetery—Locate it a short distance off of the main path. Clear a four-by-eight-foot area and enclose it with a simple, one-foot-high pole or split-rail fence.
Tombstones—Cut up wood scraps and drive nails through the bottom edges of the "tombstones." This helps support them when they are set into the ground.

Marking Pen—Do not use water-based markers. They will bleed on the tombstones when it rains.
Party Hats and Noisemakers—Make sure every kid has one. Store them in a waterproof sack or container.
Trowel—A simple, inexpensive garden trowel is adequate.
Coffin—Paint a cigar box black and waterproof it.

GENERAL NOTES:
1. Don't bury the coffin, just the leaves that were placed inside it. Suggest that the box may get in the way of natural decay.
2. If the kids can't find a seed right away, suggest that they search their pants cuffs and socks for "hitchhikers."
3. Let the tombstones accumulate from day to day or week to week; they add character to the cemetery.

On the Street Where You Live

PROPS:
Survey Markers—Red or yellow survey tape can be bought in twenty-five yard rolls. Flagging tied onto stakes and posted about the area sets the stage for the activity. Write street names on a few stakes.
Census Taker Badges—"Census Taker" printed on a heavy piece of posterboard makes a simple badge. Attach a large safety pin to each one.
Tally Sheets—These can either be mimeographed or constructed to be reused. Permanent tally sheets can be made by attaching 8" x 11" data sheets to light pieces of cardboard and then covering each with adhesive acetate. List and number the job descriptions on the reverse side. (In this way, kids can enter just the job number in the "Job Role" column instead of writing in all of the titles.) Leave the last couple of numbers blank for individual discoveries. Have plenty of grease pencils on hand. The tally sheets can easily be erased with a sponge and pail of water at the prop box. In this case, it is probably a good idea to have a master tally sheet compiled first, which could be posted later in the dining hall.
Map—Draw a simple map showing the different streets in the area. The maps can also be covered with adhesive acetate for permanency. Clue the kids in on which direction is north so that they have a point of reference when locating themselves on the map. Lay out the maps and the streets as simply as possible.
Caution Signs—These can be printed on school bus yellow poster board and cut out in the traditional diamond shape.
Weatherproof them and tack them on tall stakes. Leave some signs blank for the kids to fill in.

GENERAL NOTES:
1. Establish the development area where lots of critters are likely to be found. Keep the area small and centralized. All "streets" should be visible from a central location.
2. Remind the kids to replace any overturned logs or rocks after checking on residents in the "basement level" of the community.
3. During the activity emphasize those jobs that different residents of the community perform and where those residents live. De-emphasize any suggestion that the developer is a shady character—he just may not understand that a natural community already exists here.
4. Demonstrate for the kids how to record information on their tally sheets and refer to the job descriptions on the back.
5. Have a few caution signs already in place. Position others as you circulate with the kids.

Guess Who's Coming to Dinner

PROPS:
Coyote Tails—Make these with old, knee-high socks stuffed with newspaper. Tie off the top of each tail with a long piece of cord.
Mouse Ears—Disney-produced "Mickey Mouse Ears" are perfect. Black cardboard ears inserted into a beanie are second-best.
Mouse Tail—Roll a piece of chicken wire (2' x 3") into a long cylinder and cover with black cloth. Attach this "tail" to a belt and bend it to curve upward.
Dinner Bells—Real dinner bells are best, but less expensive models can be fashioned with #10 cans filled with pebbles or tacks. Secure a single pull cord through the bottom of each and hang them from limbs or stumps with wire.

GENERAL NOTES:
1. Choose an area that is lightly sodded and full of obvious places for hiding and sneaking. Clear out branches that will trip up running coyotes.
2. Locate the "mouse's home" in a central area. Look for a fallen log or mark off the area with string to define its limits.
3. The leader should play the role of "referee." His or her main job is to help confirm sightings made by the mouse and make sure the coyotes leave the game (to "die of starvation") if they are sighted.
4. Set up four bells near natural hiding or "sneaking around" spots. These should be just barely visible to the mouse so that the coyotes will have to be stealthy. They should also be located fairly close to, but an equal distance from, the mouse's home.

Mr. Sun's Restaurant

PROPS:
Table—Cut a triangle out of a piece of 4' x 8' plywood and attach it to the top of an old table. The table surface should be smaller than the plywood.

Tablecloths—Cut red and white checked cloth to fit the table top. Divide the triangle into five horizontal sections. Mark off each section with a strip of tape, and provide enough space so that each section can hold progressively fewer plates as one moves from the base to the peak of the triangle. The plates must just fit into their taped-off section (see figure).

Plates—Paint each set of plates with a color representing a particular plant or animal in the food chain:

      1 Plate-Brown-Bear
      2 Plates-Orange-Salmon
      4 Plates-Blue-Minnows
      8 Plates-Green-Water Insects
      16 Plates-Gray-Algae

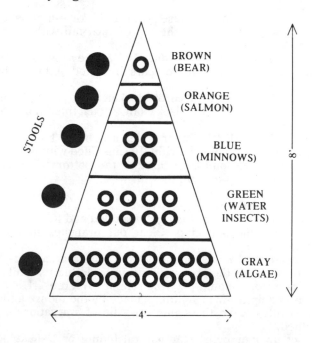

Write on the bottom of each plate the name of the plant or animal represented.

Stools—Saw logs.

Chef's Hat—Popular restaurants are happy to donate these. Novelty shops also sell them.

Character Cards—Fold 3" x 5" cards in half and after drawing the appropriate item on each one—plus its name—color code the tops of the card with waterproof markers:

Sun	Brown
Grass	Green
Grasshopper	Blue
Frog	Yellow
Snake	Orange
Hawk	Gray

The color code is for the second round, when the character cards become the "banquet tickets." (The frog will become the guest of honor or "Mr. Sun" inside the banquet hall, and thus has no corresponding color on the plates.)

GENERAL NOTES:

1. If kids have trouble arranging themselves, offer a couple of hints about who might eat whom.

2. Counselors may have to play the role of one of the characters if the group size is too small, and if it is too large, the kids may have to double up.

Peanut Patch

PROPS:

Peanuts—Buy in bulk quantities, and if you find your supply being depleted, get the unsalted kind. Store them in real squirrel-proof, waterproof containers!

Thumbless Gloves—The best buys are inexpensive garden gloves or small cotton gloves. They will fit most kids' hands. Snip off the thumbs and stitch up the opening with heavy-duty thread.

GENERAL NOTES:

1. Choose an area (about thirty feet across) for the peanut patch, a spot that is good for crawling on all fours.

2. Deposit discarded shells in a container before leaving the station. Take them to the compost pile at the end of the week.

3. Toss the peanuts carefully and slowly while kids play their "human roles" to ensure that they will be successful in catching the nuts.

CONCEPT PATH B

B-1   "DECLARATION OF INTERDEPENDENCE"

"What are all those crazy signs hanging around here?"

"Oh, wow! This must be the place that we heard about just before we took off; where the evil dictator lives and it's really dangerous to be. Let's go see what they say; I'm not afraid."

Bill, the leader, is not quite so bold, however. "Hold on a minute, friends. I've seen what that evil King Snoid IV and his ideas can do to unsuspecting souls; let's look things over pretty carefully before we get in over our heads."

"Aw, come on, we're just going to read the signs."

"O.K., but be sure you understand one thing. Those are not just ordinary signs, they're *edicts*."

"Edicts? What are edicts?"

"I know. They're like laws, things you have to do."

"Hey, that's right. Which also means that as soon as you've read them you can no longer say, 'Well, *I* didn't know; nobody told *me* about the rules!' And it also means that if you believe these edicts are wrong you may have to do something about it. And that could be *dangerous*. Remember, before we even started this morning we were all warned that there was some unrest in this area and talk of revolution. You people may even be asked to become revolutionaries!"

"All right! That'll be far out!"

"Far out? Oh, youthful innocence! No, it won't be easy. It's a long hard struggle against dangerous ideas, and the path is never easy. I just hope you folks can measure up."

"Geez, you sound like an old man. Let's do it!"

The kids bound over to the area where King Snoid's edicts are found as Bill trails along behind muttering vague pronouncements about the good old days and the exuberance of youth.

"Holy cow, look at this picture! Is this King Snoid? Is he ugly! That guy does look baaad!"

"Yeah, and listen to this edict. 'KING SNOID IV SAYS: ALL THINGS ARE SEPARATE. ALL SUBJECTS SHALL OBEY.'"

"Listen to this one. 'KING SNOID IV SAYS: NO THING SHALL DEPEND ON ANY OTHER THING. ALL SUBJECTS SHALL OBEY.'"

"That's nothing. Listen to this! 'KING SNOID IV SAYS: THOU SHALT NOT WORK TOGETHER NOR SHALL ANY LIVING THING IN MY KINGDOM. ALL SUBJECTS SHALL OBEY.'"

"Forget it, man. That's crazy. This guy is a maniac."

"Here's another one. 'KING SNOID IV SAYS: THOU SHALT DO IT ALONE. ALL SUBJECTS SHALL OBEY.'"

"Boooo! No way I'm going to obey."

"SSHHH! Listen, everybody come over here. You know what King Snoid and his goons would do to you if they heard you saying that kind of stuff? Whew, I hate to think; I HATE to think! But I must say I'm impressed with your spirit. In fact, I'm going to stick my weary old neck out and ask for something which is prohibited by that final edict right over there. Somebody read it.''

"KING SNOID IV SAYS: THOU SHALT NOT ASK FOR HELP. ALL SUBJECTS SHALL OBEY."'

"Yes, you have all probably guessed it. I'm going to ask you to join the battle against these twisted ideas. Now, before all of you jump on the bandwagon, give it a little thought. There's nobody putting any pressure on you. Don't feel like you have to . . . "

"Forget it, man, DOWN WITH KING SNOID!"

"DOWN WITH KING SNOID!"

"And now in unison, 'DOWN WITH KING SNOID!'"

"Crimonies! Hold it down. Hold it down. Your enthusiasm is great, but we have to use our heads. This is a battle to the end, and I'd better explain how we can best prepare for victory.''

Bill leads the way over to a small parchment sheet well hidden behind a tree.

"Now take a look at this, and don't read it too loudly.''

In unison again, the kids read, *"HEAR YE! HEAR YE! HEAR YE! WE DO HEREBY PROCLAIM IN DEFIANCE TO KING SNOID IV THAT MANY THINGS ON OUR SUNSHIP DO DEPEND ON EACH OTHER AND ALL THINGS ARE INTERRELATED. FURTHERMORE, WE HAVE ALL FOUND SOLID PROOF OF AT LEAST ONE EXAMPLE OF THIS DEPENDENCE AND IF KING SNOID DOESN'T BELIEVE IT HE CAN TAKE A LONG WALK ON A SHORT PIER!"*

"Good job! And you'll notice that below that there's a place for everybody to sign. *But* the last thing you want to do is sign your name unless you have some good proof of something around here that depends on something else. It's even better if you can think of two things that depend on each other.''

"I know . . . "

"Ah, ha! Words are not worth anything in this battle. You have to go out and find an example in nature, if possible, something you

can hold in your hand. It's kind of like Dracula and the silver cross; as long as you've got your example in your hand, that's your amulet and you're safe from the King. And if you're brave enough, you can even sign this declaration.

"So take a couple of minutes right now and go out by yourselves to find your examples. They have to be good or else . . . "

"He'll send you to bed early?"

"I wish that would be all, Carrie."

"Listen, that's pretty bad where I come from."

"O.K., then, the time can't be put off any longer. Off on your missions. Be careful and good luck!"

The kids are off, but it's not long before a couple of them have returned.

"Hey, listen, I just thought of something. Does King Snoid eat?"

"Well, he's a pretty weird fellow, but I guess he must eat."

"Well then I'm gonna sign the declaration, 'cause even he depends on plants to get his energy from the sun. I'll bet he eats meat, too, and that comes from animals."

"How about wood? Does he sit in chairs? Does he use a table? What about pencils?"

"Well, I guess you've got him there, too . . . but what we really need are things that we can see. Things we can show him if he ever shows up, which I sure hope he doesn't! Can you find some stuff out there?

"Try and find two things which depend on each other as well. If we can do that, we're golden."

Things are beginning to look bad for King Snoid IV. In fact, Bill comments that the wind murmuring in the trees overhead could be Snoid's fearful gasps.

Almost immediately after those two are off again, Carrie is back with the first concrete evidence. *"I've got it. I'm safe. I found a stump full of ants. Those ants depend on that stump for food and also for a home. Down with King Snoid!"*

"O.K., I knew I could count on you. That's great! Just one thing, Carrie, if we could find something that has things depending on *each other*, we'd be in even better shape."

"Yeah, I can see what you mean; I'll see what I can find."

Carrie hasn't taken more than three steps when she slowly turns around and comes back. *"This stump depends on the ants to help break it up and put it back in the soil . . . or at least the soil is depending on the ants at the same time that the ants depend on the stump."*

"Nice work. That's beautiful! I think you're ready to sign the declaration. Fill in the date there and sign your name, that is, if you really want to."

"You bet I want to. Down with King Snoid!"

"All right, that warms my old heart. Now let's see what you have, Gordy."

"See that little tree over there. The seed it grew from could have been planted by a bird who was going to eat it, but dropped it

instead. Birds carry a lot of seeds around like that. So the bird and the tree are really helping each other."

"Good, Gordy. That's a bombproof example. Even the evil King can't touch that one. Want to sign the declaration?"

"Darn right!"

Finally Carlos and Doug are back after looking for something a little more tangible than the King's need for wood and food. *"We've got the perfect thing,"* they yell, *"and it doesn't make any difference if he hears us or not 'cause we've got it right here in our hands!"*

"You mean to say you think you've found something we can all use as an amulet to protect us against the King?"

"Yeah, and it's gonna freak him out all the more 'cause it looks just like his hair in the picture," they say brandishing a tuft of old man's beard lichen. *"We learned about this stuff at the Outlook Inn yesterday. It's two separate things living together. One gives the other a place to live since it can fasten onto things, and at the same time, the other gives the first food since it's got chlorophyll and can get energy straight from the sun."*

"I think you guys have the answer, at least one answer. This is tremendous. This is going to be the end of the King. He can't touch us now. Show this to the others while you sign the declaration."

The declaration is soon signed by all, a brave and capable crew. Doug notices with a laugh, however, that Carrie, upon filling in the date in the declaration, entered: UPON THIS *SUNNY* DAY OF JUNE 1976. And so it shall be remembered for ages to come as indeed a sunny day. For on this day King Snoid and his evil misconceptions were finally put to rest by five courageous and spirited sunship passengers.

B-2   "CLIFFHANGERS"

"According to the map, there should be something neat around this corner. It says 'two-in-one tree!' What could that be?"

"I'll guarantee you one thing," replies Bill, *"We'll find out when we get there."*

"If we get there. I'm not so sure Doug can follow the map."

"He'll get us there. You just have to remember not to lose the key to the prop box. We'd be in big trouble at this station without a couple of things which we'll find in there. We're going to try to get a foothold on a big boulder at a place called 'Cliffhangers.'"

"Cliffhangers" is located alongside a small, low-angle rock outcrop. At the top of the rocks, about four feet above the ground, is a classic example of plant succession, lichens are making visible inroads on the upper level, with deeper mosses right behind them. Farther back, grasses and ferns are growing on the areas which have a little soil base.

The kids have just read the passport statements for the concept of change. They are mystified by the large wooden ramp inclined at about a forty-five degree angle which stands opposite the small cliff.

"You know, the changes on our sunship which really end up being the biggest and probably the most important are almost totally invisible. They happen so slowly and our time on earth to watch them is so short that we can't believe they're happening at all. A change is taking place right here that's even slower than the one happening to the rock mentioned in the passport. We'd find that hard to believe except for one thing; we can duplicate it ourselves and see how it works."

"We're gonna be here quite a while then. I think I'll put my jacket back on."

"No, the nice thing about this is that we can also speed the process up by hundreds of years. It won't take us long at all, if we can figure out how to do it." Bill leads the group over to the rock. "All we have to do is turn this rock into soil so that small shrubs can grow on it."

"Oh sure! That's good. Turn the rock into soil."

"That's right, except we aren't going to do it here. We'll let time do its own work here. We'll do our work over there at that smaller 'boulder' we've built, but we'll use the same process, with just a couple of changes."

The "changes" are the actors in the process. In "Cliffhangers" the kids play the roles of the various plant "characters" in the process of succession. The leader explains to the group that their job is to establish enough of a foothold on their "boulder" so that grasses will be able to grow. He explains that at one point there was no growth at all on top of the rock outcrop which the group examined. However, eventually the entire pile of rocks will be covered with soil and plants. The group moves up close to the example to see the various roles they will be playing. By looking closely they can all see that the mosses need a small layer of soil on

which to grow. The grasses by comparison need considerably deeper soil.

Roles are then assigned. Three of the kids are to be mosses and two will be grasses. Again focusing on the example of the cliff, the leader points out that the mosses can be seen moving ahead of the grasses in their encroachment on the rock. With this particular group he is able to draw on their experience from the previous day at "Cradles to Coffins" in his explanation of the soil-creating role of the living and dying mosses. (He feels a little guilty at not explaining the crucial role of the lichens, but that's part of the game.)

Bill now directs the team back to the ramp, or "boulder." "You have your positions and you know your job. We have to accomplish *succession* on this 'cliff.' All you need to do is to get the 'mosses' onto the 'boulder' so that the 'grasses' can grab onto them and 'grow' on the 'boulder' themselves. Mosses need to make it up there first and then the grasses, but everybody's got to be *off* the ground. One last catch, you can only use the face of the ramp, not the edges or the top—just like on the real boulder—and no running starts!"

"Whew! That's going to be really hard. That thing is steep."

"Just like a real boulder. Go for it."

The ramp is angled so that it is just barely too steep to stand on. Every attempt by the mosses leads to a slow slide back down. The grasses offer much verbal assistance, all of it futile. They are not permitted on the ramp until the mosses have been able to stick there themselves and thereby given them something to "grow on."

Finally after a period of frustration, the leader suggests that something must be missing. There must be some stage in this succession that the group overlooked. They return to the boulders. A bit of close examination reveals the role of the lichens on the rock surface. Bill explains that they can grow in areas with no soil whatsoever, using their dual ability as both a fungus and an algae to cling anywhere while producing their own food supply. The two huskiest kids are then selected to play the key roles of the "lichens" in the action which follows. They are given small hooks with wooden handles. These hooks enable them to "grow" on the ramp because of tiny holes drilled near the top. By reaching up the ramp and hooking into the holes they are able to gain a solid hold on the "rock." Two "mosses" then find it easy to stick to the ramp by holding onto the lichens. Finally, the "grass" is able to find enough to grow on as well.

"Hey, we did it!"

"Nice move, everybody. We've portrayed hundreds of years of succession in just a few minutes. Maybe we should stay here for a while so the next group can see the stages involved. I mean, here we are poised in a moment of timelessness: lichens, mosses, and grasses, each taking a turn in the never-ending process of soil building and the ongoing breakdown of ancient, solid rocks . . . "

"Hey, uh, that's all great but I'm beginning to fall off this . . . "

"Ye-eeooow!"

B-3   "FOOD FACTORY"

When the group arrives at their third station of the morning, they are more than a little surprised. Expecting to find the usual prop box, they are greeted instead by a number of signs warning them that they are in a top secret area restricted to "authorized personnel only." Finally, they arrive at a large cave-like structure with a rounded, low profile. From one end a tube-like tunnel enters the main compartment, an oval room about seven feet across. The entire edifice is constructed with green canvas and thatched with branches.

"What in the world is that?"
"That, friends, is the most important thing on this planet."
"You're kidding."
"Nope, I'm not. It's a leaf."
"Oh, well, that makes a little *more sense."*
"Even though it's just a leaf, it is still the most important thing on this planet. We're about to find out why. We call this model leaf the 'Food Factory.' It's going to give us all a chance to get the inside story on just how we get our energy from the sun. Picture in your mind what happens to some people when they sit out in the hot sunshine for the whole afternoon."
"Yeah, I did once and I got really burned."
"But I bet you still wanted to eat dinner."
"Yeah, I guess I did, but what does that have to do with anything?"
"*That* has everything to do with everything. We can feel the sun's heat, but we have no way to turn sunlight into a form we can eat. Only the plants can do that.
"You are all going to get a chance this morning to go inside a food factory and see just what goes into the making of the sugars that we all depend on for our energy. But no one really knows exactly how it's done. This is a very important mission, and you must be pledged to complete secrecy."
"My lips are sealed."
After the reading of the passports, the leader takes the group over to a nearby area enclosed with canvas curtains. On the outside is a sign saying "Molecule Messengers." He points out that only half of the group will be inside the food factory at a time. The other kids will have the very important job of delivering the ingredients with which the leaf works its magic. He points out three pouches hanging on a branch in the molecule messenger waiting area. They are labeled "Air," "Water," and "Sunlight." Very sneakily he reaches for one of the pouches and pulls the group together for a glimpse of what is inside. The kids are then informed that periodically a voice will come from "Chlorophyll Control Center" asking for one of these ingredients. At that time one of the messengers should take the correct pouch over to the food factory and pass in one of the envelopes found inside the pouch. The messenger must then return immediately to the waiting area; the messenger's turn will come to go inside. The

waiting area is decorated with drawings and signs outlining some of the amazing facts about how much energy plants are able to capture and how many leaves there are on a tree, etc., as well as a complete set of instructions for the molecule messengers (enough to keep them busy between calls to "send in some water or air").

The kids are now beginning to get curious about the interior of the leaf itself . . .

"What does this stuff have to do with the inside of the 'factory'?"

Bill responds in a low voice, talking out of the side of his mouth. "What you've seen so far is what everyone knows about this factory. Scientists know what goes into the leaf, and they know what comes out of the leaf, but *nobody* knows exactly what goes on inside the leaf itself. Carbon dioxide and water go in and sunlight is around, too, and then after a while sugars come out and we eat them. But inside something is happening which is a real mystery. We're going to send you in there to find out what the secret process is which can combine these things and turn them into our precious source of energy.

"In just a few minutes, each and every one of you is going to get a chance to be a 'chlorospy,' which is to say that you are going to enter this leaf wearing these green hats."

"Green hats! I'm not going to wear one of those ugly things."

"Ah, but you'll need a green hat because you'll be spying on chlorophyll, which is as green as a leaf (in fact, it's what makes the leaf green), and you're going to need camouflage."

"O.K., as long as there's a reason."

"Let me tell you something else about chlorophyll while you have me on the subject. It's the stuff we're really interested in here. As I said before, we know that leaves are what makes our food and we even know what part of the leaf does the work, the chloroplast. And now I want you chlorospies to go in there and find out just how it's done."

"Doug and I'll go first!"

"Well, wait just a second. We're almost ready, but we need a little training before you can go in. You see, I'm not going to be around. I'm not authorized to go in there, so you need to know a few things before you go."

By now their curiosity is thoroughly aroused . . .

"What's going to happen when someone gets in there in a chloroplast hat?"

This, Bill explains, is when it starts to get really tricky. He is not sure that he knows what they are to do inside. All he knows is that the rest of the group will be outside the leaf, passing in the necessary ingredients. The carbon dioxide and the sunlight will be coming in through the walls of the leaf just like in the real thing. Water will also enter in the same way it does in a real food factory, up through the stem. The person who carries the water will only be able to go up to the curtain at the top of the stem. Since that person won't have security clearance, he'll have to pass the water molecules (inside the envelopes) through the curtain to the undercover chloroplasts who have infiltrated the inner recesses.

On the next page the diagram will give the reader a chance to see all of the molecules found inside the envelopes. Consider yourself lucky; the kids never get this opportunity until they get into the leaf itself (in order to avoid accidental photosynthesis outside of the real chloroplasts and the resulting confusion.)!

Carbon Dioxide+Water+Sun Energy   = Sugar

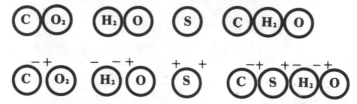

(+ = hooked velcro/ − = fuzzy velcro)

Strips of velcro on these "molecules" made from Ping-Pong balls will enable the undercover chloroplasts to unfasten the component parts of water and carbon dioxide in order to form the sugar molecule as illustrated. The resulting free oxygen atoms (O_2) can then be pushed out of the leaf as the by-product of the secret process. Since the actual molecules are inside envelopes, those outside are unable to do any "spying" before it is their turn.

What actually happens inside the leaf? Once they enter the interior, which is lit only by the narrow beams of the flashlights they carry, the chlorospies are greeted by a number of short, but foreboding, signs. Some are directed to the pledge of secrecy to which workers are bonded, or bear instructions to talk only in whispers. Other signs, however, are all clustered in the farthest corner of the leaf, around a large green box with a slot in the top. These signs inform the chlorospies that this is the super secret chlorophyll box. One large sign says that they are to await further instructions. At this point a muffled voice comes from a previously unnoticed tube lying on the floor.

Gordy looks around, then picks up the tube. A deep voice comes through, "Can you hear me? This is Leaf Control."

"Wow, yeah, I can hear you."

Bill, of course, is hidden behind a large clump of bushes, where the other end of the buried speaking tube surfaces and where he can still call out directions to the molecule messengers outside who will supply the special envelopes to the chlorospies.

At this point the action begins. The kids outside pass the first molecule envelopes into the leaf, where they are received by the chlorospies. Inside, the spies have already been given vague instructions by "Leaf Control" on how the parts inside the molecule envelopes fit together, so they set to work trying to make "sugar." Communication through the tube centers on clarifying the parts of each molecule. ("Oh, so you have *hydrogen* and *oxygen*, huh?")

The "sun-energy ball" is not passed in until the infiltrators have had a chance to try to fit the other components together without it. Of course, due to the placement of the velcro on the balls, this task is impossible. Finally, a sun-energy ball is handed in through the wall of the leaf.

"Pssst," the voice comes through the tube. "This is Leaf Control. Figured it out yet?"

"Yeah, Maria just put it together. We've got carbon and oxygen atoms from the air and hydrogen atoms from the water stuck together with a sun-energy ball."

"10-4, good buddies, that's sugar! When you're finished you can return through the stem tunnel."

When the first team emerges, Bill appears to ask if they found out the secret, but several of the other kids have questions of their own:

"Did you get it?"

"What's it like in there?"

"Did you bring the sugar?"

"Hold on. Just a minute," Gordy says. *"We couldn't bring the sugar because we had to leave it in this special box."*

"That's right," Maria adds. *"There's a sign in there which says that for the final step we have to put the molecule models into this chlorophyll box."*

Looking a bit disappointed, Bill suggests that another team give it a try. So Maria and Gordy take the supply jobs, and the others get a chance to infiltrate and attempt to discover the secret.

When all are through, Bill gathers the group in a circle and explains that he was, in fact, the voice on the tube. (This, of course, comes as no surprise.) What he wanted to know was how the chlorophyll did its job. So he had decided to send them in, disguised as chloroplasts, to see if they could figure out how food sugar was really made.

After a review of the process inside the leaf, and after some prodding and subsequent sighs of dismay over their inability to figure out the real secret of the bond itself, Bill says: "Well, friends, don't feel too bad, because you're not the only ones who can't figure it out. In fact, there's not one person on the whole planet who knows completely, not even the hottest of the hotshot scientists. We all rely on that chlorophyll, but we don't know how it works! But since you all did such a good job of trying to figure it out, I think we should partake a little of the product of this process. I just happen to have here . . . "

"An orange!"

B-4   "SUN'S BUCKET BRIGADE"

Bill is rambling along with his group, looking for good picture possibilities, when all of a sudden they come upon a prop box surrounded by six buckets. Since they are all down by the river and it's a nice sunny morning, there is an immediate flurry of questions centered on the chances of a little water fight.

"No, folks, sorry. We'll be using those buckets, but not for anything you might have imagined. You know this sunshine has made photography great this morning, but beyond giving us a little light, the sun's really pretty lazy. Just gets up in the morning, floats overhead, and sets at night. The sun doesn't even work that hard, really. It's the earth that turns. The sun just *seems* to move overhead. So the sun is just a lazy faker."

"No way, Bill. Think of all the energy the sun sends down to the plants to make them grow and everything, like what we just did at the factory."

"Yeah, I have to admit that you have a point there, Gordy, and I hope the sun doesn't do *too* much work, because we're going to do just a small part of its job this morning, and I don't want to get worn out before lunch. Right now we are all going to become members of what we call the 'Sun's Bucket Brigade.' It's quite an honor; you should all be very proud."

"Oh, no, I think maybe I want to just disappear."

"Hey, Maria, in a way that's what we're all going to do. You couldn't have asked to do a more fitting thing. Why don't you read us the key idea before we all disappear, though."

"Me and my big mouth! Let me find it. 'THE BUILDING MATERIALS OF LIFE MUST BE USED OVER AND OVER.'"

"Thanks. Now who would like to read the sunship understanding this time?"

"I've got it. 'We would soon run out of clean water if our Sunship did not have a way of using it over and over. Water on the earth is moved by the heat of the sun through a great cycle. Evaporation and the filtering action of the soil are both important water purifiers in this recycling of the earth's supply of water.'"

"Oh boy, I think I have an idea of where we're headed."

"Well, I'll tell you where we're headed first, Gordy. We're headed down to the stream. Everybody pick up a bucket and let's go."

"Don't worry; we're not going *in* the stream. We're just going to move a little bit of it."

"Move it? Are you loco?"

"Nope, not that I know of. At any rate, as of right now you people are all clouds. That's what it means to be a member of the sun's bucket brigade. There's one big difference, though. Clouds don't have buckets to fill themselves up with. Instead they use a method which just happens to be something similar to what Maria wanted to do a minute ago."

"Disappear?"

"That's right. Let's give it a try and see if it works. Everybody stick your hand in the stream and get it good and wet."

"Yah! That's cold."

"Sure is. Now take your hand out and wave it around. Faster, in big circles."

"Hey, it's getting dry. It's almost dry already."

"You must be a good waver. Mine's not dry yet, but it's getting there. Now, that water isn't just disappearing; it has to be going somewhere . . . "

"It's vanishing into thin air!"

"Into--the--air, and we're headed that way ourselves. It's time for everybody to fill up their buckets and truly become clouds. The sun's warmth does more than just evaporate the water, although it does a mighty good job of that. In fact, on a really warm, windy day, the sun could evaporate one inch of water off the top of our pond over there—and that's *thousands* of buckets. But evaporation's only one part of the story. That water takes quite a journey once it's evaporated into the air. Let's make that trip ourselves. Fill 'em up. Right to the brim."

Soon the crew is ready for the great trek which follows. "One last thing before we start out on this cycle ourselves. As you may

have noticed, there is a very distinct rise in front of us." (Bill has a wry grin on his face.) "We are clouds, and we are going to have to go in that direction because that's the way the wind blows. Anybody here ever see a cloud go right through a hill?"

"Of course not, we'll have to go up and over just like the real clouds."

"Right you are and let's go!" Bill is off, and at a brisk pace.

"Hey, can we be careful clouds? I'm starting to spill."

"That's perfectly all right. In fact, every self-respecting cloud does that quite a bit."

The brigade is about halfway up the trail and the cloud-buckets are splashing out "rain" at every step. Bill stops at a wide spot in the trail where there's room for everyone to gather.

"Whew, this is hard work. I'm pooped. This water isn't light, you know."

"Nope, it sure isn't. One thing to keep in mind though: think about the thousands of buckets the sun's carrying right now, invisibly! However, there is a point at which the water that the sun moves through the air becomes visible."

"Rain, right?"

"Well, sure. Rain is visible, but the clouds that appear before the rain comes are pretty visible, too. In fact, we can see how they become visible right here." At this point Bill pulls out a metal mirror from his pocket. "You know you're all carrying a lot more water up this hill than just what you've got in your buckets. Maria, how much do you weigh?"

"About sixty-five pounds, I guess."

"Well, about fifty pounds of that is water. In fact, we're all almost all water. Let's have a look and see if we can't turn some of the water you've got in the air in your lungs into a sort of a cloud, in the same way that the clouds in the air are formed. Breathe out on this mirror. Everybody else move around behind her so you can see what is happening."

"There's the water, except it's steam."

"Yeah, the mirror is clouding up, like a steamy window."

"It's just like the clouds in the air. What's causing the air to condense on that mirror is the same thing that happens in the sky. The glass is colder than the air inside Maria, so when the air hits the mirror, the water in the air changes from gas, which we can't see, to liquid, which we can see."

"Yeah, but there's no mirror in the sky."

"No, but it's colder up where the clouds are, and that's what causes the change. Picture in your mind what it's like up on a mountain."

"It's cold up there."

"Sure is, and snowy, too."

"Well, the air and clouds rise up along mountains and hills like we had to do here since we couldn't go through this one."

"Up to where it's colder."

"That's it, but let's go, we're not there yet." They're off. Some of the clouds even seem to be raining intentionally now.

"Man, I'm really starting to sweat."

"Well, (pant, pant) *you're part of the cycle, too."*

Finally, and none too soon, the procession, which is now strung out all along the trail, reaches the top of the hill.

"Whow, that's incredible. Where do we go from here? There's no more up."

"I guess there's only one place for a cycle to go—back to where it came from. It's time for the big rainstorm. Carrie and Gordy, give us a big rainstorm, over in that direction."

"Yay, sploosh, splish, splash!"

"Now that was simple, but think about how much energy you used to get your bucket of water *up* here. Pretty tiring, huh? From now on every time it rains, think about how much sunlight energy it must have taken to get all that water into the sky.

"However, there's a little more to it than that. If you'll remember the statement in the passport, we didn't need just *any* water."

"It was CLEAN water."

"Exactly. The sunship has to have some way of continually renewing and purifying its limited supply of water. Just to make a point, let's get everybody else's water real muddy. Mix a little soil in your buckets and stir it up."

"I don't have too much left."

"I see what you mean. Let's use your bucket to watch what happens when the rain falls on the ground . . . ooops! Right over here in the middle of our circle."

"It's soaking right into the dirt. I thought you said we were gonna clean it."

"Ah, ha. This is one of the craziest and most magical things about the whole water cycle. The *dirt* is going to *clean* the water. Come on over here. It just so happens there's a tank of sand behind this tree. It'll work perfectly for our purposes. Can you guys take the last two buckets and pour that mucky water into the top . . . slowly?"

"There's a hole in the bottom, it's coming out."

"Good. Doug, why don't you take your bucket and catch the water as it comes out."

"It's clean!"

"This is the world's greatest filter and it's always at work. We never even notice. Dump your bucket into the soil, too, Carlos. Now, can you lead us to where that water is going to end up?"

"Back where it started—in the river!?"

"Let's go!"

They're off again. This time they go back down the hill, but Bill takes a little detour just before they reach the bottom of the trail. A beautiful spring flows out of a mossy escarpment.

"Wow, here it comes!"

"No, it couldn't come that fast, could it?"

"No, it couldn't. That water is from the spring rains, but your water will follow pretty much the same path. By the way, the cycle flows through us, too. Let's have a drink."

B-5   "THE ROOT SELLER"

When Bill and the kids arrive at the morning's last station, they find not only the usual prop box, but also a rack of green umbrellas.

"Umbrellas? There's not a cloud in the sky."

"Yeah. I wonder what this is all about."

"Can't you tell? Those aren't umbrellas. Those are the leaves of plants. In fact, you're all going to be their stems in just a moment. But first, I should introduce myself. At this station, I'm known as the old Root Seller. That name may not make much sense right now, but I think you'll figure it out as we go along. After we read the passport entries, I am going to help you get to know some very special parts of most plants."

The key concept statement and explanation are soon read, and the group takes a quick look around to check out the tremendous variety of plant life that grows in the area. The leader mentions that because there is so much variety, no one usually has a chance to get to know individuals. However, he explains that they are going to change that around a bit this morning.

The group forms a circle around a black cloth, which obviously hides a pile of objects. The leader explains that under the cloth lie the "deeper personalities" of some of the plants which are found in this area. "Most people know a few plants' faces, but very few know the hidden side of them—their roots. Since roots are so important to plants, you are going to have a chance to meet a few of them right now."

Bill removes the black cloth revealing a tangled pile of plant roots, in several shapes, sizes, and textures. Everybody is told to select one for close examination, and then share any discoveries made with each other.

As the kids begin to notice the obvious characteristics of the roots, Bill suggests various ways of getting to know them better: "Rub them on your arm or against your cheek. Are they soft or hard? Waxy or velvety? Long or short? How about their smell? Are there small fibers, giving them a fuzzy character, or are they smooth and shiny? Do they feel spongy or tough? You know, these things are all similar in some ways because they are all roots, but each one is also different from all the rest."

The kids are soon satisfied with their level of familiarity, and the roots are returned to the center of the circle. Bill explains that now they are going to get "deeply" involved in the functioning of roots as well.

"Now, friends, you are about to have the rare opportunity of being watered yourselves, just like real plants."

This last comment is illustrated by a pirouette-like demonstration of the proper use of the umbrella "leaves" which Doug noticed earlier.

"Hey, Bill, you look just like a daffodil."

"I've been practicing a lot. Anyway, everyone is going to be a plant, so I'd like all of you to come over here and get two things you need, an umbrella for your leaves and one of these big sponges for a root. These sponges do a great job of collecting rainwater. Once you're set with these things, you'll need to plant yourselves somewhere. Everybody should find themselves a spot on one of these 'planting bed' boards lying around here."

It's not long before the kids have all found their places and are doing flower impersonations of their own. Bill continues, "O.K., you're all doing a good job of flowering. Really get into it. Remember, you're rooted in one area and can't move your feet. You can take your 'root' in your spare hand and hold it out there where the rains can fall on it."

"What rains? There's still not a cloud in the sky!"

"Ah! So you plants are thirsty? I thought you'd never ask. It just so happens that there's a whole streamful of water over there, and I have here a . . . sprinkling can."

"Oh, no."

"Before the rains come, however, I need to explain what you're trying to do here as plants. You are very interested in getting enough water to stay alive. In addition, just as the passport stated, we're trying to keep some plants growing here all of the time. As you stand rooted in your places the seasons will pass very quickly. Each time I come around with my sprinkling can, we will be going through one full year. Sometimes there will be a lot of rain; at other times there will be great dry spells. Some of you may dry out and shrivel up. In that case you will have to fold up your umbrella, move out of this area, and stand over there in the 'shrivel circle.'"

"How do you know when you're shrivelled up?"

"Good question, Carrie. When I come around, if you can't show me some water by putting it in my collection cup, you're finished for the year. Now if *all* of the plants die, that would mean our community had lost its struggle with the conditions here. Since nature is always trying to cover the land with living things, we have to figure out how to keep at least one plant alive in all kinds of conditions."

"One question, are you going to sprinkle right on us?"

"Let's start and you'll find out. You might want to put up your umbrella of leaves though."

The leader begins his rounds, passing from one plant to the next, watering each "leafy canopy" and the sponges thrust out from underneath them. The kids notice that he is not only watering their leaves and their roots, but also making a definite point of watering the ground as well. When asked about this peculiar behavior, he asks rhetorically if rain falls only on the plants and not on the area around them.

The first year brings good rains and after passing around this time with his collection cup, Bill comments that it appears as if everyone will survive this unusually wet year. A somber warning follows, however, "Things can't always be this good."

The second year starts very slowly with only sporadic rains. The plants begin to look worried. Out comes the cup. As it makes the rounds, two of the plants are unable to produce enough water to convince the Root Seller that they are alive and must "shrivel." Finally, after a long dry period lasting several years, the remaining plants are forced out as well. Mother Nature has lost her battle to keep green things growing on this piece of land.

Take heart. This is not the end of the story. The plants do not just hang up their umbrellas. Instead, the group circles around the prop box and is given a chance to make good.

"You know, you were all pretty good plants, but that's not all that counts. We have to figure out a way to keep some plants here that can survive all kinds of problems."

"Well, what can we do? When there's no water, there's no water."

"Now wait just a second, Doug. Remember all that water that went into the ground? Maybe there *is* something we can do here. In fact, if you all remember the roots you examined back there, they might give us a clue. Let's go have another look at them."

Looking at his root, Carlos remarks about its long and stringy appearance. *"This root doesn't look like a sponge. It's long and thin."*

"All right. That's a good point. In fact, if you remember, the main thing about these roots is that they're all *different*."

"Yeah, but our sponges are all exactly the same."

"We need something different!"

"O.K. I think the old Root Seller has the solution to all your problems. What we need around here is some *diversity*. We need a variety of roots, so that they don't all get their water in the same way. That way if there is a change in the amount of rainfall, the chances are much better that at least one plant will be able to make it through the crisis."

"I want to be long and stringy, I have a feeling that maybe there's water I can stretch out for in one way or another."

"Great, Carrie. I think I have just the root for you."

The Root Seller pulls out of the prop box a whole bundle of "roots." There are three basic kinds represented. The sponges are already familiar. The leader suggests that they might belong to a plant which is able to gather its water from the surface of the ground and which is able to stand great amounts of water such as would be found in a low area or during a rainy season. "The problems we may find are not only those of too little water, you know, so don't be disappointed if you get a sponge." A second type of root is now introduced. This one the leader equates with a cactus, for it has the ability to store water. A small sponge is combined with a tin can. Although the sponge cannot catch as much at one time as the larger "surface root" (it's cheating to catch the water with the storage can), its ability to store water over dry periods is an obvious benefit.

The third type of root brings a roar of laughter from the kids, except for Carrie, who has been waiting for her "stretchy" root. Bill seems to be a little unsure about the value of this root, too. It consists of a wire-cored, hook-shaped piece of sponge on the end of a long piece of string.

"Hey, Bill, that's not fair. This thing's no good."

"Gee, I'm sorry, Carrie. It does look a little funny, but it's the 'stretchiest' root we've got. We'll just have to see what happens."

And on that note the action begins. The rules remain the same: at least one plant must survive in order to keep life going in this area. The kids take their places on the "planting boards" again, and the rains fall. This time the first year is a year of average rains with a tendency to scattered showers. Although the cacti busily try to squeeze water into their storage cans, they can't do quite as well as the "surface roots" with their wide-reaching big sponges. As for Carrie, well, she best sums up her own situtation:

"Hey, this is lousy. This stupid root can't do anything. All the water runs off my umbrella—I mean leaves—and just soaks into the ground!"

Gordy replies: *"You asked for it."*

But silence falls on all as the measuring cup comes around. Carrie, of course, fails and so do the cacti, much to their dismay. The cacti are permitted, however, to retain the water in their storage cans, since cactus can store water for a long period of time.

Finally, Bill arrives at the surface roots, on which the whole area now depends. And they survive. Whew!

The second year is not so easy, however. Not much rain falls and things look bad. The surface-rooted plants are not able to catch the scarce moisture as it rolls off their canopies. Carrie has given up all hope by now. But, by combining the water from the two-year accumulation in their storage cans, the cacti survive.

"Saved again. Good thing we had a little diversity around here.

Those cacti were able to do what the surface-rooted plants couldn't," Bill sighs.

"Yeah, but it better rain this year 'cause now you took all the water we stored up so carefully."

"Well, that's how it goes. You save it up but eventually you need to use it to survive. Let's see what happens this year!" Alas, *nothing* happens this year. A few showers here and there, but none on our plants. And this is followed by another dry year, and another!

"Hey, I feel like I'm wilting up. I need water."

But Bill just can't help, and finally he comes around with the cup.

"Surface-rooted plants?"

"Nothing."

"Cacti?"

"Nothing."

"Well, I don't know if I even need to check Carrie. All the water that's fallen on her has just dropped down into the ground and sunk away . . . lost. Wish we could get to it."

"Maybe we could dig a well," suggests Doug.

"Plants can't dig," laments Carrie.

At this point Bill's face lights up. "No, but maybe there's a plant that can send its roots down to reach the deep ground water that's not affected so much by periods of drought. Carrie, lift up your board!"

And lo and behold under Carrie's feet all along there's been a three-foot-deep hole with a bucket of water at the bottom. Inside this bucket, there's a smaller bucket with a wire handle.

"Ground water, a third source!" shouts Bill.

Carrie then lowers her "tap root" and pulls up the smaller bucket, with just enough water so that one plant has enough to permit life to go on.

"Yeah, Carrie, your root isn't so worthless after all."

"Of course not, but remember, although she helped us this time, the important factor in the long run was that even though we're all similar, we're all suited to different conditions, which allowed us to survive. Let's hear it for diversity!"

CONCEPT PATHS—
GUIDELINES

Declaration of Interdependence

PROPS:

Edicts—Paint the edicts on 16" x 12" pieces of narrow width plywood. Drill two holes in the top edges, about four inches apart, and add a coat of varnish for protection. Run pieces of cord through the holes and tie the finished edicts to trees or hang them from branches. Place them so that the edict, "King Snoid IV says: 'Thou Shalt do it alone,'" is found last.

Declaration—Print enough declarations for each group. Keep a supply on hand in the prop box. Be sure to leave enough space for the kids to sign their names. Attach the finished declaration to a tablet-sized piece of wood with map tacks. These can be displayed later in the dining hall.

Quill Pen and Ink Bottle—A quill pen or a ballpoint pen with a feather attached adds to the theme.

GENERAL NOTES:

1. Ask the kids to enter in their passports the examples they found disproving the King's edicts.

Cliff Hangers

PROPS:

Cliff—The cliffhangers' ramp can be built with two 4' x 8' pieces of 5/8'' plywood. The climbing side of the plywood should be smooth and splinter-free and painted to look like the surface of a rock. Attach the two plywood sheets together using 2 x 4s. Bolt the 2 x 4s to the plywood with round-headed carriage bolts. You should lean the ramp against a couple of trees so its pitch can be changed when needed. (Find the angle of pitch that is just too steep for the kids to be able to stand on the ramp.) Anchor the bottom with stakes.

Drill two 3/8'' holes in the top of the ramp for holding the hooks held by the "lichens." Large 'S' hooks attached to the handle of a water-ski towrope make good hangers.

GENERAL NOTES:

1. Locate this station near a good example of plant succession: boulders with lichen, moss, and grass growing on them.
2. Be sure the kids don't take running starts up the ramp; they must begin from a standing position.
3. Have the largest, strongest kids be the lichens.

Food Factory

PROPS:

The Leaf—Build a wood frame in the shape of a leaf, then tack burlap or canvas over it. Include a curtained doorway where the stem tunnel meets the main body of the leaf.

Chloroplast Hats—Green beanies are simple and easy to make.

Chlorophyll Box—Paint a wooden box green and label it "Top Secret."

Molecule Models—Attach velcro to Ping-Pong balls as shown in the diagram (sun—hooked, hydrogen—fuzzy, oxygen—hooked, carbon—fuzzy). Paint them (hydrogen—blue, oxygen—white, carbon—black) and label them with large letters (C-carbon, O and O_2—oxygen, H_2—hydrogen). The sun balls should be painted yellow and labeled with a large "S."

Envelopes—Each is labeled "Air," "Water," or "Sun-Energy" and filled with the appropriate molecules. Have enough prepacked sets on hand to last throughout the morning. (Manila envelopes are strong enough to hold the Ping-Pong balls.)

Speaking Tube—Bury an old piece of garden hose running from a nearby hiding spot to the inside of the leaf.

Pouch—The different sets of envelopes should be stored in a special cloth pouch or an old side pack. The pouches should be hung in the molecule messenger waiting room. Each should be labeled "Air," "Water," or "Sun-Energy."

Orange—One orange can be peeled and divided up among the members of each group.

GENERAL NOTES:

1. Assign the molecule messengers specific envelopes to deliver to the leaf. Show them where the slots in the leaf are located for inserting their envelopes.

2. When speaking into the tube, you must cup your hands around the end of the hose, then speak into your cupped hands. Instruct the "chlorospies" inside the leaf to do the same thing. (Also, avoid speaking to only one of them.)

3. Explain to the molecule messengers that they must remain in the waiting room at all times unless they have been called to make a delivery. (Locate your end of the speaking tube in a hiding place where you can see them without being seen yourself.)

4. A "speaking script" for the crew counselor might look something like this: (static)

"Attention, attention! This is Chlorophyll Control Center. Do you read me?" (Make sure they cup their hands around the end of the speaking tube and talk to you.)" "Thanks for coming to work on the production line at the Food Factory. You're going to have to follow my instructions carefully, O.K.?

"Now, here in the Food Factory we need some important ingredients in order to make food-energy, or *carbohydrates*. Together, call to the molecule messengers for the first important ingredient, AIR." (You may have to say, "On the count of three, call for AIR. One, two, three . . . ") "Tell me when you've got it. What do you find in the envelope? That's carbon dioxide—C for carbon, O_2 for oxygen—and at the Food Factory we get our carbon dioxide directly from the AIR.

"O.K., call for the second important ingredient, WATER. Got it? Great. What's in the envelope? That's hydrogen—H_2, and oxygen—O, the parts that make up WATER.

"Now listen very carefully. Pull off the carbon, C, from the CARBON DIOXIDE and pull of the hydrogen, H_2, from the WATER. Try to stick the carbon, the hydrogen, and the *single* oxygen ball together to make a carbohydrate, the food energy for all life. The three balls should all stick together like links in a chain.

"How are you doing? What!? You have the hydrogen and oxygen stuck together, but the carbon won't stick to the hydrogen?

Something must be missing, huh? (If necessary, repeat the key concept statement.)

"O.K.! Call for the sunlight.

"Using the sunlight, try to stick the carbon and hydrogen together. Got it? Congratulations! You've just completed the process known as photosynthesis. That's the process that takes water, air, and sunlight and makes energy-rich food for all life.

"Just put your completed carbohydrate into the Chlorophyll Box and your work shift is over.

"Oops . . . there's one last thing you need to do. Push your leftover oxygens (O_2s) out the 'Oxygen Exit Tube.'

"Well, thanks for helping out on the production line here at the Food Factory. You can go out now. Be sure to take your flashlight.

"This is Chlorophyll Control Center signing off." (static)

Sun's Bucket Brigade

PROPS:
Buckets—Gallon-sized buckets insure plenty of water and weight for each brigade member to carry.
Water Filter—A steel drum at least two feet wide by thirty inches high is needed for the filter. Fill it with at least seven cubic feet of sand (with a layer of pea gravel on the bottom). Attach a pipe or hose to a small hole beneath the drum and set the whole thing up on blocks.
Mirror—A pocket-sized metal mirror (the kind used for camping) works well. It holds up better than glass mirrors.

GENERAL NOTES:
1. Select a hillside trail that is steep, but graded to prevent erosion.
2. Keep the "clouds" together while "rising" up the hill. Caution the brigade about "racing"; they have a very important job to perform.
3. Avoid "raining" on the same area all of the time.

Root Seller

PROPS:
Umbrellas—Rummage sales and flea markets are good places for locating these props. Paint them green and attach overlapping oilcloth leaves.
Tap Root—Cut out a hook-shaped piece of sponge. Form a large hook out of a piece of heavy wire and push it into the sponge. Although in this case the sponge hook does not actually absorb the water, it makes a visual connection with the sponges the other kids are using for their "roots." This connection can also be strengthened by using the same kind of small wire-handled cans for both the "tap root's" inner bucket and the storage containers for the cacti.

CONCEPT PATH C

C-1   "MISSING PASSENGER HUNT"

A particularly energetic group is making its way down the trail, when all of a sudden Seth stops and asks the kids how often they watch detective shows on television.

"If you watch TV, you have to watch detective shows."

"Well, I'm going to give you folks a chance to be detectives and I mean really great ones. You now have a chance to outperform any of your favorite television characters. You see, we have a missing passenger report on our hands. It was called in from right around here just a few minutes ago. Furthermore, there's a reward offered. I just saw Sergeant O'Malley posting a sign a little bit farther up this trail."

The group is now quieter than they've been all morning as Seth continues, "Since this case may be able to show us a bit about how things work in this part of the forest, there is one task we have to do before we head on up to the scene of the crime. Who would like to read the key idea in the passport that has to do with interrelationships? Anybody have that stamp yet?"

"Yeah, we got that stamp yesterday in the battle with King Snoid IV. Give me a second here and I'll find it . . . ah, O.K., 'ALL LIVING THINGS INTERACT WITH OTHER THINGS IN THEIR SURROUNDINGS.'"

"Rhonda, would you read to us the understanding paragraph right below what Willy just read?"

"Sure, 'All plants and animals living on our sunship are related. Some are involved with others around them because they compete for the same needs. Others work together or cooperate to meet their needs even if they don't know it. All of them depend on one another to maintain the conditions suited for life on earth.'"

"Thanks. Everybody follow that?"

"Yes, but what does that have to do with our missing passenger?"

"Excellent question. I told you you'd make great detectives. We'll see what the connection is when we get up to the scene, but it's a big hint."

The group moves quickly and quietly up to a large tree. From one of its lower branches hangs the following poster:

WANTED!!

INFORMATION LEADING TO
THE DISCOVERY OF ONE
MISSING
PASSENGER!!

REWARD OFFERED

(See other side for details)

"Whew! Looks serious. Somebody read the other side."

"The family of a kidnap victim offers a reward of ten thousand solarians to anyone who can give information leading to the return of their beloved son . . . "

"Ten thousand solarians! How much is a solarian, Seth?"

"Don't know, Rhonda. I'm not sure, but it must be the kind of money they use in these parts. Whatever it is, ten thousand of them must be a lot. Read on, Willy, read on."

"'Should you accept this case you must continue on up this trail. Along the way you will find clues which will help you in your search. These clues have been left by things with which our missing passenger INTERACTED while he lived in this forest community . . .'"

"Wait a minute, what does interact mean again?" asks Jackson, who was less than totally absorbed when the passport entry was read the first time.

"It's like when a thing does something with something else, or I guess really when it does something that affects something else. Right?"

"Sounds good, Gail."

"Hey, there are more instructions here. Let me go on. 'On the back of every clue card the identity of the informer will be given. You should also stick together as a group; many heads are better than one. GOOD LUCK!'"

"One suggestion I might add is that every time we get a clue we will probably want to see if we can narrow things down a bit. The best detectives use the process of elimination! O.K., detectives, let's go!"

The patrol stealthily moves down the trail until suddenly Jackson notices the first clue hanging from the end of a branch. *"Over there, look! Is that what a clue looks like?"*

The group is soon circled around the card, which reads: *"He always gave me carbon dioxide."*

"What does that mean? That doesn't make any sense!"

"You have to see who's talking, Mary Ann. Let me look at the back of the card . . . 'THIS PLANT.' So the plant is talking. Oh, I get it. The plant got carbon dioxide from the missing passenger. So the missing passenger must be an animal."

"Yeah, because animals breathe out carbon dioxide when they take in the oxygen the plants gave out."

"All right, you sleuths are really on the ball. So we can eliminate everything that doesn't breathe oxygen. Let's go."

As the group moves on in their search for new evidence, an important point is brought up. *"It could still be a person, right, Seth?"*

"Sure, I guess so."

"You mean it doesn't have to be a person?"

"Are people the only passengers around here?"

"I guess not, but . . ."

"Good detectives always check out every possibility."

"Hey, here's another clue!"

"First, let's see who's talking this time."

"It's the soil talking."

"So I guess that means that soil INTERACTS with our missing passenger," slips in Seth.

"Yeah. See what it says."

"'When your subject dies (if he hasn't already) he will add to my overall formation.' I know, that means that he'll rot and make fertilizer for the ground here. It's an animal!"

"Cool it, Willy. It could be a plant, too. Plants go into the soil, too, you know."

"Yeah, but it gives off carbon dioxide so it's probably an animal."

"Zounds, you kids are sharp. Let's move on. There must be more ahead. Don't go too fast, though. We can't afford to miss a clue."

"Here's one! The branches say, 'He uses me to make his nest.' I've got it: it's got to be a beaver. It's a beaver. I know it!"

"Right, beavers use sticks, beavers interact with sticks," Gail says, and then with a triumphant look at Seth: *"Fork over the solarians."*

"Whoa, maybe you all are not quite as sharp as I thought you were. Sure it *could* be a beaver. A beaver interacts in all those ways, but all the evidence isn't in yet. Couldn't there be more clues?"

"He's right. Come on, Kojak; let's move out."

"Roger."

"The owl's talking here: 'I'd love to interact with him but he's asleep when I'm awake.' That means he's only out in the daytime!"

"So, it still could be a beaver."

"No way! Sorry, but we were over at a beaver pond yesterday and beavers are mostly nighttime animals."

"Yeah, he's right. Now we're back where we started. It's an animal which is out in the daytime and uses sticks to build its nest."

"Let's go!"

"Not too fast, friends: you could miss a clue." And sure enough, there was another clue right behind a tree which the group was passing by.

"Wow, you have sharp eyes, Seth."

"Well, I've been on this beat for several years. You kids are just rookies. What does it say? And who is our missing passenger tied up with this time?"

"The tree limbs say, 'He uses us as stairways.' Maybe it's a bird."

"Hmmm, let's keep checking it out."

"I have one! Over here. The ground says, 'He used to dig a lot of holes around here.'"

Jackson, who has been pretty quiet, blurts out, *"It's a mole and they killed him. I just saw a dead mole up the trail a little ways."*

"No, it can't be. A mole isn't related to branches. I think we can still find the passenger alive and collect our reward."

Finally, the case starts to break. The next clue, given by a sapling, says, *"He planted me about fifteen years ago."*

"I've got it! It's a squirrel. He was burying the nuts and they grew."

"A squirrel? That's an interesting theory. Does it fit all the clues we've come up with so far?"

A quick run-through of the available evidence seems to corroborate the conclusion, but the squad has by now learned some of the finer points of detective work.

"Let's not decide yet; maybe there are more clues."

"It's not over yet," announces Rhonda. *"Here's the next one. 'He often eats at my restaurant,' and it's the tree talking."*

"Yeah, and that's not all," murmurs Willy, who is busily sifting through some fresh evidence on the ground under the tree. *"Look at these pieces of pinecone down here. They've been all chewed up by something . . . and I bet that something was a squirrel."*

"That *is* quite a piece of evidence, but I see one more clue up ahead, very near the end of the trail."

"Let's go."

Ignoring the advice of the wanted poster, Mary Ann has run ahead and, immediately after reading the clue, flashes a deeply saddened glance back at the other sleuths, who are right at her heels.

"*We're too late. It's from a hawk and . . .* "

"*Oh, no, don't tell me, after all this work.*"

"*It says, 'He was one of my favorite meals.*"

"Bye-bye solarians," advises Seth.

"*Poor squirrel,*" moans Mary Ann.

"*Lucky hawk,*" quips Willy.

"I guess when two things interact in that way, one of them is the meal," Seth notes, with the resigned air of a seasoned detective. "Everybody get out your passports and let's try to find some 'clues' to interrelationships in the natural world right around here."

"*Wow, we already saw a whole bunch of them investigating that case.*"

"You're right, but see if you can come up with the interactions instead of just figuring out who they happened to. That takes some pretty good detective work itself."

"*Hah, not really. I just read the key idea again. It says all things are related. That means everything must be an example.*"

"You people *are* slick. Well, look around and pick one out which seems really neat to you."

All of them soon have their examples entered in their passport, but upon sharing ideas one stands out as the most appropriate item to leave for other groups to find as they arrive at this point. Jackson, who had strayed away a bit in his search, happened to catch sight of a bird disappearing into a small hole in a nearby tree. After checking up on this passenger, the group decides to leave a sighting scope lashed to a nearby branch. It is far enough away from the nest so as not to disturb the comings and goings of the birds as they feed their young, but close enough so that the nesting materials which the birds have collected are also clearly visible to anyone looking through the tube.

C-2   "TOOLS AND TASKS"

Seth's group is stumped by a sighting scope left by another group on their walk from the "Missing Passenger Hunt" to "Tools and Tasks," the next station. They've figured out many scopes during their mornings on the other paths, but this one seems to be especially tricky.

"First of all, why would they have waited until they got here to leave a sighting scope? They're supposed to put them up right after they leave the station, aren't they?"

"Yes," Seth replies, "everybody does it the same way. They pick the best of the examples that everyone puts in their passports, then they find a good instance of it somewhere along the way and point the scope at it. It's the same as we've been doing all along."

"But look, this one is stamped 'adaptation,' isn't that the understanding for the next station?"

"Sometimes the scopes come loose and end up pointing at something that they're not supposed to."

"Yeah, but this thing's solid as a rock, and it's definitely pointing at that tree over there."

"What's so special about that tree except that it's all bent over like that?"

"Nothing, so that must be what they're talking about. I wonder why it's bent over anyway?"

"Good question, but I'll bet that whoever put this scope up came back here to do it. May be we should come back here to figure it out after we do 'Tools and Tasks.'"

"I guess we could do that, but I think I know what they are talking about."

"What, Willy?"

"I want to wait to be sure. Let's come back."

"O.K., let's go. The station is just around the bend. Keep your eyes open, though. There are often some great spider webs along here. We could check out one of the spiders with our bug boxes."

As the bunch rounds a bend in the morning's trail, they are greeted by a large cardboard flower perched on top of an old stump. Inside the flower is a deep vessel containing nectar, in this case lemonade. The task is soon clear: get the nectar out of the flower. However, the kids find that it is not as simple as it sounds. The leader goes to the prop box and pulls out five papier-mache masks, one for each member of the group. Each mask is in the shape of a different bird's face. The beaks of the masks are designed to represent well-defined and divergent adaptations to different food gathering tasks.

The kids soon line up at the flower, ready for their chance at the sweet reward. The "hawk" is unable to fit his sharp beak, adapted for tearing, into the flower. The stubby, seed-cracking "sparrow beak" has the same problem. Three more attempts are made with similarly frustrating results: neither the "pelican," the "shorebird," nor the "woodpecker" is able to adapt its physical features to the flower's peculiarity. Finally, just in the nick of time and with a great flourish, the leader produces the perfect tool, a hummingbird mask complete with a long penetrating bill. Furthermore, the bill is equipped with a central straw, enabling the leader to approach the flower and draw a great slurp of lemonade. As might be expected, this act is met with a healthy amount of criticism from the maladjusted birds.

"Hey, that's no fair! Your mask fits right in there like a straw."

"Don't blame me. Everything fits where and how it lives. I guess I'm just adapted to getting the nectar out of flowers."

"You're not adapted to do that. The hummingbird is adapted to do that. You just put on the hummingbird mask."

"Well, you each had a mask. Your birds are all adapted to a certain kind of life, too. In fact, let's have a look at this box over here. Every animal has a task in life, like getting a certain kind of food. And for every one of these tasks there's a tool that fits its job."

The leader takes the group to a large toolbox. On the inside of the lid are placed drawings of a number of different birds including the five that the kids have just met. Each bird is portrayed in the act of using its beak. Inside the box are found the tools which correspond to the functions of the bird beaks illustrated:

Pelican: Strainer
Hawk: Pruning Shears
Sparrow: Nutcracker
Spoonbill: Salad tongs (interlocking spoon and fork)
Warbler: Needle-nosed pliers
Woodpecker: Geology pick
Sandpiper: Long tweezers
Bittern: Ice pick

Each youngster tries to select a tool from the box to match the beak on his or her mask. The extra tools found there provide for some challenging problems. Finally, the leader suggests that all should have a try at the hummingbird's role. As the kids wait their turn for the nectar, the leader brings out some animal and bird skulls to examine. (Each has been selected for its obvious adaptive structure.)

"O.K., let's see if we can find some examples of things with special adaptations right around here and describe them in our passports. Remember, you can either describe your example in words or draw a picture. But, if you draw a picture, be sure to put in a caption explaining it. I'm not saying that you're not all great artists, but even artists sometimes forget what they were trying to say, and you'll want to be able to use your examples when you get back to school."

"What if we can't find enough animals right around here for everybody to come up with a different example?"

"Do they all have to be animal adaptations? What about that tree that we went by before we got to the flower?"

"Ah, ha, Willy. I didn't think you'd forget that. Still think you know what they were talking about?"

"Yeah, now I'm sure, because I had an example of a plant

adaptation yesterday. That tree is adapted to be able to bend over and grow in certain directions in order to get to the light. Probably there was a bigger tree growing up over it for a while or something like that.''

"Good work. I think you *all* have picked up quite a few detective skills. Let's see everybody use them in the search for examples here, too. Then we'll get stamped in."

Now that the kids are thinking about both plant and animal adaptations the examples roll in. When they show Seth their work, he checks them out and then for each person repeats the key idea as he stamps the passports with the concept word: ADAPTATION.

C-3   "CHAIN GANG"

Seth's group rambles along to the next station, commenting on the way about the warmth of the morning. Just as they round the bend in the trail which leads to the end of the pond, Seth mentions that they couldn't ask for a better day to complete the activity at the next station. "It is *possible* to get a little wet there, even though the wetness will mostly be in your minds. But that will make more sense later. Right now who wants to read the sunship understanding from the passport?"

"Which one? We don't know what we're doing yet."

"Oh, that's right. Does anyone have any stamps for energy flow yet?"

"Yeah, I've got two already."

"O.K., the one we're interested in right now is on page eight. Who'll read the statement in the box on that page?"

"I will. 'THE SUN IS THE SOURCE OF ENERGY FOR ALL LIVING THINGS.'"

"Do you remember Mr. Sun's Restaurant, where you were all plants and animals at the banquet of sunlight? Well, here we're going to be seeing a different part of the same understanding. If you read further in your passport, I think you'll see what I mean. Who would like to read aloud? O.K., Gail, take it away."

"As energy moves along from the sun to plants and on to animals, much of it is lost. Before they are eaten, plants use up much of their energy just to grow. And a lot of sunlight energy is required just for animals to move around. Because of this energy loss, a lot more sun-energy is needed to feed a meat-eater than to feed a plant-eater."

"Good. Thanks, Gail. Now, in just a minute we're all going to be taking part in a great race. We call it the 'Chain Gang.' However, in this chain gang you folks will be carrying buckets instead of chains. The chain we'll be seeing in action is a *food chain* similar to the one at Mr. Sun's Restaurant. But this time we'll be seeing how energy is lost as it moves from the sun to whatever finally ends up eating it. In fact, this great race is going to be from the sun to a burger."

"A burger?"

"Yep, a burger. In this race we are all going to be carrying energy through a food chain. But one team is going to be carrying energy from the sun to a *ham*burger, and the other is going to be carrying energy from the sun to a *soy*burger."

"What's a soyburger, Seth?"

"I know; it's a burger made from soybeans."

"Exactly. Now, it's a little difficult to actually carry energy, so we have to find something to take its place and that something is going to be water. In fact, the pond over there is going to be the sun in our race, and both teams will get their energy from the 'sun-pond.' There will be a tub for each team at the end of the course. For one team, this tub will stand for a soyburger, and for the other team, it will be a hamburger. I'll be interested to see which team will be able to fill up their burger bucket first, or in other words, which team will be using sun-energy most efficiently."

Willy, who has been doing a little investigating, suddenly calls out, *"Hey, wait a minute. These buckets have got holes in them."*

"Ah, ha, that's a good observation. Remember what was said in that sunship understanding in the passport."

"Something about energy being lost?"

"Right, and since most of the energy is lost as it moves through the food chain in the natural world, that's exactly what may happen here. We'll just have to find out as we go along. So let's get on with it. We need two teams, and each team will have different people playing different positions in the food chain. Now, let's just see who would like to be what and divide it up that way. I have here the name tags for the different steps in the food chain. Who wants to be a Sun?"

"I do!"

"Me, too!"

"O.K. It just so happens that each team has to have a 'Sun-person,' since that's where it all starts. So both of you can be 'Sun-people.' Now where do you suppose the Sun-people will have to be in this race?"

"Down by the edge of the pond, since that's the sun and water is energy."

"Great! Take a bucket marked 'Sun' and one of you stand on either side of that string down there. That's the line that divides the soyburger team from the hamburger team."

"Do we have any budding plants in this group?"

"I'll be a plant."

"O.K., anybody else? We have to have two plants. They're the only ones who can take energy right from the sun. This is a very important role to play in this race."

"Yeah, but both of use want to be animals."

"Hmmm, that's a problem. We have the Sun-person for each team down there, and here we are going to have a *soy*burger and a *ham*burger. We seem to be missing some links in our food chain. Let's see what we need to end up with one hamburger and one soyburger."

"Hey, I've got it. Only one team has to have an animal. Soybeans aren't animals!"

"Well, in that case, do you want to be a plant?"

"Well, I guess so."

"Thanks. Now plants, let's figure out where you're supposed to play on these teams."

"We must be down by the Sun-people, but how do we get the energy from them?"

"Good question, but remember, water is energy here."

"They just pour it in?"

"Right. Sun-people get their energy from the sun-pond and then pass it on to the 'plant-people.' Then the plant-people will pass it on to wherever it goes next, just like in a relay race. There's only one person left, and he's going to be the cow."

"I eat the plants."

"That's it, more or less. Come on over, Sir Cow. Now, we have two lines, and they're both trying to fill up their burger tubs first."

"Yeah, but we have more people in our line," says the forlorn cow.

"Well, it takes a cow to make a hamburger."

"Oh, yeah, I guess so."

"And a soyburger is made directly from plants, so it looks like the soyburger team has a shorter distance to go, which brings up the last of the rules before we start the great race. Since this race is just a copy of what happens in nature, we'll play it by those rules. Now, what that means is that you can only pass energy on to whoever gets energy from the role you are playing in the natural world. Sun-people pass to plant-people, plant-people pass either to the cow or to the soyburger tub, and the cow fills up the hamburger tub. Since energy loss is something that is always

happening in the world, we can't try to avoid it here. In other words, don't try to cover the holes in your buckets, just go as fast as you can while carrying energy along the food chain. As soon as you have emptied your bucket into the next bucket in the chain, you can turn back and fill it up again. We'll see which team fills up their 'burger tub' first.

"One last thing, when I say 'stop action,' that means everybody stop right where you are, and we'll have a look at what's happening to the energy as it moves from the sun to the burgers."

"What if you're pouring energy right then?"

"Sorry, but you have to stop right then."

"What if it's going on your foot?"

"Then since it's a warm day, your foot gets an energy shower. Everybody ready? Remember: water is energy. On your marks! Get set! Go!"

The action is fast and furious. Since the buckets are set at distances which approximate the conditions in a food chain, the Sun-people are moving back and forth at a great rate while the plant- and cow-people are doing proportionately less work. It soon becomes apparent that the soyburger team has a definite edge over the hamburgers. Of the two tubs at the goal line, neither of which have holes, theirs is filling up about twice as fast.

"Stop action!"

"Whew! This is crazy. The energy is escaping almost as fast as you can get more."

"True. It's a tough life carrying energy. About nine-tenths of the work is wasted. Take a look and see who is doing the most work here."

"The Sun-people. At least I sure am," announces a panting sun.

"Can you all see who's winning the race?"

"Yeah! We are!" yell the soyburgers.

To this the cow responds, *"Yeah, because we have to carry the energy through more steps. But, if I could squeeze the water out of my clothes and put it back in my bucket, we'd be winning."*

"O.K. Let's start the race again. Go!"

It doesn't take long until the soyburger tub is completely full. "All right! We have a winner. This team has moved enough energy to make a soyburger while the hamburger bucket is only half full."

"We protest! We want another chance," yells the cow.

"Forget it, Jackson. We can never beat them. They have less work to do and fewer places to lose water . . . I mean energy."

"That's right, folks. I'm afraid the deck was stacked against the hamburger team, so shake off the water and come on over.

"It's time to get out your passports and find some examples, then I'll stamp you in. Everybody try to find a natural example around here of energy being lost just like we saw it get lost in the race."

"Boy, that's tough, because you can't see energy really."

"That a good point; energy is slippery stuff. But look around and see if you can find energy being used up by anything or any *things* that are gathering energy right now."

"Hey, the fish in the pond are using up energy while they swim around."

"Dynamite, Jackson. Figure out some way to put that in the example section of your passport. Either draw a picture or write it out. Everybody else take a minute and look around here for other examples."

One finds an ant crawling along, one notices decaying blackberries, another points to a bird chirping, and one notes that *they* just used up a lot of energy running around carrying leaky buckets!

"We sure have. We'll be extra hungry for lunch today; we'll have to get lots of energy from other plants and animals in order to be ready for our big event this afternoon."

C-4   "SOIL SINKS"

Seth and his group are fascinated by an iridescent blue insect, which they have discovered and placed in one of their magnifying vials.

"The color on that thing is unbelievable."

"It seems like it's going to crawl right up into your eyeball when you look at it through this end of the tube."

"And those eyes seem like giant globes on the side of his head."

At this point, Seth joins the conversation: "It's incredible how we overlook all the insects around us when, in fact, they're probably the most unusual and interesting of all the passengers on the sunship. What's even more amazing is that four out of every five of the animals on our planet are insects, and we don't even see most of them!"

"I can't say I'm too sorry."

"They sure are neat when you get a close look at them, though, aren't they, Gail? Perhaps this guy might win our weird insect adaptation of the day award."

"Hey, that's true."

"Another amazing thing about insects is that many of them spend a large part of their lives in the soil. The next station on our map today is going to give us a good chance to check out some of that soil. Maybe we'll find some more of these little beauties.

"You know, soil is a thing that most people overlook in the same way they overlook insects. Everybody calls it dirt and tells you to wash it off your hands. Well, pretty soon we're all going to have a chance to switch that one around a bit. But first, let's read what the passport has to say about soil."

After checking the entry in the passport, the kids pick up handfuls of soil and sift through them, trying to imagine what could possibly have gone into its formation. Seth produces a hand lens for each so they can see the minute particles: "I wonder what's in that handful of soil you're examining? Most of this forest soil was formed right here—it didn't come from somewhere else—so the things it's made of must be around here somewhere."

Seth suggests that they try to do a little soil building on their own. It will be tough, he comments, since about two hundred years are required to build an average inch of this rich soil, and the group will only have a few minutes to create their masterpiece. This brief announcement sends everyone scrambling to collect the ingredients for their soil recipe, turning up and discarding various items.

Each youngster is given a sturdy denim bag to use as a "time capsule" in which the long-term effects of weathering and erosion can occur. The kids are then assigned the roles of great storms, seasonal freeze-thaw patterns, and chemical and bacterial actions in the slow-motion drama of soil formation. (The group's drama is faster paced, however, since mallets are used to pound the bags in imitation of these natural forces.)

After thousands of mini-years have passed in the guise of a few minutes, the contents of the bags are opened on a cable-spool table situated in the center of the work area. Products are compared in relation to the ingredients used in their creation. And some of the soil makers decide to make a few last minute additions in light of recipe hints shared by fellow "chefs."

Of course, denim bags and mallets cannot be expected to duplicate the work accomplished by more subtle forces over far greater lengths of time. For this reason the group leader suggests that they take a tour of nature's "soil kitchen" in order to get a stop-action view of a few of the many stages found throughout the thousands of years of soil creation. *"But,* upon entering any kitchen and particularly after doing such 'dirty' work, we must wash our hands." The group files past a sequence of four old kitchen sinks placed on the ground and filled with four stages in the development of soil. Parent material, subsoil, topsoil, and duff are all represented in the separate sinks. The group "washes up" in each sink sampling the color, texture, dampness, and smell of each layer of soil.

Seth suggests, "As you file by, keep your own sample in mind. Which sink comes closest to being the same as the soil you made yourself?"

"This first one has sticks and leaves and stuff just like the one I made."

"Yeah, it seems like when you get to the next sink those things are much more mixed in; you can hardly tell they're in there any more."

"Go back to the recipe table, grab a little bit of your concoction and bring it over. Check it for feel and smell against the soil in the sinks."

"I sure never thought I'd be smelling dirt, but you can really tell the difference. This stuff, the real thing in the sink, smells much older or something than mine. I know. It smells much moldier."

"It seems damper, too; sticks together more. But it's even more different from the soil in the end sink than it is from the stuff that I made. This soil in the last sink is a completely different color. It's much rockier and drier, too. It's really rough when you wash up in it—like the Lavaiest soap in town!"

Finally, after sampling the soil layers firsthand, the kids head down for a tour of the master chef's kitchen. A soil profile pit has been dug so that the group can see the four layers of soil in their natural position and sequence. Everyone is encouraged to feel carefully (and smell) each layer and compare it with the soil in which they washed their hands. Measuring just the duff and topsoil "frosting" on the soil layer cake, the group is able to figure out roughly the time involved merely in the formation of the few inches on top of the profile. Even more impressive is the notion this gives of the incalculable number of years lying between the soil's parent material and its distant relative in the fertile topsoil.

Up to her elbows in the "layer cake," Mary Ann sums it all up: *"You know, it's true: 'EVERYTHING IS BECOMING SOMETHING ELSE.'"*

C-5   "THE BEST DEAL ON EARTH"

After having washed off the residue left from dipping their hands into the "sinks," the group spends a few quiet minutes soaking their feet in the stream all the while looking for snails. They then proceed along the shore toward the next station, about which Seth is being decidedly uncommunicative. "All I can tell you is that you are going to take part in the best deal on earth. I'm going to make you *such a deal*, you won't be able to resist it.

The group is curious, but not overly so; this is the last station, the last of fifteen stamps. By now, they know better than to anticipate the upcoming action.

All of a sudden Rhonda notices a sighting scope improbably suspended over the water and pointed straight down. A couple of light-footed hops place her close enough to the scope to read the key idea stamp, "Change."

"The darn thing is pointing right at that boulder in the middle of the stream. What could possibly be changing about that?" asks Rhonda.

"That's a great scope," Gail replies. *"That rock is changing, but not very fast! The water's wearing it away. I wonder how in the world they got that scope up there? Somebody must have been on somebody else's shoulders."*

"Good point. That *is* quite a placement. Beautiful. Well, friends, we're just about there, the last station. How would you all feel about taking a trip to see what the twenty-first century might be like?"

"I thought you were going to make us such a deal . . . "

"Well, that's all part of it. This place is not necessarily what the cities of the twenty-first century are *going* to be like, but it's easy to imagine that the situation *might* be something similar. So let's enter my time machine up ahead."

"What's this thing?" Jackson asks as the group passes an old bicycle with several strange tubes draped over it.

"Oh, that old thing? That's my 'air cycle.' You may get a chance to ride it a little later. First, who can read this sign for us?"

Rhonda reads aloud a sign which explains to the group that each step they take down this "time trail" is ten years into the future, and *there's no turning back!*

The leader guides the group down the time trail and into a small tent. As soon as they all have a place to sit and the passport entries are read, he proceeds to light an extremely cheap and foul-smelling cigar. Over their protests, he reminds them that they all had agreed to this trip to a city of the future, and now they have arrived.

The stench begins to get more and more overbearing. Before the situation is truly noxious, two gas masks are pulled out from the station prop box, which is inside the tent. Five voices simultaneously raise the same protest, *"Why only two?"*

"What I'm going to offer you is the best deal on earth, but I have only been able to contract for a small part of it. It's a trade that goes on all the time, but which we all take for granted. Here in the twenty-first century they took this deal a little too much for granted, and that's the situation we've all got ourselves into by agreeing to go on this trip into the future."

"Hey, Seth. How about letting us use those masks. At least two of us could be breathing!"

"O.K., I'll tell you my sad tale then while we share the two masks we have.

"As you know, the good clean oxygen we need to breathe comes from green plants." (He draws a deep breath from the mask.)

"Yeah?"

"Well, it just so happens that it takes quite an area of green plants to produce enough oxygen for just one person. I was only able to make a deal with enough area of forest for two masks. These hoses we're breathing out of run outside to a certain amount of plants. This deal I made, and which we're all making, is a two-way deal. For the oxygen we *get*, we repay the plants with the carbon dioxide that we breathe out."

As the masks continue to be passed around, Jackson asks, *"So these tubes run out to the plants and we're trading off with them every time we breathe?"*

"Exactly. The problem is that it takes about 625 square meters of forest to supply enough . . . sputter, sputter . . . air for one person. And . . . cough, cough . . . these tubes only draw from 1250 square meters, so I think we'd better . . . get . . . out of here!"

The group hastily exits from the tent, closely pursued by a purple haze. Everybody is curious about the course of the tubes leaving the tent. One hose is seen to end right outside the wall of the tent. The leader then points out two cords which outline squares of forest twenty-five meters on each side, one for each hose. The kids are amazed at the size of the area. It seems incredibly large for just one person's air supply. They then step into the area and exhale mightily, helping in a small way to repay their end of the deal.

The leader now brings the group over to the "air cycle." He explains that the deal they just made with the plants would certainly seem more than fair; after all, the plants give us exactly what we need in exchange for exactly what we want to get rid of, oxygen for carbon dioxide. However, the story gets even better, as they will all see by taking a ride on the "air cycle."

The kids all agree that it takes oxygen to ride a bike, even a bike like the "air cycle," which doesn't go anywhere. If you ride hard enough, you'll be short of breath. The "wheeler dealer" then explains that we need to take oxygen in so our muscles can burn up the food and release the energy which it takes to move that bike around in the first place. He then produces a candle and a small glass jar. This is used to illustrate how the candle needs oxygen in order to burn. Removing the candle's oxygen supply causes it to burn out.

The first rider is now ready to hop on the "air cycle." It then becomes apparent why the bike is placed right in front of a blackberry bush. Before the subject can ride, she is given a small sample of berries from a jar hung in the bush. She now has the food she needs to pedal. The only thing lacking now is the oxygen needed to enable her to release that energy. Of course, this comes from a mask which has a hose running up into the leafy branches of the tree.

As the kids all take their turns on the cycle, Seth proudly stands alongside the bike. "I *told* you I was going to make you the greatest deal on earth. My friends, the plants are not only the ones who give you the food you burn, they also give you the oxygen to burn it with. Such a deal. Such a deal. Just be sure to keep breathing out."

There is no problem getting examples here. Almost everyone in the group soon has a picture of a leaf—colored a natural green—in their passports. As they leave their sighting scope along the trail, Rhonda gives it a spin, *"They're everywhere!"*

CONCEPT PATHS—
GUIDELINES

Missing Passenger Hunt

PROPS:

Clue Cards—Write the clues on one side of a 5" x 7" index card, and the identity of the informer on the reverse side. (Laminate them or press them between adhesive acetate sheets to increase their durability.) A six-inch piece of red surveyor's tape slipped through a hole punched in the card adds visibility and keeps the "detectives" on the right trail.

Set the clue cards up along the trail, starting with those that offer the most general information and progressing to those that contain more revealing information. Place the cards so that the trail forms a loop. The activity begins and ends near the prop box, where the cue cards can be returned.

GENERAL NOTES:

1. Deputize the detectives by having them swear an oath that they will not run ahead to the next clue until each bit of evidence is thoroughly investigated, and that upon completing the investigation, they will keep all information from future detectives. This discourages the detectives from running ahead from clue to clue and encourages the kids to put their heads together while working out a slow and thorough investigation.

Tools and Tasks

PROPS:

Bird Masks—Construction of the bird masks might be a creative project for the local high school's art class. Begin by salvaging old wire strainers that have handles, then fashion bird faces around them using papier-mache or plaster cast material. The individual beaks hold up better if they are supported with chicken wire or light woods. Once dried, the masks can be painted to resemble the faces of the birds they represent. Attach a hook to the top of each mask so they can be hung inside the prop box when not in use. (Be sure to leave a hole in the mouth of the hummingbird's mask that is large enough to slip a soda straw through.) Cover all the masks with a waterproof finish.

The Flower—The flower can be made with a gallon-size glass jar. Paint it a bright color, punch a hole the size of a straw in the lid, and decorate the top with colorful papier-mache flower petals. (A gallon jar holds a large residue of nectar for many hummingbirds). Set it up on a stump or a special post.

Straws and Cups—An ample supply of these items should be stored in the prop box. A separate straw should be available for each student. Limit each person to one "strawful" of nectar. (Although it is true that hummingbirds have a high metabolic rate, the flower may become "overworked" if excessive sips of nectar are taken from it.)

Toolbox—An old footlocker or similar container can be converted into a toolbox. Inside the lid post pictures showing different birds actually using their beaks.

Chain Gang

PROPS:

Relay Buckets and Burger Tubs—Number ten cans make great "energy" carriers. Paint on the cans the different names of the items represented in the food chain—two "suns," two "plants," one "cow." Punch holes in the bottom of each can. Use larger cans for the burger tubs.

Name Tags—Cut up pieces of wood about mousetrap size. Drill holes in the top and lace string through them so they can be hung around the neck. Inscribe each with the name of the role to be played.

String Divider—Take a fifty-foot piece of string and tie it to stakes between the relay runners. (The players' positions can be indicated on the stakes.)

GENERAL NOTES:

1. Occasionally the hamburger team might win due to an exceptionally fast "cow" or "plant." To account for this factor, position team members a little farther apart or punch a few extra holes in the cow's bucket.

2. You may want to use a second tub of water for your "energy" source. In this case, the teams try to move their whole tub of "energy" down to the burger tub. The winners are the ones who move the most energy in the time allotted (which can be until the first supply bucket is emptied), and it is easy to make the point about what percentage of energy gets from the sun to the burger.

Soil Sinks

PROPS:

Sinks—For a nice surprise, real kitchen sinks make great soil containers. Try rummaging through secondhand stores. Place the names of the layers on the sinks. Be careful. A good rain can destroy your soil samples. Cover each sink daily with a waterproof lid.

Denim Bags—These bags are subjected to a lot of "beatings!" Make them with sturdy denim material (or legs of old blue jeans) and sew in drawstrings.

Wooden Mallets—Check the secondhand stores again.

Yardstick—Use meter sticks if you are teaching the metric system.

Cable Spool Tables—These can usually be picked up free at your electric company's warehouse. (They will expect you to transport them, though.) Circular tables aid sharing among small groups and the spools hold up well outdoors.

GENERAL NOTES:
1. Set up staging areas for each part of the activity.
2. Leave the mallets and bags on the table for the following groups.
3. A large soil profile is not necessarily needed. Look for profiles that have already been cut; for example, near a roadway, drainage ditch, or building. Ask the kids to touch the layers gingerly if the cut is steep. Consider building a shelter over it to prevent it from eroding during heavy rains.

The Best Deal on Earth

PROPS:
Gas Masks—Obtain surplus gas masks to add impact to this station. Use duct tape to attach the hose from each mask to the hose leading outside of the tent. Cut off the head straps to

facilitate passing them around. Keep the masks hidden until you are ready to present them to the kids.

Hoses—Check out garage sales or the local junkyard for sections of garden hose, vacuum tubing, etc.

Tent An old camping tent, or simply pieces of burlap or canvas draped over a wooden frame, makes a good time machine. (It should be airtight.)

Incense—Incense can also give kids the impression that the air of the "Time Machine" smells foul. Burn the incense inside an incense burner or fireproof container. Light it before the kids enter the tent and keep it hidden.

Matches—Keep the matches inside a glass jar. (And keep an extra glass jar on hand for holding the used matches.)

String—Mark off areas around the tent with flag-draped string to indicate the amount of forest needed to produce enough oxygen for one person.

Air Cycle—Again, check the local junkyard. Elevate the rear wheel by lashing the bike up between two trees or make a simple stand.

GENERAL NOTES:

1. Ask the kids to eat their "plant energy" just before riding the air cycle. Review with them the trade between the plants and animals before each ride in order to reinforce how the air cycle works. Be sure to point out that this is not an even trade. We return carbon dioxide to the atmosphere, but the plants do not depend on us for it.

2. Keep the length of rides on the cycle to a minimum—encourage the kids to put out a quick spurt of energy by peddling fast.

Chapter Eight

INTERPRETIVE ENCOUNTERS

Understanding a concept is somewhat like building a house; you have to start with a solid foundation. And like a well-built house, the whole of the concept is much more than scattered pieces of lumber and masonry.

On the Concept Paths, the crew members take part in a series of activities which demonstrate the meaning of such concepts as energy flow operating in the food chain, or change occurring in a particular area. In the "Interpretive Encounters," they participate in activities which take a single concept from a concrete level to a more abstract level of understanding. The Concept Paths serve as the foundation; the Interpretive Encounters build the walls and complete the roof.

The well-built house is a simple, but useful, analogy. The Interpretive Encounters are like the "walls" that provide definition for the structure. By setting the limits for new data relevant to a particular concept, they establish a distinct place for separate pieces of information to come together in strengthening the concept both now and in the future. The "roof" provides dramatic closure. Each Interpretive Encounter ends with a punch, an attention-getting bit of action which vividly completes the essential structure of one particular concept.

Obviously, one of the criteria for an Interpretive Encounter is an unbroken block of time of at least an hour and preferably more. During this time, the activity focuses on a single concept, and there is a central problem-solving story line which is carried throughout to help with the flow. There are two Interpretive Encounters in the Sunship Earth program. They serve as culminating activities for the concept-building portion of the program. Both of them deal with concepts which seem particularly to incorporate all the others: Community and Interrelationships. In

"Border Dispute," the plot involves a war between the inhabitants of neighboring communities. In "Model Planet," described in the last section of the book, the action revolves around the creation of interrelated, self-sustaining systems of life in a model solar system.

"BORDER DISPUTE"

The group is gathered in the "Troll Capital" awaiting the arrival of a messenger. The "Wizard" arrives in a tall pointed hat, breathless.

"A terrible thing has happened! I need your help! Let me explain. You are sitting in the capital of a large community. The citizens of this natural community are in great distress because of the horrible conflict they are having with a neighboring community. The problem arose because the people who live here, who are known as Trolls, have never been able to get along with the inhabitants of the nearby community, the Elves. In fact, for years and years their motto has been heard throughout this land: 'Never trust an Elf.' The situation is made even worse by the fact that the Elves, who live high on the hill at the end of this road, the 'Greenway,' have long had as their motto: 'Never trust a Troll.' All this time, the Wizards, like myself, who have the power to bestow temporary peace on the area, have roamed these communities, trying to establish lasting friendship between the two peoples with no luck. For although the Elves and Trolls are usually peaceful, the Wizards have had no success in bringing them closer together for very long. Now, I'm sorry to have to tell you that I am the last of the Wizards, and in hopes of ending this problem, I am going to turn you into Elves and Trolls to see if you can find a solution. What is so sad about this situation is that, although you may find your best friends in the opposite group, they will have to be your enemies until you find permanent peace."

Amid much protest the Wizard now divides the group into Elves and Trolls, taking care to split pairs of friends. He then has them face each other, glaring.

"Trolls, look around you. This is your home. What is it like?"
"It's kind of open and sunny."
"It's grassy. There aren't any evergreens like over at camp."
"The trees don't have any leaves."
"Lots of bushes."
"Yeah, berry bushes."
"O.K., you have the idea. It's very OPEN . . . in fact, the name of this place is 'Openland.' Everybody get a good look at this area. Fix it in your mind because now we're going to be heading up the Greenway to the Elf capital, a place called 'Forestland.' Notice as we go that there are mileposts along the trail. As we move up, you may see that things change. We're going on a seven-mile hike and we will stop at Milepost Seven, where we'll pull together one more time before the GREAT CONFLICT."

With the atmosphere punctuated by rumblings about a

seven-mile hike, the kids head up the steep hill towards Forestland. Pausing to catch their breath, they notice the changing vegetation.

"This is still open land. Look at these bushes."

"Yeah, but look at the big trees . . . it's getting darker."

Finally, all arrive at the tall cedar-enclosed campfire circle which marks the capital of Forestland, and where they are relieved to discover that the miles they covered were only "elfin" miles.

"Hey, man, this place is beautiful! I'm glad I'm an Elf."

The Wizard asks: "See any differences between the two communities?"

"It's much darker here."

"I'm cold, even though we just came from the open trail."

"Everything's wet!"

"There's nothing growing on the ground!"

"O.K., it's obviously different from the Troll's community. The problem isn't there, though. Both Trolls and Elves know where their territory lies. They know where their home is and what kind of natural community they like. The problem is they don't know where one begins and the other ends. The conflict involves the exact location of the border between the two."

"Oh, that's easy. Just draw a line halfway between the capitals."

"Ah, sorry, but that's just the catch. What's happening, and it seems fair to me, is that both sides are trying to claim as much land as they can. And they both think they have a right to more territory."

"Yeah, Trolls need more land!"

"Hold it, hold it. Here's how it works. As you walked up the Greenway, you noticed the mileposts. Those give us a way of estimating our claims. *But*, since this isn't a war of violence, both groups must use special 'weapons' to back up their claims."

"I know! The Elves can plant seeds of these big trees down in Troll territory. The Elf kind of stuff will grow there."

A Troll responds quickly: *"Well, how come they're not growing down there already? Seeds move around anyway, you know."*

"Ah! Good point!" comments the Wizard. "There must be some other things that play a part in what can grow. Let's compare the two areas, looking for differences between them."

"There's more sun down there."

"Forestland is much higher up and colder 'cause there's more wind and everything."

"Hey, the ground's not the same."

"Yeah, the soil."

"Great, good . . . lots of differences. Now all those differences have something to do with backing up the claims of the Elves and Trolls. It's evidence, like in a trial. And it just so happens that I have here in my bag some things to help you collect this kind of evidence. These are the weapons of this war. It's a war of *proof* . . . a war of wits. Now you'll need a good *solid* proof because Trolls are very hardheaded."

"Yeah, really!"

"And Elves are stubborn, too!"

"Sooo, I think we're ready to go. First you may want to get a little more famliar with your own capital. Then you can try to press as far as possible into the other community . . . as long as you can get proof to back up your claim."

"How can we prove anything about the plants?"

"Don't ask me," says the Wizard. "I'm impartial. Anybody got any ideas?"

"We could bring back some plants as proof."

"O.K., fine. But just take small bits of the most common plants, just enough to indicate what kind of plant you found.

"Now we're ready. At three o'clock we'll hold a high court at Milepost Four, halfway between Openland and Forestland. You'll both be able to present your evidence then. Both Elves and Trolls are reasonable people, so any decision made will depend on which evidence is most solid. Your field commanders (formerly known as crew leaders) will be around to help you out with the different "weapons," if you decide you need to use them to find proof. Trolls, here's your armory and your Openland flag. Fly it proudly and never trust an Elf. In fact, you've got just ten seconds to get out of Elf territory!"

As the Trolls leave, the Wizard turns to the Elves, warning

them: "Believe me, I've said it a thousand times before and I'll say it again: 'Never trust a Troll.' They'll grab all the area they can. You'll need solid proof to make your point. They might even try to claim this capital since there *are* a few Openland leafy bushes here."

"Impossible."

"Well, O.K. That will depend on your evidence."

After carefully studying their own capitals, both groups now begin to press into each others' territories, looking for indications of conditions similar to those they found at home. Milepost Four is the halfway point between the hearts of each natural community, but as the two groups push past it, they continue to find evidence supporting their point of view. Even as they reach Milepost Five, high up in the Forestland community, the Trolls are satisfied with their findings.

"Look, we've still got deciduous trees and shrubs with old man's beard in 'em."

Yeah, and the soil temperature's only dropped one degree from down in Troll Capital."

The wandering Wizard comments, however, "Be careful. You're in the opening by the trail. It's sunny here; that may not be typical of the whole Forestland community."

"Whoa! Yeah, let's check farther back in the Elf woods, you guys."

Before they can do that, however, a hummingbird whizzes by.

"Hey, that's evidence for us. That guy mostly hangs around in the area near our capital. Write that down."

The Elves are not idle either. And the inevitable passing on the Greenway takes place peacefully under the supervision of the Wizard.

"O.K., pass in peace, Elves, but don't look at our chart."

The Elves continue to find their Elf plants all the way down the Greenway. They also find no sudden change in soil temperature, but they wisely observe: *"Sure, but that could be good for either us or the Trolls."*

"The soil looks and feels different, too, but it doesn't change suddenly. It's redder and clayier up in our capital."

The appointed time comes for the high court to be held at Milepost Four. The Elves arrive to find the Wizard basking in the warm sun.

"Hey, isn't this sun great?"

"No, it's terrible. I like cool, moist, shady forests."

"Oh, sorry . . . forgot you folks were Elves."

The arrival of the Trolls incites some hostility: *"You Trolls stay away!"*

The Wizard begins the proceedings: "First let's hear the claims of the Elves."

"We proudly announce our rights all the way to Milepost Three!"

"Forget it!"

"Yeah, wait a minute!"

"Now, I can see that we'll need a way to keep track of who's claiming what and on the basis of what evidence. I have this map/ scoreboard here just for that purpose.

"Trolls, how far are you going to claim?"

"Well, there's proof, even at number seven, but we'll be nice and only claim six."

"Whew! This is terrible . . . if Elves are claiming to Milepost Three and Trolls to Milepost Six, that's a lot of area we are fighting over."

"Yeah, everything from six to three, but it won't take long 'cause we Elves have scientific proof for our claim."

"Well, so do we!"

The Trolls win the toss of the coin and so have the first turn at presenting one piece of evidence.

"O.K., look. See this leaf from a bush that grows all over down in Openland? We found it clear up at number six."

"It's all wet, though. See, it's wet in Elf country."

"Ah, ha, Elves, that's a good point, but I'm afraid we'll have to give the Trolls the credit. That plant mainly grows in the community around Troll Capital."

"I guess so. He's right."

"O.K. One for the Trolls. I'll draw that leaf on the map at number six. Your turn Elves."

"Take it away, Carrie."

"I've got this evergreen sprig here that we found right in Troll Capital."

"Hey, hey, but there's not much of it down there."

"Now, Trolls, you would have to admit under oath that this cedar is found in your natural community, and it is mainly a Forestland plant. I'm afraid that's a point for the Elves."

The battle of plant evidence continues, until finally, a Troll remembers the hummingbird that buzzed by him while he was doing a soil test at Milepost Five.

"It's not only plants, you guys; that hummingbird had its nest near Milepost One in Openland."

"Yeah, there are mountain beaver all the way up to number five, too."

The Elves enter the chickadees they found in Openland, even though the whole group saw flocks of them as they sat under the fir trees at Elf Capital.

"Well, folks, this is getting pretty complicated," comments the Wizard. "You both will admit that the other group has a definite natural community they're defending, but we're all finding examples of each in the other's territory. Maybe we'd better look to our scientific data for a clear border. What did you find?"

Although valiant (and sometimes devious) attempts are made to prove otherwise, air temperatures, soil pH, soil temperatures, and soil profiles do not lend much weight to the argument for a clear border. All show a gradual change from one community to the other. Again the Wizard speaks, "Perhaps now we can see why this conflict has been so hard to resolve for so long. Look around;

even as we stand at Milepost Four, halfway between Elf Capital and Troll Capital, which evidence do we see here?''

Both Elves and Trolls speak out . . .

"Alas, perhaps there is no simple solution. Perhaps there is no *clear-cut* boundary."

"Let's just have a war," Willy says, brandishing a glinting soil auger.

"How about just sharing the whole place?"

The Wizard responds, "Yeah, but we know there's a difference between the natural communities, and you've seen how Elves and Trolls get along."

"Well then, let's share the mixed-up place."

"Yeah, let's have a NO MAN'S LAND."

"You mean you think we'll never find a clear boundary?"

"Naw, it's a blur, a blend."

"We'll have an EVERYMAN'S LAND, where the two communities blend together.''

"Wow, that's great, and henceforth, by the powers invested in me as a Wizard, I hereby call the land from Milepost Three to Six an EVERYMAN'S LAND.''

(Elves and Trolls line up and ceremoniously bow to one another.)

INTERPRETIVE ENCOUNTERS
GUIDELINES

Border Dispute

PROPS:
General Equipment
   Flags
   Day Packs—to carry equipment in
   Easel—to mount negotiation chart on
   Grease Pencils—to record data on chart
   Sponge and Water Pail—to erase figures on chart
   Milepost Signs

Data Gathering Equipment
   Data Sheets and Clipboards, one for each group
   Soil Augers—to check soil moisture, depth of duff, soil
      coloration
   Soil Thermometers
   Air Thermometers
   Light Meters—to measure degree of sunlight intensity
   Rulers—to measure depth of duff layer
   Soil pH Kits—to check soil acidity
   Nets

Wizard's Negotiation Chart
   Heavy poster board covered with acetate. Sketch the Greenway,
Capitals, and Mileposts on the poster board before covering.

GENERAL NOTES:
1. Technically, the term community is used only to describe the
living things in an area. When both the living and nonliving things
are considered, the proper term to use is "ecosystem." However,
at the Sunship Study Station we may examine some of the
nonliving aspects of a community without distinguishing between
these two terms.
2. Prior to the "Border Dispute," crew counselors should be
briefed on how to use the different measuring devices, how to
interpret the information, and approximately where to take the
measurements.
3. The Greenway should cover about one-quarter of a mile.
Mileposts should be set out at equal intervals along the trail.
(Remember that the seven miles are only "elfin miles.")
4. Crew counselors should assist the Elves and Trolls in
establishing their claims.
5. Explain that all measurements should be taken in
representative areas near each milepost. However, measurements
taken on the Greenway or in meeting places will be invalid.
6. Data doesn't need to be gathered from all the milepost areas.
For example, the Elves might decide to skip measurements at
Milepost One—the Trolls' Openland Capital, since the capitals are

OFFICIAL DATA

DOMINANT PLANT

List Two:

MILEPOST #1 _____ _____

2 _____ _____

3 _____ _____

4 _____ _____

5 _____ _____

6 _____ _____

7 _____ _____

DOMINANT TREE

List Two:

MILEPOST #1 _____ _____

2 _____ _____

3 _____ _____

4 _____ _____

5 _____ _____

6 _____ _____

7 _____ _____

DUFF SOIL DEPTH

MILEPOST #1 _____ '' inches

2 _____

3 _____

4 _____

5 _____

6 _____

7 _____

SOIL TEMPERATURE

MILEPOST #1 _____ ° degrees

2 _____

3 _____

4 _____

5 _____

6 _____

7 _____

SOIL MOISTURE CONTENT

Check One:	Dry	Moderate	Wet
MILEPOST #1	_____	_____	_____
2	_____	_____	_____
3	_____	_____	_____
4	_____	_____	_____
5	_____	_____	_____
6	_____	_____	_____
7	_____	_____	_____

AIR TEMPERATURE

MILEPOST #1 _____ ° degrees

2 _____

3 _____

4 _____

5 _____

6 _____

7 _____

SUNLIGHT INTENSITY

MILEPOST #1 _____

2 _____

3 _____

4 _____

5 _____

6 _____

7 _____

SOIL pH

MILEPOST #1 _____

2 _____

3 _____

4 _____

5 _____

6 _____

7 _____

located where features of the natural community surrounding them are most evident.

7. Elf and Troll groups should elect a scribe to record the data they gather.

8. Other kinds of data can be collected depending on the setting and the equipment available. For example:

Frisbees—to check vegetational density. Check how many throws it takes to fly a Frisbee carefully through a given area and compare it to other areas.

Increment borer—to check sunny-shady/wet-dry growth patterns in the trees of one community and compare them with the patterns in another community. Use with caution.

9. Check all thermometers to see if they register the same temperatures before distributing them.

10. Instead of writing all of the data on the Greenway Chart, a more visual alternative is to have the Wizard use small red and blue splotches of paint for recording the points made by each group. In this way, when he is finished, the kids can squint and see the "purple" area of "Everyman's Land."

Chapter Nine

DISCOVERY PARTIES

The sense of wonder through which a youngster sees the world is a fragile lens, easily shattered or worn away during the process of growing up. The child with that sense of wonder still intact is capable of walking home from school on a "shortcut" that goes the long way around, perhaps climbing a fence to gain access to an open field. Engulfed and captivated by life's myriad forms, that child can poke along silently just absorbing the feel and smell of the place, or lie down and contentedly watch the journey of an insect as it zigs and zags on its way, or run exuberantly through wild open spaces for the sheer joy of it all. Time has no hold on such a free spirit. Eventually, the youngster wanders home, where parents are waiting to ask what took so long. They are worried, anxious, angry, and do not ask about the sightings and feelings, but only voice a perfunctory where and why. Out of their concern, they unknowingly damage that delicate lens.

Later, the young person becomes too busy to follow the wild things, too much in a hurry to get somewhere else. One day, however, the adult may feel a twinge of remembrance when he or she watches another kid exploring a similar field. And perhaps the lens clears for a fleeting moment to recapture that sense of wonder which lay dormant for so long. Sigurd Olsen, writing about his beloved north country, describes this loss and recovery: "While we are born with curiosity and wonder . . . I know such inherent joys are often lost. I also know that, being deep within us, their latent glow can be fanned to flame again by awareness and an open mind."

To rekindle a lost sense of wonder, or nourish a dying one, requires the vital elements of opportunity and encouragement. So our "Discovery Parties" offer these: opportunity to explore and to wander, to just plain poke around, and encouragement, both from the activity itself and from the leader's own enthusiasm, to enjoy the freewheeling experience. They are parties because they are gatherings with a festive atmosphere as well as groups working together to accomplish a task. Superficially, they appear to be goal-oriented, but that goal is actually just part of the means to the real purpose: an open-ended experience in uncovering the simple marvels of the natural world.

Discovery is an important part of the entire learning process at the Sunship Study Station. Individual discoveries are not found and forgotten, but entered in the passenger's personal Logs, posted on the "Discovery Board" at the Outlook Inn, or both. In addition, such items often provide another opportunity to apply the understandings acquired on the Concept Paths during the morning.

For the leader, Discovery Parties offer a chance to respond with both wonder and knowledge. The natural history lessons are not doled out in large chunks, but shared in small morsels. A youngster finds a snail and the leader responds with a "Wow!" and perhaps comments that the snail has 14,000 teeth; or another kid finds a bright yellow dandelion and is encouraged to taste the edible flower. Such "finds" provide an opportunity for the leader to pass on small bits of knowledge about the natural world, but eliminate the "show and tell" format. Instead it becomes "share and do." These are multifaceted activities—the kids sharing with the leader and with each other, and the leader sharing with the kids, Discovery Parties are vehicles to be ridden, not ones to be pulled or pushed. They are rafts of adventure to climb on with the kids and be swept away by the tide of enthusiasm.

"LOST LETTERS"

Doug and his group of youngsters sit in a circle around an old leather pouch. Inside the pouch are nine envelopes, one for each of nine letters. The envelopes should contain enough copies of the letters so that each child will have a complete set of the nine at the end of the activity. On the side of the pouch is the title, "Lost Letters."

"A terrible thing has happened," Doug says sadly, shaking his head. "I met an old man in the mountains last summer, and he told me that at one time the letters in this pouch spelled out a very important word. It was a word spoken by all the great explorers of our world—by those who searched the jungles looking for lost civilizations, who first crossed the oceans and mountain ranges, who probed the deepest caves and the longest rivers. And he said it came from the lips of the great scientists, too—from those who first peered into a microscope to examine a drop of rainwater, or lived with the animals in the wild, or uncovered a fossil in a deep canyon. In fact, he said a lot of ordinary people, like you and me, used this word, too. But lately its meaning has been lost. This bag has the letters of the word, but they just don't mean anything anymore. Now we're not even sure how to put the letters in here back together again.

"The old man who gave me the pouch claimed that this word was a password, a password for revealing the secrets of the world. He said that there were all kinds of treasures to be found for those who could figure out the meaning of these 'lost letters.'"

"Treasure! What kind?"

"Whoa, Willy. We have to figure out what the letters mean before we can find any treasures. There is a way, though," he adds, pulling out a folded note that is at the top of the pouch contents. "The old man put this note in here: 'Find something that starts with each of the letters—but one at a time; you must be go-getters.' I wonder what that means?"

"We gotta find stuff that starts with the letters. Which ones?"

"Reach in here and pick out a packet," Doug suggests. The youngster reaches in, pulling out a packet for the letter *D.*"

"Hey, it says, 'Find something for a D, but not for a list; it has to be something you see through your fist.'"

"Like this," another suggests, holding his hand up to his eye with the fingers curled around like a tiny sighting scope.

"Let's give it a try," Doug says, holding his slightly opened fist up to his eye and peering through it. "Wow, that's kind of a neat view, almost like a little telescope." The kids all try it, and go off in search of things that start with the letter *D*.

"Gordy, since you read the clue, why don't you be keeper of the letters. When somebody finds something, we'll show it to you, and you can hand out the *Ds*," Doug suggests. Everyone, including Gordy and Doug, is soon peering around for things that begin with a *D*.

The first ones to finish want to start on the next packet, but Doug cautions, "We'd better be sure we have plenty of *Ds* first. Maybe you should help the others find their *D*."

"Here's a drip of sap," says one kid, dragging Gordy and the others over to see it.

"Wow," says Doug, patting it with his finger. "It's kind of sticky. I wonder what it tastes like? You know, sap is a plant's blood, but it's not like our blood. In fact, it's like sugar water. If we boiled away most of the water from this sap we would have a sweet syrup."

"Hey, I've done that. That's what they do with maple trees. They stick this pipe in the tree and the sap flows out and then you have to boil it all day."

"Hey, there's a dead log over here. That's a D for me!" exclaims Carrie. Gordy isn't fooled, though.

"You gotta look at it through your fist," he reminds her. *"Like this. Look at the crumbling wood close up."*

With help from their friends, it doesn't take long for everyone to find a *D* and to share in the discoveries of others.

Gordy announces that everyone now has a *D*. Doug puts his in his pocket, commenting that he wants to make sure that he doesn't lose it. He then asks Mary Ann to read the riddle on the next packet. Each time a letter is completed, a different youngster is named to read off the next letter's clue.

"C *may be big or it may be quite small, as long as you see it from down in a crawl.*"

"V *is a very good letter for you—find a high spot and look at the view.*"

"S *is a letter that stands for smell; you must find it first, then find someone to tell.*"

"*Overhead is the place to look for an* O; *so lie down on your back to get very low.*"

"Y *is the toughest, but couldn't be neater; it just means you have to be within a meter.*"

"E *is for ear, but have no fears—for an* "H" *will do too since you hear with your ears.*"

"R *is a letter for many a thing, but you must have everyone 'round it in a ring.*"

"I *is a letter you'll like very much; use your nose and find something to touch.*"

And so it goes: dead logs, dry pine needles, something to duck under, deer trails, and dew drops; things that are icky, icy, ivory, and iron-hard, or an insect or something itchy; sweet and sour and spicy things, and even things that smell sick or strong or swell. There are climbing vines, cup-like flowers, and cottony, course, cracked, craggy, and colorful things, and things with claws and cuts and curls. There are orange leaves and oval shapes, odd and old things and open spaces, and even stickers that make you say "ouch" and one sharp rock on the ground, which is opposite overhead. Next come a variety of vegetation, and vines and valleys, violets and veins of a leaf; echoes and eeks and sounds that are eerie, then hiss and hum and honk and holler and howl; ribbed and ragged stumps, roots, rusty colors, and rough, round, and red things. Finally, there are the yellow or young, the yawning and a yard, and something a year old or something that yips or

yelps. The letters spur the discoveries, and the discoveries lead back to the letters.

When they have completed the task on the last packet of letters, Doug asks everyone to form a circle, and sit down on the ground.

"O.K. Let's get out all of our letters. Get out your Logs, too. We can use them for small tables to lay our letters on. Let's see if we can figure out what they spell.

"Hey, I've got a 'dove.'"

"Yeah, but you have to use all *of your letters, Carrie."*

"O.K."

"Huh, mine spells civredsoy."

"Wait a minute, just a minute, I think I've got it. D-I-S-C-O-V-E then R and Y. That's it, Doug! DISCOVERY! *See, you guys, it spells discovery."*

"O.K., way to go, Gordy! That's the word, folks. And just so we won't forget it, let's peel the backs off of these letters and stick them on the covers of our Logs. If the old man was right, we should be able to find a lot of treasures."

"Hey, Doug, that's right. I thought you said we were going to get some treasures."

"Hmmm . . . Willy's right, but maybe we have already got some and didn't know it. Look at this note which I just found in the bottom of the pouch.

"Congratulations. You have not only rediscovered *discovery,* but while doing that, you have found the *treasures,* too."

"ARTISTS AND SCIENTISTS"

When the kids arrive for lunch on Wednesday, an assortment of large, old-looking maps decorate the dining hall. By supper, each will be literally covered with small pieces of paper in various colors and shapes. Some will have numbers, some drawings, some bits of poetry. Right now, though, the maps have just a few landmarks sketched in—a creek, a boulder, a tall tree. "Land of the Giant Boulders," "Valley of the Lichens," and "Enchanted Forest" are some of the names of these strange places. When they see the maps and ask, *"What are those?"* the kids are told that these are wild places no one has ever really explored before.

Later that afternoon, Helen's dozen "discoverers" set out, maps in hand, heading for the Enchanted Forest. The maps show a mossy stump near a tall tree on the southern border of the forest, with a fallen tree nearby. Helen says, "I've never even been in this place before—just these landmarks are known, and I know that it's someplace in this direction. But when you spot these landmarks, we'll know we're there."

One of the kids is carrying a red pack titled "Artist's Discovery Kit," and another is carrying a blue pack labeled "Scientist's Discovery Kit." The group of twelve discoverers have been divided into six "artists" and six "scientists." Both groups have a copy of the same map from the dining hall, but each will be examining this "unexplored" place from a different perspective. One of the maps has a caption reading, "The Artist's View," while the other reads, "The Scientist's View."

"Hey, there's a moss-covered stump!" exclaims one kid.

"Yeah, but where's the tall tree?" asks another.

"Wait—over here," says a third. *"Here's a tall tree." "Where's the fallen tree?"* Soon a fourth finds the second landmark, and the discoverers are convinced they've found the Enchanted Forest.

After the initial wave of discovery has died down, Helen has the two pack-carriers place the packs on the ground and open them up. Inside the red pack they find small free-form pieces of white, yellow, light blue, and light green paper, plus charcoal, fine-point colored pencils, white glue, watercolor paints, and colored chalk. The blue pack contains tape measures, compasses, clipboards, sweep nets, hand lenses, psychrometers, soil thermometers, collecting jars, and tiny vials and soil test kits, plus an assortment of colored paper tags.

Helen explains that the scientists and artists can take any of the tools or materials they want—one item at a time, of course—and use them to gather information about this wild place in order to help fill in the blank spots on the map. They can write the scientific data on the tags provided in the blue pack, and use the cutouts in the red pack for poetry, drawings, paintings, or collages that help describe the Enchanted Forest. "We want to do such a neat job of describing this place that everyone else in camp will want to search for this special place that we found." Helen also explains that they can trade the tool they've used for any that isn't being used, and can always ask her for help figuring out how to use any of the tools, such as the soil test kit. Soon the scientists and artists are combing the area and sharing their finds.

"Hey, here's a passenger," comments one, watching a spider spinning a web. *"How can I put him on the map?"* he asks Helen. She suggests a sketch, a painting, or a haiku for an artist, or a measurement or biological drawing (the spider as seen through a hand lens) for the scientist.

Helen spends most of her time circulating among the discoverers, pointing out new perspectives and sharing bits of information. She pauses to help someone use one of the tools, explains to another how tree rings are formed, and tells an Indian story about the fungus one group is admiring. One "scientist" measures soil temperature and writes, "Soil 70 degrees" on a tag; another decides to measure the distance and take a compass bearing from the boulder to the tall tree; still another prepares a tag with descriptions of some of the passengers she's collected in a sweep net. Meanwhile, the "artists" are busy sketching trees, insects, fungi, birds' nests, and flowers to add to the Enchanted Forest map. One of them is using some cutouts to make rubbings of the various textures found in the area. Another one puts

together a collage showing the different shades of color found on the forest floor. Finally, some of the discoverers decide that they want to do both: estimate the height of a tree *and* draw a picture of it.

"Helen, can't we be both artists and scientists?"

"Yeah, I want to try the soil thing, and Jackson wants to use the paints."

"Well, I don't see why we can't do both. After all, many explorers are really a little bit artist and a little bit scientist. I guess we could be, too.

"I tell you what, let's have the scientists share something they're using with the artists and then the artists can share something they've done with the scientists."

"O.K.! C'mon, Jackson."

Helen is soon besieged with requests to "come look at this" as the artists and scientists together explore the Enchanted Forest. A red wildflower, clusters of white berries, the symmetry of a leaf, the shimmering wings of an insect, the delicate beauty of a web, the mystery of an unknown animal's home, and the grandeur of an ancient fir tree are among the artists' subjects. They see a tiny insect dangling from the tip of a blade of grass, listen to the warblings of birds invisible to them, watch one lone leaf drift slowly to the floor of the glade. The artists begin transforming their map into a hobbit-like rendition of a sensory adventure. The scientists are discovering soil depth and layers, temperature and humidity differences, and a variety of sizes, types, and numbers of plants and kinds of animals. They poke around in a layer of fallen leaves, check wind speed and plant height, peer into the hollow of a tree, examine a brightly colored caterpillar. The scientists soon turn their map into a quadrant study, keying their data to the squares they have marked off.

All of the kids listen for the excited calls of others and hurry over to see what's going on. They cross their arms to analyze an "artist's" sketch of a tiny ground pine. They watch quietly, fascinated by a "scientist" who is removing a small cylinder of wood from a tree with her increment borer. They begin to realize that they don't have to pursue art or science; they can, and should, pursue both. At the end of the hour, they attach their tags and cutouts to their maps with pride, ceremoniously roll the maps up again, and return to the dining hall.

"It looks to me like we've done a great job," says Helen, looking at the maps side by side in the dining hall. They're covered with tags and cutouts: numbers and words and sketches and patches of color. "It looks to me like we learned a lot about this natural wild place by using the tools of both the artist and the scientist. Our maps show that many secret beauties and understandings can be found in a wild place once you have set out to discover the unknown."

"You know," Rhonda says, *"when you put them together, they sort of make a whole."*

"Let's see what some of the other groups have come up with," Helen suggests. "Perhaps some of you would like to try to locate one of these other wild places during 'Time Out' this afternoon."

"All right! I'm going to see if I can find 'The Land of the Giant Boulders'!"

"Bet nobody ever finds our place. We'll be the only ones who've ever really been there."

DISCOVERY PARTIES—
GUIDELINES

Lost Letters

PROPS:
Pouch—Print "Lost Letters" on the side.
Nine Small Manila Envelopes—Print riddles for each letter on the sides of the envelopes.
Message Notes—To be stuffed in pouches.
Self-Adhesive Letters—These should spell D-I-S-C-O-V-E-R-Y— enough to make one set of letters for each student.
Toothpicks
Day Pack

GENERAL NOTES:
1. The DISCOVERY letters can be printed on sheets of self-adhesive paper. If all the letters are printed in straight rows, it doesn't take long to mass-produce a large supply of individual letters by using a sharp paper cutter. The size of the letter should be small enough to fit on the Log covers.
2. Carry a batch of toothpicks to help peel the adhesive backing from the letters. Be sure the backings get tossed back in the day pack.
3. If possible, arrange for the teachers to conduct the Discovery Parties, with assistance from the station leaders.

Artists and Scientists

PROPS:
Butcher Paper—Cut four-foot squares and antique with tea staining.
Poster Paper—Cut in small, free-form pieces of different colors.
Day Packs
Charcoal Sticks
Tape Recorder (for natural symphony)
Fine-point Colored Pencils
Roller and Printer's Ink (for leaf prints)
Water Colors and Brushes
String (for mobiles)
Water Containers
Glue Stick
Increment Borer
Tape Measures
Compass
Clipboards
Water pH Kit
Sweep Nets
Soil Thermometers and Psychrometers
Soil Auger and Soil Test Kit

GENERAL NOTES:
1. Areas should be predetermined by the station leaders. Within each area the kids can choose the specific places where they would like to set up shop. Let the kids decide who will be the artists and who will be the scientists.
2. Teachers should help organize all the "Artists and Scientists" equipment for each group in a central "supply depot." They should take charge of passing out and collecting the different tools the kids will be using.
3. Ask the kids to record the date and their names on the maps. Post the maps in the dining hall, then send them back to school with the kids at the end of the week.
4. For a small group, use a large old stump for a "wild place."

THE FEELINGS

Touch the Earth

"Bug's World"

"Share a Shadow"

"Touching Trail"

"Magic Paintbrushes"

"Bloodhounds"

"Magic Planet"

"Giants and Leprechauns"

Magic Spots

Immersing Experiences

"Micro-Parks"

"Curious Heron Walk"

"Earth Studios"

"The Nightwatchers"

Chapter Ten

"TOUCH THE EARTH"

The new arrivals at the Sunship Study Station have just come out into the sunlight after the Welcome Aboard session, where they were urged to go out and "touch the earth; see it with new eyes." The crew counselors divide the large group of youngsters into two groups. Each is led to one of two hub areas to begin the "Touch the Earth" activities. On the way, the crew counselors lead their kids on an adventure in diversity. Their task is "simply" to count all the things in the world. Each group is equipped with a small grocery counter, and everyone has their senses alert for every kind of different natural thing they can see, smell, hear, feel, or taste along the way. On a rotating basis, one kid in each group uses the "counter" to keep tabs on how many things they have seen. At the beginning of the walk, only the obvious items are spotted, such as grass, trees, and soil. But soon the kids notice that within these major categories lie many subtle differences. They don't worry about names, just variety. Colors, smells, and sounds lead to many new discoveries.

Upon reaching their destination, the kids use a simple equation to estimate the number of things in the world. It was one-quarter of a mile from the sunship room to the hub, and they found 250 different things. The earth is about twenty-five thousand miles around, so that's one hundred thousand times larger. Thus, if they had walked all the way around the earth, they might have seen 100,000 x 250 things. The kids realize that there's a limit to their accuracy, but twenty-five million represents a lot of things.

At each hub, there is a wooden post capped with a large globe, which shows the continents in relief. From the post, signs point in different directions and bear the names of the activities that are about to begin: "Magic Paintbrushes," "Share a Shadow,"

"Bug's World," "Leprechauns and Giants," "Touching Trail," "Bloodhounds," and "Magic Planets."

The Touch the Earth activities encourage various means of making contact with the natural world: heightening senses, changing perspectives, breaking down barriers, seeking patterns, sharing appreciations, and looking for small things. Each activity helps the youngsters get to know their planet. Each group chooses a different activity with which to begin. Each activity is self-contained, so there is no need to complete them in any particular order. Because some of the inquiries take more time than others, two counselors lead those activities in order to minimize the waiting time.

The kids begin their first activity with the crew counselor who brought them out to the hub. When they are finished, that counselor returns them to the hub, where another counselor will meet them for the next activity. If there is a short wait until the next crew counselor is ready, a station leader is there to host a sampling party. Old weathered boxes positioned around the hub display an assortment of natural foods from which to choose. There are small cups of mixed seeds and nuts, fruit cups of berries and rosehips, candied clover and garnishes of dandelion head, fresh-picked salads of cattail, bead lily, and arrowroot, and teas of sassafras and sumac. These serve as a quick afternoon snack, and at the same time heighten the senses of taste and smell and increase the contact with the earth and its products.

"BUG'S WORLD"

When Bill and his group reach the North Hub, he quickly leads them over to an isolated spot and explains, "Listen, this is a very high adventure mission we're about to take off on. It's a once-in-a-lifetime opportunity for you kids, because here at the Sunship Study Station, it just so happens we have the world's only shrinking machine."

Although he receives some rather skeptical looks, Bill continues, "The problem is that this machine is only a prototype."

"You mean it's a new thing, like they're just trying it out?"

"That's right. This machine is on loan to us from the International Science for Youth Laboratory. They were looking for some guinea pigs to try it out on and we figured we could use it. Does anyone have any suggestions about what we could use a shrinking machine for here?"

"To shrink big trees so we could look at them more closely?"

"Not bad, but I have something a bit different to suggest."

"What are we going to shrink then?"

"You."

"We're going to get shrunk?"

"Right. Come with me."

As the group goes with Bill out to the site of "Bug's World," he says, "I want you to note your brightest item of clothing. The machine might break down while you are in a shrunken state, and if it does, you should wave a piece of clothing and hope that somebody can see you. Furthermore, you should stay off the main trails to avoid being stepped on."

The inevitable question is finally asked: *"What's the point of shrinking us in the first place?"*

"Well, it just so happens that some of the most amazing citizens that we have on our sunship are so small that they are almost always overlooked."

"Bugs, right?"

"Exactly. When we heard about this shrinking machine we all said, 'Hey, this is a perfect chance to see what a bug's world is really like!' Now, before we go I want to give you people a little pre-shrink information. Let's form a circle around this old log. Can anyone find a bug in there?"

After a little fingertip investigation a small red ant is found. *"You mean to tell me I'm gonna be that small? You must be crazy."*

"Give it a try. You won't believe how incredible that little guy's world is. Just feel those little pebbles in there. What do you suppose those are like to our little friend here?"

"They'd be like boulders."

"No way, man. They'd be giant mountains."

"Right. And feel those little blades of grass. What would they be like?"

"They'd be like giant trees. That whole place would be like a big jungle."

"O.K., now there may be something to learn from that ant before we enter his world ourselves. Let's have a close look at him. How is he getting around?"

"Very carefully."

"Ah, good point. Remember that when it comes your turn to be shrunk. See if the ant has any more tips he can give us about how to move around."

"Well, he seems to be finding his way around mainly with his feelers."

"Yeah, he really checks out stuff with those antennae."

"O.K., that's important. Because when you folks go into the bug's world, you'll be wearing a special mask which is designed to keep out the rays that the machine gives off. Fortunately, this mask also makes it impossible to see, and that's just fine because most bugs can't see very well, either, so actually you'll be getting a better idea of what it's like to be a bug."

"Hold on just a minute. We don't have any feelers."

"Exactly, you're all catching on real fast. You will have to use your hands and arms as feelers, like this. Everyone try it . . . Now, just a couple more points and we're off. We have a little trail that you'll all be following. You'll be able to feel your way along it with your feeler-hands if you really concentrate. But that's not all you want to do. As you move along be sure to explore around you and above you with your feelers; see what that bug's world is all about. I guarantee you will be amazed! . . . Oh, one last thing: insects don't walk on their hind legs!"

"Oh, no, you don't mean . . . "

"Yes, ma'am, that's why everybody has old pants on. The best bugs always have the dirtiest knees."

"Bugs don't have knees."

"Oh, well, we can't do it all for you, you have to put a little imagination into it."

Bill pulls out the special masks. "We'll put these on here. The location of the machine is top secret, so I'll guide you all over together then send one person through the shrinking process at a time."

Finally the great moment has arrived. Helene seems to be an enthusiastic "bug," so Bill guides her over to the "machine" first. The kids are able to walk in, and there is enough room for them to kneel down as the shrinking process occurs. Once shrunk they are able to crawl out through the other side and can easily find the beginning of the trail.

Helene is now inside the stump so Bill explains that he's got the key ready and hopes that everything works. "As you hear the machine shrinking you, you should get in your bug position and move out the door. As soon as you're out the door turn right and you will pass by a series of rocks and pebbles. As you move past the rocks they will seem to get bigger and bigger. Actually of course you are only getting smaller and smaller. Remember to explore your world as much as you can; you'll probably never get this opportunity again."

The machine slowly starts to make a strange whirring sound. A slide whistle is actually the "key" to this machine. By buzzing and varying his breath Bill is able to create a sound which is very much like what one might imagine a shrinking device would produce. He also climbs up on a stump as Helene "shrinks," thus enhancing the effect.

Helene leaves the machine and finds her way to the beginning of the trail. The trail itself has been laid out in an area with a terrain conducive to the "insect experience." There is much heavy growth around and above the actual path. This makes it difficult for the bugs to stray very far from the prescribed course. The whole trail is visible to the leader; so that directions can be called out to errant insects. Several spongy and slimy rotten logs are located along the trail as well. Startling "feeler" discoveries are definitely in order. A small rise, and later a small drop, are also incorporated into the forty-foot loop which constitutes the path.

As soon as Helene is far enough along the trail not to cause any traffic problems, Bill directs John to the machine. John is soon shrunk and is asked in a low and slow voice: "How does it feel down there in the grass, John?"

"Well, it feels weird."

"What's weird about it?"

"Well, you don't know what to expect."

"Oops, Helene, where are you?" Bill asks. "It looks like you're getting a little off the beaten bugway. Use your feelers."

Everyone has soon been put through the machine, and Helene is just about back to the start-finish of the path. "O.K., you're just about there, Helene, a little more to the right, good. Let me guide you over to this spot, right . . . over . . . here; you can investigate this area with your feelers until the others have returned."

As soon as the whole group is gathered in the same area, Bill announces that he's about to try something totally new. He is

about to try to bring them all up to size at the same time in order to save energy. It could be tricky, though. After much sputtering and screeching of the slide whistle, the tone rises, signifying the restoration of the whole bunch to their original sizes. "Whew, that was close, but I think you're all just about the same size as you were when we started—close enough, anyway. You can take off your masks."

"*Wow, that was something. That giant mountain we had to go up was amazing.*"

"Gee, I'm sorry I can't show it to you. It was so small that you would hardly be able to see it now."

"*I came face to face with a giant millipede. He was reaching out for me with his feelers.*"

The comments continue. One thing is certain—bugs will never be the same again, and the kids' world has become larger because they learned about small things.

"SHARE A SHADOW"

The leader holds up a piece of white poster board and says, "I'll bet you think this is just a piece of poster board, but it is really a shadow catcher." He then explains that although there are shadows all around on a sunny day, we never really notice them. "Look around right here at all of the shadows, just in this area. Let's divide up into partners, and each pair will get one of these shadow catchers to look for the neatest shadow they can find."

The group stays in one defined area, not too large, so that discoveries can be shared. The leader can help trigger discoveries by suggesting different methods of shadow catching, but most groups will experiment on their own. They'll notice that shadows have focal points; if they move the poster board closer to or farther away from the object that is casting the shadow, they will be able to bring it into or throw it out of focus. "Try moving the poster board back and forth in the shadow," the leader might suggest. Another discovery is that a shadow reveals details of an object that one doesn't notice otherwise—tiny projections on a stem, unnoticed on the plant, show up in the sharp silhouette on the "shadow catcher." Finally, objects can be poked into lumps of modeling clay to make shadow collages, or other objects can be piled up to create sculptures which produce interesting shadows.

To record their shadows, the kids can try to capture the shadow that they like best, then fill in the shadowed area on the poster board with charcoal or colored chalk. They will soon discover that they have to be quick. As the earth turns, the shadow changes. The kids can easily tell where the shadow has been moving, however. The sunlit ground is warm, and the shady ground is cool, but there are also areas recently warmed that are now in shade, or recently shaded and cool that are now just beginning to warm up in the sun.

Sharing is a major part of this activity, as each pair notes what others are doing and tries to improvise new methods for shadow catching. The leader congratulates each discovery and offers help that can lead to still more discoveries: asking what the same shadow would look like from a different angle, suggesting how to "follow" a moving shadow by outlining some of its different positions, or challenging them to find the smallest or roundest or most intricate shadow. At the end, each pair props up their poster board so that one of the shadows they liked best is "captured" for others to see on the "shadow trail." Even then, the shadows keep moving and are never quite the same.

"TOUCHING TRAIL"

The group is divided into pairs. One member of each pair is blindfolded. The other's task is to lead his or her partner to leaves, stones, bark, plants, and other natural objects to feel different textures: rough, smooth, silky, slimy, feathery, velvety, bumpy, spongy, solid, sticky, spiny, soft, wet, brittle. Being sightless enhances the sense of touch. The leader shows the guides how to direct their blindfolded partners by holding their left forearms.

The "Touching Trail" is laid out with special markers for neat things to feel. Cutouts of a hand, a nose, even a bare foot, are placed on interesting and unusual objects along the trail as suggestions for the guides to follow. The markers provide the guides with ideas for neat ways of helping their partners make contact with the surfaces and textures and patterns around them.

The guides direct their partners to crawl along the trail in order to touch soil, plants, or a piece of decomposing bark. They shape the others' hands around a pinecone, tickle cheeks with a fern frond, or rub a leaf against the lips. The guides must walk slowly and watch carefully for obstacles, but their main job is to help their partners "get in touch." After about ten minutes, an owl hoot or other signal from the leader means that it's time to change roles.

"MAGIC PAINTBRUSHES"

When the group returns to the hub, their dirty knees are proof that they've been visiting Bug's World. Jim, wearing a French beret, greets them: "*Bon jour!* I am zee artist for zee expedition. Come with me, *s'il vous plaît.*"

It doesn't take long to get to a beautiful, dense grove of trees. Below the tall trees, the ground is covered with lush ferns and mosses. A moist feeling pervades the whole area.

"Everyone take a seat on this big log and I'll clue you in on the great chance you're about to have. I can only explain a little bit, since words cannot express the magnificence of what you're going to see, but I'll try to demonstrate for you."

With this, he pulls from his pocket an ancient-looking glass bottle stoppered with an old cork. The bottle contains a liquid

which is clear, but which has the smell of cloves and licorice.

"Zis is a very special fluid," he begins. "Seth and I spent all last winter wandering in the high mountains of Tibet and Nepal in search of it. Only after discovering zee secret monastery were we able to purchase any—at one hundred dollars an ounce. This flask contains just one quarter of an ounce." By this point, the kids are beginning to exchange furtive glances.

"Why ees eet so rare, so precious? Because it is *magic* paint. With just a little dab of this stuff, anyone can be a great artist. In fact, it is rumored that the great artists of history were really the ones who knew the secret of this magic paint. And now, you, my friends, are going to have a chance to see our Sunship with the help of this fluid in the every same way the great painters did."

Explaining that he'll just have to show them how it works, Jim asks the group to wait one second while he goes to find an appropriate canvas. With sweeping gestures he wanders about peering here and there around the area, all the while muttering vague phrases of artistic balderdash, such as "Ah, not quite enough depth," or, "There, there, such color, but not quite up to my standards!"

The kids, meanwhile, although curiously watching this exhibition, have a few comments of their own:

"It sure looked like water to me."

"Yeah, but what about that smell?"

"He must be crazy; look at that hat."

Finally, with a great outburst of superlatives, Jim exclaims that he has finally found the proper canvas. The kids, unable to see the actual spot, watch as he paints with large, broad strokes, and then switches to tiny pokes and dashes.

"Come on over and see my masterpiece," he proudly announces.

"Hey, wait a minute! You didn't paint that," Judy accuses, as she sees the beautiful patch of wet moss that Jim is still busy embellishing.

"Sure I did; I'm still painting it. Look how I heighten the depth in these parts by painting around them, using only one or two bristles. See how I created all those different shades of green? Actually, of course, I can't really take credit for it. It was the paint. And now every one of you will have a chance to do at least as well. In fact, I'm sure you can do better. The trick is to find just the right canvas, one that suits you perfectly.

"Here's a brush for each one of you, and . . . here are your berets. You must have a beret. And most importantly, of course, here's your paint. Please, just barely dip your brush into it. It is very precious, very precious. Now look around. You'll probably want to do several canvases so that you get the hang of it."

After distributing brushes and berets, Jim gives them some pointers on selecting a canvas. He gestures toward a lichen-covered rock, the bark of a tree, a leaf just beginning to turn color, a rotting stump from which fungi are sprouting. At first, some of the young artists attempt to apply a great deal of magic paint to their canvases, but are quickly admonished for wasting the priceless commodity.

"Just a little bit," Jim cautions. "Even Rembrandt used only a trifle. Use just a little paint and a lot of technique."

Although a few begin with some hesitation, the rate of production increases after a few words of praise from Jim. Soon, masterpieces have appeared all over the grove. The artists are "creating" with great flourish. The tiny brushes and small amount of paint means that they must work slowly and carefully, gently brushing the pistils of a blossom or probing the crevices in the bark of a tree.

"It's almost time to begin the gallery tour," Jim announces. "Finish the canvas you're working on, and then select your best painting.

"All right, let's start here at Dick's creation; then we'll move up the row one by one until we get to Judy, way down at the other end of the great hall there.

"Well, Dick, what have we here? Wow! Now I see where you were working. That's spectacular. Give us a little rundown on your techniques. What should people be sure to notice about your masterpiece?"

"Aw, it was nothing really."

"Nothing, huh?" Jim comments incredulously, looking at the phosphorescent green lichens that constitute Dick's canvas. "Tell us something about how you got that great detail on those fine hairlike strands there."

"I'll show you. What I had to do to get that real fine effect was to

use just a few strands of the brush. See how sharp the detail is there? See how it stands out against the dark bark behind it? Something else you'll all want to notice are these little yellow dots in among the green down there by the bottom. See how they stand out? That took a lot of work, I'll tell you.''

"Wow, Dick, that is pretty good.''

After all of the selected masterpieces have been viewed, Jim suggests that all of the artists deserve a round of applause, which they duly give themselves.

"But we should really be applauding all the great canvases,'' Judy comments, as they head back to the hub.

"BLOODHOUNDS"

For this activity, the kids crawl along the trail on hands and knees to sniff out discoveries. The group is first divided into "dogs" and "trainers," who will help the dogs with their discoveries. Down on hands and knees, the dogs are put on "leashes," pieces of string attached to a belt or tied around the waist. The trainers lead the dogs out, then hold one of several cloth bags up to the dogs' noses. Each sachet contains some natural substance that has a distinctive smell (balsam, cedar, rotting wood, wintergreen, cottonwood seed husks, mint, moist soil, milkweed, grass) and can be found along the trail they will follow. Crawling along, the dogs sniff along the ground and in the brush, searching for the natural object that creates the particular scent found in the bag. Noses to the ground, they discover that by concentrating on the smells, they are able to notice many more besides the one in the sachet. In fact, just about everything has a smell, from mossy rocks to fallen leaves. The trainers are allowed to help the beginning bloodhounds by peeking into the bag and then gently guiding them to a place where the object can be found. The dogs can only bark when they think they have found the object similar to what is in the bag. It's up to the trainer to praise the good work or to help the dog find the right scent.

When the kids return to the hub, they are told that they've become better prepared to learn more about the sunship. They have learned that their noses can tell them a lot about this planet.

"MAGIC PLANET"

The site is a windfall, stump, or large boulder, covered with all kinds of different tiny plants and animals. It has been specially selected ahead of time as the "magic planet." The youngsters are each given a hand lens and told that if they hold the lens up to one eye and close the other one, they will be ready for a space flight. The lenses will be their portholes, to see through when they land on another planet. They are led slowly, single file, to the stump or boulder and taken around it for one orbit. Through the lens, at this distance, everything is blurry. But after they are instructed to begin landing in order to search for evidence of life on this "planet," they move closer and closer to the magic planet until, suddenly, everything comes into focus, and they see the magnified lichens, fungi, insects, and larvae which live on it

A tiny rainstorm can be simulated with an eyedropper or spray bottle; an exhaled breath creates a puff of wind; standing between their planet and the sun, the kids can cast shadows over the little world. As they explore this wonderful planet, they see the residents going about their daily business, but it all seems so extraordinary. This activity acts as a reminder that size is relative, because the view with the naked eye and the view through a hand lens are two quite different perspectives. It is also another reminder that small things count.

"GIANTS AND LEPRECHAUNS"

"What do you see when you look around at the forest here?" asks the leader, stopping at the site for Giants and Leprechauns. There are tree trunks and bushes and ferns and any number of things, but the eye-level view is a fairly familiar one. "Now, I wonder how it would look if you were only a foot tall, like a leprechaun? Everyone find somewhere that would be a good place for a leprechaun to sit, just about a foot or less off the ground." They scatter, finding small fallen branches, rocks, and low tree stumps. "Okay, now lie down on your back right there and look up." After they've had a chance to look up through the forest from this angle, they are asked to turn sideways and look out, from ground level. It is a completely different view of the forest floor, the thickness of undergrowth, and the many kinds of objects that lie close to the ground.

"Now, I wonder how this would all look to a giant?" the leader asks. He leads the group over to a tall tree where a bosun's chair has been securely set up to rise about twenty feet off the ground, using a block and tackle. Each youngster in turn is hoisted up to the "giant's-eye view," watching as the ground drops below him. Some of the others help pull slowly on the rope to hoist the chair, while others are occupied with "steadying" the tree so the giant doesn't tip it. Of course, the tree is actually quite sturdy, but by hugging it and leaning against it, they, too, get a different perspective on that one tree. Meanwhile, the kid up in the chair is describing the giant's-eye view of the forest and what lives in the upper level of the forest. From this angle, the neighboring trees form a kind of latticework wall, while the ground looks different than it did from the two other perspectives.

TOUCH THE EARTH—
GENERAL GUIDELINES

Leaders

Crew counselors are each trained to lead one Touch the Earth activity. During the course of the afternoon, the counselor may lead four to five groups through the same activity. The counselor receives a day pack filled with an activity's props upon arriving at the hub area. Cue cards are included inside the bag.

The station leader's job is to coordinate groups coming in and out of the hub. He or she assigns incoming groups to new crew counselors. If one group has a short wait, the station leader invites them to sample the wild edibles.

Hub

This area is the central meeting place. It should be located where many paths could lead off to different activity areas. Each path should be designed to handle the traffic moving in and out of the hubs. To avoid noise and distractions, the activity areas should be separated from each other. (See the layout for the Sensory Loop Trails in the chapter, "A Beginning, Not an End," in *Acclimatization*.)

Each activity takes from fifteen to twenty minutes. Five minutes before closing all Touch the Earth activities, the station leader should sound a signal indicating to crew counselors that they have a few minutes to bring their activities to a close. Use a conch shell horn to sound the signal.

Groups

During the first Quiet Time on Monday afternoon, the teachers should arrange their classes into subgroups of about five to a group. Names should be assigned to each group: the "bugs," the "leprechauns," the "shadows," the "bloodhounds," etc. At the same time the station leaders will tell the crew counselors the name of the group (bugs, bloodhounds, etc.) they will be taking to the Welcome Aboard presentation. The counselors have several responsibilities: (1) to enter and sit with the kids during Welcome Aboard; (2) to guide them through the diversity activity on the way to the Touch the Earth hub; and (3) to take the group through a Touch the Earth activity, then return to the hub for another group.

TOUCH THE EARTH—
GUIDELINES

Bug's World

PROPS:
Masks
Slide Whistle

GENERAL NOTES:
1. Slide whistles can be purchased at a novelty shop and should occasionally be lubricated with vaseline.
2. Locate the activity in a dry area with a variety of undergrowth to feel along the "bug trail."
3. Instead of blindfolds, use simple Halloween masks and tape over the eyeholes. Paint them with stripes to add to the effect that they are really radiation masks.

Share a Shadow

PROPS:
Poster Board
Tongue Depressors
Glue
Colored Pencils
Charcoal
Clay

GENERAL NOTES:
1. Use white poster board for shadow catchers. Glue tongue depressors to the boards to make handles.
2. Crew counselors should pick up all shadow catchers along the shadow trail at the end of the Touch the Earth activities.
3. For cloudy days see the chapter, "The Quiet Walk," in *Acclimatizing* for additional activities.

Touching Trail

PROPS:
Blindfolds

GENERAL NOTES:
1.   Check out the area for poisonous plants and other hazards.
2.   The leader should demonstrate how to guide a partner, holding the forearm of the person firmly with two hands and walking slowly. It is very important to set a serious tone for this activity.
3.   Be firm with pairs who tend to roughhouse. Keep an eye on all of them.

Magic Paintbrushes

PROPS:
Small Water Color Brushes
Berets
Glass Bottle (with cork)
Oil of Cloves

GENERAL NOTES:
1. Inexpensive berets can be purchased in novelty stores.
2. Mix up "paint" with water and a few drops of oil of cloves or anise.
3. Have the kids dip their brushes into your bottle of magic paint and come to you if they need more. This way you can keep in touch with their work and they are automatically encouraged to use only small amounts of the "paint."
4. Ask the kids to share the special techniques they discover.

Bloodhounds

PROPS:
Small Cloth Bags
Leashes
Items to Smell (packed in bags)

GENERAL NOTES:
1. Locate items to be "sniffed out" along the trail before conducting the activity.
2. Encourage the "dogs" to search out the smells while crawling like four-footed animals. Don't forget to have the kids switch roles.

Magic Planet

PROPS:
Hand Lenses
Water Spray Container

GENERAL NOTES:
1. Ancient stumps with rotting walls are fragile and naturally invite small fingers to pick them apart. Before orbiting, explain that the planet is fragile and challenge them to leave the planet and all living things on it in the same way they discovered it.
2. For the best effect, press the hand lens up against one eye while masking the other eye with your hand.
3. Select a log or stump that is large enough for the entire group to observe at one time. Circle it while "coming in for a landing."

Giants and Leprechauns

PROPS:
Block and Tackle
Strong-test Rope
Bosun's Chair
Safety Line

GENERAL NOTES:
1. The bosun's chair can be a salvaged swing set seat or a seat fashioned from a piece of wood.
2. A safety line should be tied with a prussik knot to the main rope. This knot is moveable and can be slipped along the main rope by the leader. The safety rope should be anchored to a nearby tree or large boulder. The safety line with a prussik knot will grip the main hauling rope and prevent it from slipping.

ROCKS

No two rocks have the same personality. Some make you sad, some old, some excited, and some glad. The rock I have before me is small, lightly bumpy and is of five different colors: black, orange, white, blue and red. All these colors are faint. It looks as if it had lived a hundred thousand years, yet it seems still to be a child. "Why a child?" you ask. Because it hasn't smoothed down completely, it hasn't rounded off yet, and it has a sense of excitement in it.

Scott Gilbert
Sixth grade

TREES

*The trees dance to the wind. And the branches play tag with each other.
The scent of the pinecone lurks about.
The clicking of the woodpecker's beak stops.
The moment's still*

Open up your senses...

Jeff Terhaar
Sixth grade

Chapter Eleven

"MAGIC SPOTS"

The youngster sits alone, leaning comfortably against a tree trunk. He is by himself, but he knows that his friends and counselor are not far away. There is no sound of human voices, no noise but the murmurings of the branches in the wind, birds singing, a stream meandering on its way, a single leaf scuttling along the ground. He comes here each day to his own special spot in the forest to pause and rest, to ponder and dream. He looks up to see the pattern of the branches of "his" tree against the sky, leans back to feel its bark against his skin, reaches out to touch the soil at its roots. This is his Magic Spot.

Magic Spot time provides the opportunity for each youngster to develop this easy, quiet relationship with one particular place in the natural world. To help the kids along, there are suggestions in their Logs for what they could do each day during the fifteen minutes or so that they spend at their spots.

On the first day, each youngster selects a personal Magic Spot, a secret place known only to the kid and the counselor. After Touch the Earth, the youngsters go out by class groups, each to a different area. A counselor takes a smaller group of five youngsters from the class to help them find their spots. The counselor will return with them to this area each day.

Before they select their spots, however, the idea of the Magic Spot is carefully explained. They are cautioned to be very careful about selecting one small spot from so many possibilities. "Your spot should be out of sight and hearing from spots chosen by others, if possible," Jim suggests. "It should be a place where you can sit comfortably, with a good tree or stump to lean against." He tells them to look in their Logs for a number of suggestions about what they can do during this time. "You don't have to do those things, though," he notes. "Those are to help you become familiar with your spot. But Magic Spot time is a time to sit quietly and alone—that's the one overriding guideline here."

For the first day at the Magic Spot, Jim suggests applying some of the sensing techniques practiced during Touch the Earth. Looking at small things, smelling and listening, searching for patterns of light and shadow, and looking at the forest from different angles are a few of the possibilities. Sitting there, the youngster is encouraged to imagine the full picture—a boy or girl sitting under a tree, the entire forest, the planet whirling through space around the sun, as in the movie presented in the sunship room. On the first day, the idea is to get acquainted with this one small spot and to begin to develop a feeling for how it fits in as part of the larger sunship.

Log inputs include suggestions for exercises which will help the youngsters listen to the sounds, scrutinize the small things, and focus on the many scenes of their Magic Spots. A very special technique for one of these times is called "Seton-watching," which Jim explains to his group on Tuesday afternoon.

"Today at your Magic Spot, try some Seton-watching. Ernest Thompson Seton was a great artist and writer in the early 1900s, who based his paintings and stories about nature on the countless hours he spent observing the natural world. We named this activity after him because it's a good way to get to know a lot of the plants and animals in your spot." Then Jim tells a story of a time when he was Seton-watching and a squirrel came up and sat right next to his foot: "I was so still and quiet that that squirrel didn't even pay any attention to me. When you sit very still and quiet, the natural world just sort of settles down around you like you're not even there. You may not see animals, but you're more likely to. And you're more likely to feel a lot of other things, besides.

"The best way to do Seton-watching is to find a tree or stump to lean up against so you can sit still for a long time. Sit down, then make sure you are comfortable. Sort of run through your muscles with your mind and see if there is any pressure," Jim says, demonstrating. "Then, when you're completely comfortable, take a couple of deep breaths and relax. As you breathe, settle into a state of motionlessness. Don't move at all, but don't strain. Just relax. Let the natural world sweep over you and engulf you."

Then he takes them to their Magic Spots, where they try Seton-watching. Some see birds, animals, insects; some see falling leaves. They may see what goes on in their secret places when they are not there. Most importantly, they begin to feel the flow of life around them.

At the end of Magic Spot time each day, a horn or conch shell is sounded to tell the youngsters that the counselor will soon be coming down the trail to have them join him. In the meantime, they have spent a part of their day in a quiet place, where each is alone with his or her personal thoughts. Magic Spots provide a good environment for the kids to make the connection between the problems of the entire planet and this one special place they have begun to value. The more they get to know this one place, the more they will respect and remember one small piece of the natural systems of Sunship Earth.

MAGIC SPOTS—
GUIDELINES

GENERAL NOTES:
1. The success of this activity depends upon the location of the Magic Spots. Station leaders should guide their class group to a specific area. Subgroups should be formed with a crew counselor in charge. Each subgroup should be assigned an area where individuals can choose their spots. The crew counselors should check where the kids are located, then find their own spots. None of the spots should be within view of another.
2. Before the initial Magic Spot time, the station leaders should set the stage:
+Talk in a hushed voice to set the tone.
+Ask the counselors to make a pact with their group not to infringe on the rights of fellow group members by talking, moving around, hooting, or whistling.
+Explain the signal for the end of Magic Spots. If possible, use a conch horn. When it is sounded, everyone should check in with the counselor.
+Suggest possible places to locate a Magic Spot—on a stump, up against a tree, perched in a windfall, or beside a stream.
3. Before the first few Magic Spot sessions, the station leader should discuss with the group suggestions for things they might think about or do while at their spots.
4. If the woods or fields are wet, ask the kids to bring their raincoats to sit on.
5. In some cases you may find one or two kids who aren't ready for a solitary experience. Give them the option to spend some time at the Outlook Inn instead.

Chapter Twelve

IMMERSING EXPERIENCES

Cautious footsteps riffle the long grass of a starlit meadow on a fragrant spring night. From the center of the meadow, the light of one shielded candle can be seen. Along the edges of the clearing, sheltered and hidden by leafy branches, a number of youngsters listen to the sounds of night, their eyes reflecting the tiny brilliance of that candle and those stars, their senses becoming sharper and more alert to the life around them.

The shining eyes are those of a group of kids brought to the meadow to discover the sights, sounds, smells, and feelings of a world bathed not in sunlight, but in shadow. Their footsteps rustled softly in the meadow as they sought hidden places in the night, places where a person could sit, alone, in silence, as alert as a deer and as much at home with darkness as that shy animal.

For these youngsters, night is an unfamiliar world, especially without flashlights and without walls to keep the night out. But entering it as Nightwatchers they are able to forget their fears and become totally immersed in feeling what night is like. They can enjoy a barrier-breaking experience. They stop thinking of themselves and turn their concentration outward, into the world of night that surrounds them now, the way sunlight surrounded them during the day and water surrounded them when they waded in the lake. They became part of the night. An immersing experience is one which emphasizes this total sensory involvement with the natural world, when one is caught up in the doing and being and absorbs the smell and sight and taste and texture of what is there.

"MICRO-PARKS"

Bill has led his group into a small clearing in the forest, where luxuriant moss cloaks fallen trees and lichen clings to bark.

"Wow!" he exclaims, looking around in amazement. "You folks are never going to believe where we are. We've just stumbled right into the middle of Leprechaun National Forest!"

"Where?"

"Right here, all around us, is the site for many new parks soon to be opened. Everyone link arms and form a circle. Let's sit down now, and I'll explain what this is all about." He swings the rucksack he's been carrying into the center of the circle, right in front of him, and all eyes are on it.

"What's in there?"

Bill reaches into the bag and pulls out—one peanut. "Well, here's one thing that's in the bag. We'll find out how this fits in a little later." He reaches in again, pulling out a handful of tiny flags made from toothpicks and small red squares of tape. "These parks are a bit different from Sequoia, with its giant redwoods, or Grand Canyon, with its huge canyon, or Yellowstone, with its spouting geysers. What's different is that instead of being places with colossal-sized attractions, these parks have features that are so small the casual tourist might miss them. In fact, if you aren't looking carefully, you might even step on some of the most fascinating attractions in these parks.

"What we're going to do is mark off some parts of the forest so they can be set aside as special parks. You can use these pieces of yellow yarn to lay out the parks' boundaries."

"Hey, these pieces aren't very long."

"Well, remember, Sally, these are *micro*-parks. In fact, because they're so small, I have something else here that I think you'll need."

Bill reaches into the rucksack again, this time pulling out enough hand lenses so that each kid can have one. "Some of the wonders here are so small that you may need these just to be able to see how neat they are. It's like having a 'third eye' to help out when your two eyes aren't quite enough.

"O.K., after you have laid out the boundaries of your parks, you can note your parks' special attractions by putting these miniature flags next to them. When you're all finished, each of you will be the guide for your park and take others on a tour. You can even charge admission."

"Wait a minute, I don't have any money," one guide protests.

"That's okay," says Bill. "I have some currency right here. You might say that it will only cost peanuts to get into Leprechaun Forest."

Each child gets one peanut now, with the caution "not to spend it all in one place." They will need the peanuts later to be admitted to each other's park areas.

"There are still a couple of things left in my sack," Bill says, rummaging around in it and pulling out a handful of badges, a stack of blank index cards, and one small envelope. Each kid gets a badge, which says "Park Guide," and an index card to use for an entrance sign. Bill reads the note from the envelope:

"'Caution. Since people so often step on the natural wonders of this forest, we urgently request that no one be allowed to use the bottoms of his or her feet. Hands and knees only, please. Remember, this is your forest; help keep it beautiful. Signed, Superintendent of Leprechaun National Forest.'

"O.K.," Bill says, "that sounds reasonable. It's really just as well—not only won't we step on natural wonders, but also when we're on our hands and knees, our third eyes will work better.

"Now, find an area right around here where you want to establish your own park. Look for points of interest, then plant these flags next to them. This isn't a very large park, but it has a lot of features in a small area. In fact, the best tour I ever took was in an area just a few feet wide."

The kids go off, scrutinizing the ground and shrubbery around them, noticing small things and examining them with the hand lenses. The points of interest they mark continually amaze Bill: the mountain-climbing lichen at the base of a tree, hanging gardens of moss on a small boulder, wildflower "lanterns," boneyards of insect husks and mosquito wings, sap waterfalls and bark caverns. One youngster chooses the edge of the stream for her parklet, and puts up an entrance sign for the "Underwater World of Jacques Micro." Another naturalist establishes a series of flags for "The Seven Wonders of the Ant World." Another park is dedicated to the death-defying feats of the climbing spider. The small flags are on the ground, up the side of a rotting stump, next to a tiny colored pebble, and in the scales of a pinecone.

After fifteen minutes, Bill begins the tours by giving one young guide a peanut and announcing, "Looks like Johnny's park is open for business." The kids shop around to find a park they want to visit and try to attract tourists to their own parks by announcing some of its tantalizing attractions.

"Come see the amazing dance of the ants that speak seven languages," announces one. *"See the giant snail that towers over the treetops."*

Bill, with his bag of peanuts, takes tours himself and insures that there is a steady flow of tickets. Tours are taken in small groups, so that each guide can point out to the interested tourists all of the marvels of the park. And, of course, they go on hands and knees and use all three eyes.

"On your left here, you see the doorway to an underground spider's den," one guide points out. *"Here on the right, use your third eye to see the sparkling sands (mica flakes). Here's a seed, in this nursery over here, the site of a future forest."*

"Stick your nose up here, shut your eyes, and take a big whiff of the world's smallest perfume shop," urges another. *"Now, over here, we have a delicate leaf skeleton."*

"This is a canyon made by the Bark River. Note the amazing suspension act of these tiny insects clinging to the canyon walls."

After about twenty minutes of tours, Bill announces that there are five minutes left to finish up. Then the tour guides reunite in the main parkway area to sit in a circle and talk about their discoveries as they consume the profits from their admission charges.

"Wow, we've really come across some neat things in the forest today," Bill concludes. "I hope you'll all remember your first micro-park, and keep your eyes open in the future, because the world is made up of millions upon millions of them."

"CURIOUS HERON WALK"

Sunlight sparkles on the wind-ruffled water as it laps against the shoulder of land. A blackbird whistles, a dry tree limb creaks, and the wind rustles in the treetops.

Jim has brought a classroom group of about twenty-five youngsters to this setting, the edge of the lake. Part of their anticipation is based on his warning at lunch to wear their "grubbies"; old jeans and tennis shoes are the fashion of the day. Scouting out the area earlier, Jim selected a feature of this lakeshore that he knows will capture the kids' attention: the trunk of a tree, two feet from the water's edge, bearing definite marks

left by the beaver that felled it. As they form a circle around the stump to examine it, Jim comments that this is just one of the many fascinating features of the lakeshore.

"This is a really interesting area because there is so much that lives in this narrow strip that is partly water, partly shore," he explains. Then, with no warning at all, he steps into the shallow water and begins wading over to a cattail, continuing his comments. "Right over here, for example, is a plant that starts underwater but reaches up above the water."

There's no help for it, so the youngsters follow, wading behind him to the stand of cattails. By this time, they're wet up to their knees, with a little encouragement from Jim, and they're curious about what's going on.

"We want to make sure we don't miss anything as we walk along here," Jim says. "I'll tell you what we'll do—let's divide up into two groups and cover each other's tracks. That way we'll have two chances to spot some of the interesting things along here." He divides them into two groups and explains that one half will go back to shore by the beaver cutting and walk along the shore with Doug to the point where a particular tree juts out over the lake. Then, they will reenter the lake and walk back through the water. Meanwhile, his group will start from where they are in the water and walk toward the jutting-out tree. What will happen is that the two groups will pass each other in the water just as they come in line with a specified boulder, and then retrace each other's steps.

"To help both groups spot special features here, each person will have one of these blank baggage tags and one of these bobbers," Jim says, distributing these two items along with a pencil to each wader.

"Before your group reaches the midpoint boulder, leave a clue for the other group pointing to some interesting object. If I saw a bee's nest, for example, I might write a riddle or a rhyme like 'Buzz—it's up, it's round, it's way off the ground.' Then you use this long string to tie your tag around a cattail or, on shore, a branch. The bobbers can be looped around something in the water that the other group has to reach down to feel or peer into the water to be able to see," he explains. "Then, after we cross paths, we can look for the clues the other group has left.

"Oh, there's one other thing. In order to see what really goes on around here, we can't just walk and splash around like people. We need to act like something that spends a lot of time in places like this. You've probably seen one of those tall birds that lives around here—the kind that has stilty legs."

"Herons!"

"Herons. How do they walk?"

"Stilty."

"Kind of like this," Jim demonstrates, stretching his head and neck forward, then leaning back as he takes a long, slow stride into the water. "When we're wading along here, let's be curious herons, stepping carefully and checking around for what's here."

The groups divide and start off, each person transformed into a heron with that long, careful walk. They begin spotting all kinds of possibilities to point out to the next group, and begin hanging their tags and bobbers as clues. One imaginative riddler comes up with the rhyme, *"I'm not here now, but I'll be back; you'll see who I am if you're on the right track."* If the second group is watchful, they will spy the raccoon tracks near the water's edge. Another heron ties his bobber to an underwater rock, home for a small crayfish.

Many discoveries are of small things that normally would go unnoticed: *"Look up and see a giant's foot"* is a clue pointing to a broken branch overhead, one that does resemble a foot. Another card bears the title, *"Nature's Christmas Tree Ornaments"*— bright clusters of hidden berries. *"Golf tees"* are trumpet lichen at the base of a stump; *"School's in session"* means to be on the lookout for a school of minnows.

Each group looks for discoveries of its own first, then, switching routes, looks for the other group's markers and the discoveries suggested by their clues. In the process, they scan the shoreline, peer beneath leaves, examine roots, feel moss-covered rocks, reach into the water to bring up a handful of bright pebbles, and poke and probe into the mud and sand. The clues, using colors, shapes, analogies, puns, and rhymes, are fun to write and fun to figure out.

The last person in each group collects the other group's cards as they go along. When both have completed the circle tour and are back at the beaver cutting, Jim suggests that there might be items in their Logs that they've been looking for and found during the Heron Walk.

"Yeah, like the coldest water at that one spot."

So the curious herons, having dipped into the lake and come up with their curiosity rewarded, return to post some of their "finds" on the Discovery Board at the Outlook Inn.

"EARTH STUDIOS"

Seth leads his group to a circle of trees that has been chosen for the headquarters of the art colony, the immersing experience for Thursday afternoon.

"Hey, there's some kind of drawing on those trees," one boy points out. Walking over, he comments, *"Look, it's just some scribbles."*

"Hey, I'll have you know that those *scribbles* happen to be my latest masterpiece," Seth says with mock indignation. "In fact, I was planning to work on another drawing today. If you'll notice the walls of this gallery, you can see that only a couple of pictures have been hung. This is part of an art colony, but the artists need a little help in filling up their gallery. They've agreed to let us borrow their studios for a while if we'll help express the sights and sounds and smells and textures of their community.

"We have charcoal and paper here, and if you want, you can use some natural colors as I did in this one. Note the design here. I wasn't trying to draw an exact reproduction, just to capture the mood of the place. There was a kind of breeze whispering above me in the high branches, so I drew this faint little wavy line here to represent that sound. There are a lot of shadows around, so I put these dark splotches in. Just kind of draw it as you feel it. We don't have any art critics in this gallery. The important thing is that our work should represent our feelings about the place or 'studio' where each of us will be setting up."

The artist's materials, including clipboards for easels, are distributed, and Seth takes each youngster to a special studio. Some are perched in tree limbs, windfalls, or among boulders. Others are on the ground, surrounded by moist earth, ferns, and shade. One crawls into the middle of a blackberry thicket. Another sits on a rock in the middle of a stream. The idea, of course, is that each artist is "immersed" in his or her surroundings—shoe-horned into a special niche or nook or cranny where contact with the earth will be heightened as much as possible. From this new perspective, the artists use charcoal and paper to convey what their senses tell them.

After about twenty minutes of studio time, the artists-for-the-day are led back to the gallery. Those who want to do so can pin their masterpieces on vacant trees and explain them to the others. Sharing isn't dictated by the leader; it just comes naturally as part of the setting. And since the original drawings displayed by the leader are not detailed representations, no one feels threatened by

any great standard of artistic achievement. The focus is on expressing sensations, not on the visual reproduction of reality.

"This line here is the sound—kind of a steady whoosh, but with some birds piping up—that's more jagged."

"I used some leaves to rub in green—my place was mostly green."

"I was looking out through a bush, so mine shows the little spaces of sky and the rest blocked out by leaves."

"I was lying on the ground, so this dirt stuff is for the wet smell."

When the gallery tour is over, the kids have had a chance to feel, express, share—and see that an area appears very different from different points of view.

"THE NIGHTWATCHERS"

"We've been talking a lot about how Sunship Earth gets all its energy from the sun," Jim comments at supper, talking to the assembled crew members. "But the sun only supplies energy to half of the planet at a time. The other half is in shadow. There's a shady side to the sunship, and the neat thing about that is that the sunship becomes a whole different world when it's in shadow. It's as if there's a changing of the guard when the sun goes down, when the daytime things go to bed and the nighttime things wake up. See if you can notice the changing of the guard tonight."

The next day at lunch, Jim mentions nighttime again. "Anybody notice the changing of the guard last night? Wasn't it neat the way the birds just got quiet all of a sudden, and then pretty soon the crickets started chirping? There's an old character who sometimes drops in around here who knows all about that kind of thing. I thought I'd let you know, 'cause he's a little spooky looking, but he's really a neat old man. He is one of Sunship Earth's Nightwatchmen. He'll be coming around one of these evenings, and if you're lucky, he'll share with you some of the secrets of the Nightwatchers."

Well, after all that, the kids aren't too taken aback when there is a soft knocking on their cabin door one evening just about dusk, when the first few stars can be seen. When a crew member opens the door, standing outside is a fellow carrying a rucksack slung over his shoulder. After a slight double take, the crew member says, *"Oh, it's Ed."* The reaction to Ed's appearance was predictable. Dressed in dark clothing, his face and hands smeared with charcoal, his clothing rubbed with fragrant balsam, his lantern casting strange shadows, he isn't immediately recognizable.

"What's that stuff for?" Willy asks, as Ed walks into the brightly lit cabin, squinting and blinking in the light.

"I'm going to make my rounds," replies the Nightwatchman, still shielding his eyes from the room's glare. "Can we turn those lights off? I want to show you how neat this lantern is." Someone hits the switch, and everyone huddles around the candle-lantern.

"Why do you have to look like that to watch the night?" Dick asks.

"I'm a Nightwatchman," Ed announces, in case they haven't guessed. "This is the uniform of the Nightwatchers. It helps us fit in better with the night world, the shady side of the sunship. Say there are deer grazing in the meadow. They might think I'm just part of the night, or maybe even a fir tree or another deer. That way I can watch them up close."

"Hey, that's pretty smart."

"Thank you, Dick. As a matter of fact, I came over here to ask you to come along with me on my rounds tonight. You see, I may not always be able to go, and it's important that there be other people who know how to be Nightwatchers. By coming along with me tonight, you can learn the basic secrets of my profession.

"First, though, you have to get ready. Everyone needs long-sleeved shirts and long pants and sneakers. Sneakers are good for walking around if you want to see some of the passengers who come out at night." Also important is the careful application of charcoal to faces and the rubbing of balsam on necks. When this is completed in the faint glow of lantern light, they leave the cabin.

By the light of Ed's lantern and one hooded flashlight held by one of the crew members, the group follows a trail until they come to a small red reflector about two feet off the ground.

"This is the first stop on my rounds," says the Nightwatchman. He asks the kid with the flashlight to look for a card tied to the reflector and to read it aloud very quietly.

"'This is the edge of the shadow. This is the violet time. Look at

the sky. See how the color is deepening, from blue to black. The first bright stars are beginning to come out. Night is a world of black and white. But with stored sunlight from your flashlight, check to see if the colors are still there; if the grass is still green.'"

The first kid shines his dim flashlight on the ground. The grass is green. Then he turns it off, and the grass takes on the shadowy violet hue of late dusk.

The flashlight is transferred to the hands of another crew member, who leads the group to another red reflector, finds the card, and reads it.

"'Look at the tops of the trees against the sky. You are moving deeper into the shade, but there is still light. Trace the outline of a tree with your finger.'"

The next card instructs the youngster to clap his hands, just once, as loud as he can. The sounds around the group cease abruptly and the night world becomes silent. Crickets stop chirping, then, after the silence, resume their calls.

"'Now, listen to the symphony of sounds. The Nightwatchman can help you with this.'"

Ed has the youngsters sit down on the ground, close their eyes, and listen to the sounds around them. "Don't try to identify what's making the sound," he cautions. "Just listen to each sound as an instrument in an orchestra. Listen for the soloists and the groups of instruments, the patterns and rhythm. Listen as the sounds get louder and softer. Just let the music sweep over you."

They sit, these young Nightwatchers, eyes closed and ears open to the night. The wind stirs the tops of the trees, softly, growing and dying. The crickets chirp and something rustles in the dry leaves. An owl hoots.

A fourth red reflector calls attention to an animal of the night. It could be a spider, spinning a web. In this case, it is an owl's favorite tree not far away. The kids sit and watch for the owl. *"'As you move deeper into the shadow, you meet this passenger, who prefers the shady side of the sunship. Many things live in this world of night, just about as many as prefer the brightness of day.'"*

The shadow has spread so that the group is no longer on the edge but in the middle of the darkness. Ed asks them to form a circle around his lantern, which he places carefully on a stump. He gives them each a small penlight covered with yellow tape so that the light glows yellow, and the white light comes only from a tiny hole in the tape covering. One of the lights has red, rather than yellow, tape, and the young Nightwatchers will pass this red light from one to another as they take turns at leading the swarm of "fireflies."

"Let's change lights as we go deeper into the shadow," Ed says. "Instead of that big flashlight, we'll use these little tiny lights, like fireflies, to explore farther into the shadow.

"Fireflies don't have voices either, so we'll communicate with our lights. The firefly with the red light is the leader. We'll swarm around whatever the leader finds. When you find something interesting, flick your light on and off very quickly, like this, so others will know to look there."

They begin with a stump, circling it with their tiny lights, and discover that they have to come very close and look at the small area that is illuminated by their points of light. They may see a mosquito clinging to the underside of a leaf, a tiny lichen, a shadow cast by the light shining on a miniature fungus. When they focus on a small pebble with their small spotlights, it seems to take on the depth and dimension of a giant boulder. The little things become large as the Nightwatchers peer closely. The firefly lights flicker in the night, announcing discovery. They swarm from stump to tree to fern to spider web.

"From here on, we must go with only the light of this lantern," Ed says, asking the fireflies to return their lights to him. "We are nearly in the most beautiful part of the shadow now." He leads them a few yards to a clearing, walking slowly. He sits on the ground, his lantern in his lap, and asks them to sit in a circle with him.

"To be a Nightwatcher, you must be aware. What we have been doing so far is sharpening our senses to the wonderful sights and sounds of the night. Now, to be a true Nightwatcher you must learn to be alone. Then you will know that night, like day, is beautiful and pleasant. Leave this circle and walk softly through the grass to a spot where you can still see the candle glowing here. Choose a spot and sit down. When I call, hooting like an owl, come back here to the circle."

They walk off, some a few yards, some much farther. They choose for themselves how far they will go into the night. The more timid might stay very close to the lantern, but there is still no talking, no whispering, no communicating. Each is alone with the night, watching and listening. They see shadows within shadows and hear sounds of wind and crickets and small animals. But they become more at ease, more familiar, with the sounds that are there. They no longer shudder at the rustlings. An owl hoots and each Nightwatcher returns to the glow of the lantern.

"Now comes the last stage on your journey into the shade," Ed says, once they have sat again in their circle around the small, shielded candle. "It's time to go completely into the shadow." He blows out the candle and they sit, in silence and in darkness.

"Lie down on your backs with your heads in the center of the circle," he says, doing so himself. They do so, looking up at the bright stars. "At first we used the light from the flashlight, then the firefly lights, then the candle. Now, we have those stars for our lights. I hope you're holding on tight to the ground, so you don't fall off. Right now, we're whirling through space, a part of those stars. That white band of stars is the Milky Way—our galaxy. We're on the edge of that galaxy, spinning around our own star, the sun, at more than sixty-five thousand miles an hour, as our sun itself travels through space and the galaxy whirls in a spiral. Pick out a star and focus on it. It may look like a firefly light, but that star is probably bigger than our own sun. The light from that star, lighting up this sky now, began its journey years ago, perhaps hundreds or thousands or millions of years ago. The closest star to us, the one that is called Alpha Centauri, is so far away that its light takes almost five years to reach us. When the light left some of those stars out there, dinosaurs were roaming the earth.

"Isn't it incredible?" he asks, still in a hushed tone. "Here we are, clinging to our little sunship, on the edge of that galaxy, whirling through that vast, lonely space. All that separates us from the void of space is our fragile bubble of air. People don't often think of that in the daytime, but at night, in the star shine, we can see far, far into space and feel how our planet is such a small part of it.

"Look at your star again and let your eyes zoom through space. Remember the film you saw in the sunship room. Just look at those stars!"

They lie on the ground, clinging to the sunship, watching the countless, ageless stars. They are riding on a sunship, and the stars are the view they see from the porthole.

Eventually, Ed stands up, saying that it's time to head back. "There aren't many Nightwatchers around here any more," he comments. "On the way back, you can practice, now that you've learned some of the secrets. We'll return without using any of our lights."

One of the secrets of the Nightwatchers is that the shady side of the sunship is not as frightening as it might first appear to be, and that there is always some light or some sense to guide us in the darkness.

IMMERSING EXPERIENCES—
GUIDELINES

Micro-Parks

PROPS:
Flags—Cut red surveyor's tape into one-inch squares—eight to ten per person.
Toothpicks—Use as miniature stakes for mounting flags.
Hand Lenses (one per person)
Peanuts (one per person and a few extra for the bank)
Yarn
Guide Badges
Entrance Sign

GENERAL NOTES:
1. The leader's role is to distribute props and visit the micro-parks once they have been completed. The leaders help stimulate the action by being able to take unlimited tours themselves and by reinforcing exciting micro-discoveries.
2. Set off a definite area within which the parks can be established. If the parks are too far apart, less trading of park tours will take place.
3. Leaders should announce a "five-minute call" before the activity ends. This gives the kids a chance to finish up park tours and return their lenses, yarn, and flags.
4. Approximate time breakdown:
   5 minutes—explaining the setup and touring procedures
   15 minutes—setting up trails
   20 minutes—conducting park tours
   5 minutes—finishing tours and taking down station markers

Curious Heron Walk

PROPS:
Baggage Tags—Attach strings and small fishing bobbers.
Pencils

GENERAL NOTES:
1. Prior to participating in the activity, the kids should be told to wear old clothes and tennis shoes.
2. Before wading along the shore, the kids should make a pact to refrain from splashing and curtail the urge to take a swim.
3. After the Heron Walk, time should be allowed for the kids to change clothes.
4. For safety, don't allow the kids to go barefoot on the Heron Walk. Tennis shoes (sneakers) dry easily in the sun.

Earth Studios

PROPS:
Heavy Sketch Paper
Charcoal Sticks
Clipboards

GENERAL NOTES:
1. Prior to the activity, post a few of the sketches you have drawn on the trees near the "art colony." Also, locate some particularly inspiring perches or niches for studio areas.
2. Collect the "masterpieces" after the gallery tour and post them in the dining hall.

The Nightwatchers

PROPS:
Rucksack
Candle Lantern
Candle and Matches
Charcoal
Flashlight
Reflectors
Input Cards
Penlights—Use tape to mask the lens, leaving only a small hole to project a tiny beam of light.

GENERAL NOTES:
1. Keep the evening agenda a secret. Build up the suspense during mealtimes, but don't let the kids know exactly when this immersing experience will take place, or what it is.
2. Setting the tone for this activity is crucial. Talk in a hushed voice throughout the experience. That's part of the magic.
3. The Nightwatchman leaders should decide ahead of time where they will take their groups. This prevents overlapping and crowding in one area.
4. The kids should be dressed properly for the nighttime. Apply insect repellant before going out, if mosquitoes are likely to be a problem.
5. On an evening after a rain, you may want to take raincoats or ponchos along to sit on.
6. If you think (or discover) that the youngsters in your group want to play with the flashlight rather than using it as a tool, give the role of flashlight carrier to the counselor instead.

THE CHOICES

Time Out

Games

Expeditions

Community Services

Projects

Evening Workshops

Food Projects

Tool Projects

Outlook Inn

"The 'Inn Touch' Box"

"The Note Nook"

"Old Country Store Spice Rack"

"The Morgue"

"The Discovery Board"

"Mama Nature's Pizza Palor"

"The Po-E-Tree"

"The Whiffery"

"The Color Wheel"

"The Rock Rack"

"Concept Corners"

"Corrals"

Chapter Thirteen

TIME OUT

Every afternoon at the Sunship Study Station, time is set aside for activities that are mostly just for fun and relaxation. By late afternoon, the kids and counselors have all had a busy day that has demanded concentration, heightened senses, and conceptual understanding. What they need now is a chance to unwind and relax, or simply to let off steam.

Our "Time Out" activities, like the rest of the Sunship Earth program, have special criteria. Just any game or sport does not necessarily fit into the category of a Time Out choice. Because this is a Sunship Study Station, we feel that the activities should encourage contact with the elements and consist of simple, yet appealing, pastimes. In addition, there should be choices both for those who want a quiet activity and for those who crave physical exertion. There should also be, in each of these, an opportunity for each participant to be just that—a participant. The games, for example, are not as competitive as they are fun. It's physical activity, but there is not so much pressure to win as there is encouragement to join in and have fun.

Here are the kinds of Time Out activities that we feel fit the criteria. This list should offer plenty of choices for a week-long session, as well as suggesting other activities that have the same basic components.

GAMES

Again, these are not really competitive, and the individual leader should emphasize this point. All of our games are played outdoors, of course!

Frisbee. It's simple, and its beauty is in that simplicity. All kinds

206

of variations are possible, but one of the best systems for a group of about ten is simply to form a large circle and pass the Frisbees around to various members. (Extra Frisbees mean extra action!) Everyone gets to throw, everyone gets to catch, and everyone gets to pick how far they want to throw. You might suggest some challenges: the greatest number of consecutive catches, the weirdest catch, etc.

Earthball. This game is played with a large, six-foot-diameter balloon painted to resemble the earth, and the object is simply to keep it from falling to the ground. This is a group activity, since no one can really manage the task alone. Again, there's running and jumping and heaving the ball into the air—and everyone gets involved, not just a few star athletes. Another popular approach is to have the participants keep spreading out to see how much area they can cover while keeping the "earth" in space.

Horseshoes. Keen eyes and energetic arms are the basis for this game, an old American favorite. It is a good-natured contest that literally rings with fellowship. Best of all, it is reminiscent of the simple toys and pastimes of our forebears. Many youngsters have never tried their hands at it.

EXPEDITIONS

Gold panning. "Thar's gold in them thar hills," even if it is only fool's gold. Panning for treasure in a creek puts kids in contact with nature, which is a golden opportunity in itself. The idea of finding something is always exciting, but by looking for gold they might uncover marvels they would never have thought about finding. Rocks and aquatic life, the fascination of water currents, the fun of make-believe—these are part of what panning for gold is all about. It is also a folklore lesson about how the old-timers really did it.

Skin Diving. "Who would like to go skin diving this afternoon?" is the invitation. But this kind of skin diving is a little different. It uses a basting tube and an enamel pan, nets and vials, and

involves wading in the pond or stream. Hands and feet go "skin diving" to gather small discoveries to examine with a "jeweler's monocle," or hand lens.

Indian Run. This is a cross-country run taking the group through high grasses and muddy lowlands, up and down steep hills, hurdling over pricker bushes and fallen limbs, and crossing logs over creeks. Frequent stops along the way allow everyone to catch up, then they all take off for another spurt. The idea stressed from the beginning is that the run is not a race, but a chance to feel fluid and agile, like a deer. The run is divided up into short spurts, so everyone can find their own limits and not have to worry about being left behind. The challenge is to run like an Indian, that is, to see as much as possible along the way, to remain alert to the surroundings.

COMMUNITY SERVICES

Gardening. Depending on the season, there is plowing and planting, hoeing and weeding, mulching, pruning and thinning, and of course, harvesting. Gardening is a lesson in where food comes from, as well as what any gardener knows is just plain exercise. Theoretically, each youngster could spend one hour in the garden during his week's stay, and it would be a very well-cared-for plot. The rewards are contact with the soil, a chance for building up some honest sweat or calluses, and the opportunity to sample a freshly-picked vegetable!

Food Gathering. Like gardening, this expends some physical energy while illustrating where food comes from. Natural foods such as edible seeds, berries, roots, and leaves can be gathered in baskets, and fish can be hooked with simple willow poles. There is one rule for gathering, though: whatever wild edibles the kids gather, they must eat. So even the fishermen are in it for the food source, as well as the sport.

PROJECTS

Raft Building. The same logs can be used over and over again by different groups of Huck Finn fans. Each group can lash the logs together, then experience the feeling of wind and water as they loaf on their own raft. (Since the raft can be taken apart and reconstructed next week, this project does not make any major impact on the forest!)

Kite Flying. Wind is the key to flying a kite, so the kids get in touch with this natural element while playing. Building their own kites offers them a chance to work with their hands and create something. The materials are simple, but the enjoyment can be immense.

Tree Climbing. A perennial favorite, tree climbing and tree house building also include a special kind of contact with the plant itself. This activity should be well-supervised, and you may want to provide harnesses for your climbers.

Chapter Fourteen

EVENING WORKSHOPS

Workshops are offered four nights a week, with most of them taking two evenings to complete. They give the youngsters an opportunity to learn and practice skills that are compatible with the Sunship Earth theme. Just as Time Out activities are carefully chosen to meet certain criteria, the workshops are more than just assorted crafts projects.

Workshop choices center on activities that have something to do with keeping the study station running, but they are geared to specific topics and skills rather than general maintenance. Our workshops offer a wide variety of skills to attract a range of interests, contain a bit of novelty, and above all contribute to awareness of the sunship's operating systems.

Awareness of sources is a major factor in two of the categories of workshop offerings: "Foods" and "Tools." *Food projects*, such as grinding flour to make bread, mixing granola, growing sprouts, culturing yogurt, preserving by smoking or drying, pickling, and making jellies, are all ways that kids can become more aware of where their food comes from. The results of these projects are edible, not merely decorative. They are useful, not wasteful. *Tool projects* carry the same stipulation. The items made are for use. They are practical things that the kids will be able to use, not just make and then store in a closet, because that would be a waste of important sunship materials. They might weave more cloth napkins for the dining hall, make brooms for the cabins, prepare soap for the bathrooms, produce paper for the "note nook" in the Outlook Inn, build a solar heater for the central washroom, or make pottery and baskets for food gathering. All of these projects, of course, also help the kids discover alternatives to the plasticized, consumption-oriented elements of our society. And all of them result in simple tools and simple foods that have a direct tie to the materials available on the sunship.

Evening Workshops are an ideal time to draw upon a wider pool of talents. Not only the leader and counselors, but also the teachers, parents, and individuals from the community can be invited to share a special skill or knowledge with these younger passengers. Parents are often eager for an opportunity to see what the site is like and are usually pleased to join the sharing. Don't overlook these resources, nor the inevitable area resident who is an expert in baking bread, weaving, or preparing wild foods.

Chapter Fifteen

"OUTLOOK INN"

Picture in your mind a building that is partly backcountry bookstore, part tinker's shop, part general store, and part country inn. Inside there is an atmosphere of warmth, a clutter of all kinds of interesting objects, and an abundance of nooks and crannies of every shape and size. Like an old-fashioned store, the Outlook Inn is the kind of place that invites browsing. It's a place to stop in and poke around, and a place to while away a rainy hour. There is always something new to see by reaching to the very back of the bottom shelf.

But while the Outlook Inn is indoors, the focus is on the outdoors—hence the name. You are inside, but the atmosphere and messages urge you to look outside.

From the moment you enter the door, you can tell that this is a special place. There is a smell of woods and of herb tea, of books and pinecones. There are windows in strange places, some in the ceiling and some down at hands-and-knees level, all for looking at various natural masterpieces. Mobiles and drying roots and artifacts hang from the rafters.

There are window seats and alcoves with big cushions for curling up with a book. In one corner, a cassette player offers selections of outdoor sounds: bird songs, waves, thunderstorms, wind, and raindrops. Houseplants (representing plant communities that exist in other parts of the world) are growing all over, tended and talked to by the youngsters. A wood stove in another corner heats water for sampling herbal tea in small, egg-sized gourd cups. There are bowls of fruit and seeds, prints and paintings, artifacts and collections of all kinds. But the collections and interpretive displays are far from the sterile or stuffy stereotype. They invite participation, or approach an old subject from a new perspective.

There are hundreds of possibilities for the Outlook Inn, from simple items like a puzzle table dedicated to jigsaw puzzles of natural scenes, where anyone can pause and add a piece or two, to complex exhibits that demand major construction. Each area or exhibit contains "fun fact" charts and diagrams. Here are a dozen examples of the kinds of wares that the Outlook Inn can offer.

"The 'Inn Touch' Box"

A box of weathered wood, resembling an old sea chest, can be opened only far enough for an arm to reach in. You can't see what's inside, but a chart above the box gives clues to what is in each of the compartments. One reads: "I have 14,000 teeth." Reaching inside for the cranny that corresponds with that clue, you feel—a snail! Another hint says that the compartment contains the only thing on earth capable of turning sunlight into food: a small leaf. Still another cubbyhole in the chest contains a burr; its clue reads, "I am a hitchhiker, destination unknown." The "Inn Touch" Box combines sensory experience—touching—with fun facts about the natural world.

"The Note Nook"

An old desk or library table serves as a place to write letters, using special Outlook Inn stationery that features block prints of leaves, seeds, and grasses. An extra flourish is the large quill pen, dipped in regular ink or one of the jars of colors made from barks, berries, and roots. Sample letters are pinned to the partition behind the desk to offer further encouragement.

"Old Country Store Spice Rack"

An array of glass jars in all shapes and sizes is the source of some of the marvelous aromas wafting through the room. The jars contain an assortment of herbs and spices that invite sniffing and comparing. Another set of smells drifts through the room, of course, from the perpetual tea kettle that brews herbal teas, many collected locally, for tasting by visiting crew members.

"The Morgue"

Not as gruesome as it is fascinating, the morgue is a many-drawered bureau. Each drawer contains the skull or skeleton of a different animal. "Who is the victim?" and "What might have been the cause of death?" are two of the questions raised, as well as where and how the animal lived. A plotting board shows where the "stiffs" were found and encourages additions. Obituaries, life stories of the deceased, are posted nearby.

"The Discovery Board"

"Ah, has!" are everywhere, and the Sunship Study Station encourages sharing them. The Discovery Board has hooks labeled for such discoveries as the tallest tree, the coldest spot, the smallest plant, the largest passenger, and so forth, as listed in the Logs under "Individual Discoveries." The crew members come here to have their discoveries duly noted and to hang the tear-out sheets from their Logs on the hooks that correpond to the discovery they made.

"Mama Nature's Pizza Parlor"

Everyone loves different kinds of pizza, and animals are no different. Mama Nature's establishment, however, offers a special menu. Pasted on salvaged pizza cardboards are the components of pizzas that would appeal to different animal appetites. A "Whitetail Special" pizza, for example, might include the tender leaves and twigs of shrubs, young shoots of grass, and a garnish of herbs. "Chipmunk's Choice" features a variety of seeds, fruits, nuts, and insects, heavy on the seeds. Along with the display of several such pizzas, a menu of the house specialities lists ingredients for still more.

"The PO-E-Tree"

It is always a bit surprising to find a fairly large tree growing inside, but that's what we have—the PO-E-Tree. A round bench surrounding the trunk offers work space for poets who yearn to express themselves and their feelings about the world. Poems written by others already dangle from the branches of the tree and encourage similar sharing, whether signed or unsigned. It is a good place for free verse, as well as for more conventional styles.

"The Whiffery"

This is like a perfumery of natural scents—"Essence of Clover," "Eau de Spruce Bog," "Parfum de Pine," and so forth. Flowers, berries, barks, soils, roots, and stems provide the base for the scents. A large cylinder with holes just big enough for a nose to poke through is the center. Each "scent-hole" has a different cup of mystery fragrance behind it in the cylinder. On an adjacent shelf, a row of atomizer bottles are "samplers." A spray of scent on a wrist or behind an ear is also the product of various plants.

"The Color Wheel"

One of the window alcoves is set up as a "Color Wheel," with a rainbow poster on the wall above the circular window. Rows of prisms are suspended from the otherwise empty curtain rod. Youngsters can find objects in the room that match up with the different colors of the rainbow, examine the ever-changing prisms, look through kaleidescopes attached with long thongs to hooks on the wall, or peer into the fresnel lens attached to the window. Directly underneath the window sits "Nature's Color Wheel." It is a large circular tray containing samples of naturally colored objects in pie-shaped compartments. This is a collection that invites comparisons and additions.

"The Rock Rack"

This is, and isn't, a rock collection. Different kinds of rocks are hung from a shelf in little pouches and macrame-like holders. Other rocks are displayed on blocks of wood. Each has a sign. There is a rock that floats, a rock you can see through, a rock that is soft enough to write with, a rock that crumbles in your hand. There are rocks that aren't rocks, like fossils and petrified wood, and old rocks, or sand. There are also rocks that have been cut open in slices to show the hidden patterns inside. And there is a pile of rocks which contains some that can and some that cannot scratch glass. Different characteristics of different kinds of rocks show that there are many fascinating things to learn about plain old rocks.

"Concept Corners"

Seven areas are set up for "storyboards" on the EC-DC-IC-A concepts. Each corner focuses on the story of a single concept and backs up the visual explanation with things to touch and examine and try out. While a youngster appears somewhere in each story, the emphasis is upon the overall functioning of the concept on Sunship Earth.

"Corrals"

The corrals are the Outlook Inn's outside area. Outside the Outlook Inn, two pine-pole canopied corrals serve as centers of activity for those who are wandering through in between other activities, or on Time Out and Evening Workshop time. Each

corral is about twenty feet in diameter and full of equipment and props for the type of activity indicated by its name.

Curiosity Corral. The Curiosity Corral contains all sorts of "scientific" equipment, from the barometers, thermometers, and sling psychrometer of the weather station to a table full of microscopes, tripod magnifiers, enamel pans, soil test kits, and nets and seines. There is a recording of bird and animal voices to play and to mimic. It is also the site for the "Sunship Hotel," overnight lodgings for the small passengers collected one day and released the next. The hotel is a sharing center for "Look What I Found" discoveries, so that others will have a chance to get in on the discovery experience. There are three resort sections in the Hotel: Fur and Feathers (and other land creatures), Scales and Fins (aquatic), and the Honeybee Hotel for insects and slugs. Each guest is registered one day and checked out of the hotel the next. The register notes the date checked in, the name of the discoverer, and the creature's home address and job (habitat and niche).

Still another feature of the Curiosity Corral is the "Flight Control Board," where the bird-watchers post their findings. Bird and sighter are both listed on little flags which show where the "flier" was located.

Creative Corral. In this corral, additional creative projects also help focus on the world of nature. The Natural Loom is used for making mats and wall hangings with dead leaves and grasses; one of the stipulations for collecting the weaving materials is that no live materials be collected. Each weaving can have a design or theme, and should make use of the variety of colors, textures, shapes, and patterns found in the natural world.

"Nature's Paint Box" includes an easel with tear-off sheets of paper and a box of colors made from barks, berries, rocks, soil, leaves, and roots. The artists can find their own materials or use some of the materials already gathered to express the mood of a landscape within view of the easel.

"Bottle Gardens" are made from an assortment of glass containers constructed in many shapes and sizes, all fairly small. A tub of soil and another of gravel and sand offer a start, and the youngsters can add small plants and rocks. The tools provided are small, to encourage making miniature habitats rather than massive terrariums.

Charlotte's Web. Near the Curiosity Corral is another pine-pole frame, this one strung with a horizontal replica of a giant spider web. There is a space in the center of the web for a kid to stand from which all of the strings radiate out. In this way, kids can role-play spiders. Head covered by a black bag, the "spider" stands in the center while others pluck at the strings from the outer edge of the web. By feeling the vibration of the strings, the "spider" tries to match the spider's feat of locating the section of the web that contains the "prey." The task isn't as easy as it sounds, because the interconnecting strings make it difficult to feel which string was originally plucked.

THE CHOICES—
GUIDELINES

Time Out

GENERAL NOTES:
1. Prepare a Master Sign-Up Chart which includes descriptions of the activities offered. This will give the kids a chance to see what they are buying into beforehand, as well as giving you a chance to plan ahead for staff and equipment needs.
2. Ask some of your staff to be "floaters," moving from place to place during Time Out. (Encourage the kids to spend their Time Out period outside, rather than in their cabins.)
3. See "The Ramble" in the Environmental Study Station chapter of *Acclimatizing* for an activity appealing to those who want more time just to poke around.
4. See the "New Games" and "Project Adventure" materials for other activities which may meet our criteria.

Evening Workshops

GENERAL NOTES:
1. Workshop skills should be fairly easy to master, so that the kids can learn the skill well enough to turn out a usable product.
2. Be sure to notify your teachers (and other volunteers) far enough ahead of time so they can prepare for their workshops. It takes a lot of planning and coordination to pull these off in just two evenings.
3. See the *Foxfire* books for additional workshop ideas.

Outlook Inn

GENERAL NOTES:
1. Achieving the overall atmosphere is the most difficult part of developing a good Outlook Inn. It must be a careful blend of the diverse elements that make it up. The effective use of space and light and surfaces will determine much of your success (plus a pinch of magic and a dash of clutter).
2. The justification for the "hotels" in the Curiosity Corral is that this technique allows the kids to display animal discoveries instead of hiding them in their cabins. The method of "checking the animals in" for the day assures both that their stay will be a brief one and that someone will be looking after them.
3. Analyze your building in terms of your own use (and loss) of energy. Prepare a checklist and a plan of action for improving upon your structure in terms of energy consumption.

THE ROUTINES

Routines

Community Meeting

Cabins and Crews

Empathizing

Disguise-removing

Fun Facts

Meals and Snacks

"The Packaged Sunlight Challenge"

"The Conversion Room"

"The Waste Watchers"

"Dedication Dinners"

Quiet Times

Sharing Circles

Concept Clarifiers

Values Building

SUNSHIP MONITOR

Campfires

Crew Campfires

"Journey Home"

Chapter Sixteen

COMMUNITY MEETING

The groundwork for the Sunship Earth experience begins long before the youngsters leave for the outdoor school with the visit by the staff person to their classroom for passport applications and the suggestions for preparations by their teachers, as described earlier. But when the youngsters do arrive at the outdoor school and throughout their stay, some very important program elements help make the difference, we believe, between a good experience and a great one. The nitty-gritties of meals, lodging, waking up and winding down, and spending time with other kids in cabin groups are inextricably part of any resident outdoor program. Most programs, however, separate curriculum from camping, sometimes assigning a separate staff for each. And most curriculums assume that all of the necessities of living quarters, meals, recreation, and entertainment will be taken care of by someone other than the camp counselors or leaders involved in the curriculum. The Sunship Earth program does not make that assumption. We feel it would be a mistake to ignore the importance of the resident aspect of the program and its effect on the learning we want to take place.

That poor planning and organization of the daily routines can detract from what the kids learn during the week is obvious. On the other hand, in a well-planned program, the hours that the youngsters spend at meals and in their cabins can also offer opportunities for learning in less structured ways. Our experience has been that people learn what they live, so eating, sleeping, and playing are part of the total learning process. Most importantly, the quality of life on the sunship will be determined largely by our daily life patterns, and a resident experience offers a good opportunity to convey this recognition to the kids.

The first few moments after the kids arrive are crucial. Here, the tone for the entire week is set. A station leader boards the bus the moment it enters the main gate and rides with the youngsters to the parking area. "Glad you could make it," Helene says, introducing herself and talking a bit about what will be going on as soon as they park. She explains that when the bus stops, they can just leave their gear on board and get off. They will have a chance to meet their counselors, tour the facilities at the Sunship Study Station, and then come back to move their gear into their cabins. "So don't worry about your gear right now. Just kind of relax and look around and get to know the Sunship Study Station."

They are naturally excited and concerned about cabins, counselors, and the other new experiences of the setting. But now they have already had a chance to meet one of these new people, and she seems all right. They also know what the agenda is for the next few minutes, so they have some idea of what to expect.

The entire staff is on hand to give them a warm welcome when the bus stops at the parking area. They all walk over to the campfire ring and take seats on the semi-circular benches.

"Well, here you are. Welcome to the Sunship Study Station. This spot is where we'll have our evening campfires. You might be wondering who these funny-looking people are and why they're all standing around up here," says one of the station leaders. He proceeds to introduce the staff, who ham it up as they take bows. The kids are already having a great time, and the ice is broken.

"You saw a small part of our community here as you rode in on the bus, but there's a lot more. You just left your communities at home, the grocery stores and houses and streets and factories, and here you are in another community. I think it's a great community, and you'll be learning more about it later.

"I guess you know why you're here. We call this the Sunship Study Station because the earth *is* a sunship—it's like a spaceship with all of its life-support systems, and the sun is the mother ship because it is the energy source for the earth. We're all passengers on that ship and depend on its life-support systems.

"The problem, of course, is that lately some of the life-support systems are being overloaded. In some places the air is getting a little thick and gray; in other places the water isn't as clean as it used to be. This situation is causing a lot of concern. The systems get overloaded because many of the passengers don't understand how the sunship works. You've been selected as a special crew to go through this retraining process so you'll understand how it all works and how you can help keep the ship in operating order.

"One thing you'll be doing this week is meeting some of the non-human passengers on the sunship. You should keep in mind that we humans aren't the only passengers on the ship, and we should respect our fellow passengers. A lot of things live here besides us, and other human passengers will also come here later for retraining, just like you. So one of the main ground rules here at the Sunship Study Station is to leave this area at least as nice as you found it, so that other passengers can live here and enjoy it too."

That's the end of the brief welcome message. Then it is time for crew assignments. The counselors read off the names of the kids who are in their cabins, and each group goes off to tour the facilities. They learn where the dining room, washrooms, and nurse's office are and begin to feel at home. The counselor then helps them move their gear into the cabins and find their bunks.

Then it's time for lunch, for stocking up on packaged sunlight energy for the busy afternoon ahead.

Chapter Seventeen

CABINS AND CREWS

The "crew members" are spending most of their time outdoors and very little of it in their cabins, but the fact remains that in any camp setting there is a cabin-bonding process at work. They eat together, sleep in the same cabin, and have a few special cabin activities. For all of this, the cabin itself is an important center. It's home. Our cabins, like our Sunship Study Station, are a little different from those found in the ordinary outdoor school. Some important learning devices are set up before the youngsters arrive.

Empathizing

Because kids identify with their cabin name, we name our cabins after endangered species: crocodile, condor, key deer, gray wolf, black-footed ferret, peregrine falcon, whooping crane, ivory-billed woodpecker, and so forth. A picture of "their" animal is on or in the cabin, with a short natural history of that animal—where and how it lives, some of its special characteristics, and why it is endangered.

Disguise Removing

To help the youngsters realize how their home is connected to the natural cycles of air, water, and soil, we label certain parts of the cabin for what they are, rather than for what they are not. For instance, drains are labeled "The Other End of the Faucet," to emphasize their part in the water cycle. (And a diagram nearby illustrates the idea.) Each ceiling light or light bulb has a yellow cutout shaped like the rays of the sun. A similar cutout is on the light switches, with the request to "Please Stop the Sun Leak." The reminder here of course is that the electricity used is a form of solar energy flow; when the lights are left on needlessly, a leak in the energy flow system results.

Next to the toilet, there is a diagram of the soil cycle, including a picture of a child sitting on a toilet and his place in the soil cycle. Human excrement is part of the material that is returned to the soil nutrient cycle, and that is how we treat it.

Any exposed pipes or wires are labeled with what they really are: water cycle, soil cycle, ins and outs.

Each cabin has several plants, and on each pot is the sign: "Air Conditioner at Work." This label indicates an oxygen source for the air in the cabin.

Bunks are nests and burrows (top and bottom). If there is a heater or furnace, that, too, is labeled as part of the solar energy flow.

"What's a *waste*basket?" reads the sign on the cabin trash container, to make the residents think; and there's a camp recycling center where everything from the baskets is sorted each morning. The point is that you can't really throw anything away because there is no such place as "away." Everything has to go somewhere.

Some cabins might have other homes—a bird's nest under the eaves, a spider's web in the corner—and these can be labeled, too. The possibilities are endless, of course, but we also want to leave some connections for the residents to discover themselves after getting a running start.

Fun Facts

A sign on the faucet mentions the number of gallons a faucet would drip in a year. Other signs note how many air molecules there are in the cabin, how many trees went into the cabin's construction, and how the decomposers will eventually break it all down. A few "fun facts" like these help tie the cabin in with the rest of the environment. Home, too, is part of this community.

Chapter Eighteen

MEALS AND SNACKS

We get our energy from food, and food is a tangible example of our dependence on the sun. The meals at the Sunship Study Station focus on what the food really is and where it comes from. Rather than leaving the Sunship Study Station model behind when we go into the dining hall, we use mealtime as an obvious illustration of our relationship with other passengers on the sunship.

"The Packaged Sunlight Challenge"

At one of the first meals, Bill announces that he will give Jim's dessert to anyone who can name more than one thing that they are eating, excluding water, that doesn't consist of energy from the sun. Almost everything does, of course, but there are a couple of items which we will allow: salt (a mineral), baking powder in biscuits (a chemical compound), and various chemicals that are artificial, such as flavorings, food colorings, and preservatives.

"The Conversion Room"

For one of the midweek lunches, each cabin group (crew) and its counselor are told to report to the dining hall to receive lunches to go. Each group is given a large basket, described as the complete picnic. They go out, spread a tablecloth, and prepare to eat. "Wait a minute!" they shout. "This is a basket full of leaves and grass." There's also some soil and a jar of water. But then, at the bottom, they find an instruction card. As directed, they report to the Sunship Conversion Room, where their sackful of plant material is transformed into food they can eat. But in order for the conversion to work, they have to say the magic words in answer to the question: What can convert this plant into food for you?" "A cow." "A chicken." "I know; the cow eats the grass and drinks the water and it's hamburger!" Not only do we rely on the sun for our food—we also depend on animals which convert that stored solar energy into the forms may of us prefer to eat.

"The Waste Watchers"

At the end of each meal, garbage from each table is scraped into a bucket and weighed by the official Waste Watcher, an honored appointment. The weight of each table's leftovers is then blocked in as part of a large "garbage can" bar graph showing the total weight of the group's garbage throughout the week. The goal is to help everyone focus on discarding less, and to come up with less waste at the end of the week than preceding groups. Afterwards, the Waste Watcher takes the garbage to the garden compost heap and learns how it is turned back into soil nutrients and then into food in the garden.

"Dedication Dinners"

A series of "Food Chain Feasts," beginning with a dedication speech and a grand toast are a highlight of the week. Appropriate pictures decorating the dining hall, centerpieces, posted menus, and special serving dishes and utensils add to the tone of the meal. (Naturally, the Producers' and Decomposers' banquets have more food because they are more energy-efficient.) The following menus offer some suggestions:

PRODUCERS

Salad bar, fruits and berries, bread and jam, juices
(Include a "vegetable vendor" strolling around the dining room!)

CONSUMERS

A Bovine Banquet.	Hamburgers, milk, cottage cheese, butter cookies.
Wings and Things.	Hard-boiled eggs, turkey soup, baked chicken.
Aquatic Critters.	Clam chowder, tuna sandwiches, baked fish.

DECOMPOSERS

Yeast breads, cheese (grilled cheese sandwiches),
mushroom soup, yogurt, apple cider

Chapter Nineteen

QUIET TIMES

Each day, for about an hour after lunch, a time is set aside for the classroom teachers to spend with their youngsters in quiet activities. This time gives them a chance to touch bases as well as to help the kids process what is happening during the week.

One way to help is through skill-building activities that will help the youngsters later on, such as learning how to write haiku poetry. They can use haiku for expressing their impressions of the natural world during Magic Spot time and in some of the other activities. "Quiet Time" is a good time to learn how to write haiku and practice the new skill. Here are some haiku instructions that make it simple:

1. Select an object or scene.
2. Describe it.
3. Name the setting.
4. Describe the setting.
5. Describe the mood, or the feelings you have about your subject.
6. Go back and underline the words you've written that are key words and phrases, words that describe the essence of the scene.
7. Move the words (or select alternatives) around until there are seventeen syllables: one line of five syllables, one line of seven, and another line of five.

Taken step by step, and with plenty of encouragement, the youngsters can easily use this tool for creative expression.

Another way of helping the kids sharpen their ability to observe is by reading to them from the works of some of our popular naturalists. The teacher can select short stories about animals, or portions of books by such authors as Ernest Thompson Seton, Sally

Carrighar, or Allan Eckert. One of these books may also be selected for reading to the kids in the evening just before "lights out." This helps the kids relax, setting the tone for bedtime, and gives them a continuing story to look forward to each evening. (While the crew counselors have the responsibility for reading to their cabin group, we suggest that the teachers take a turn as well, reading to a different group of their kids each evening.)

Sharing Circles
Quiet Time is a good time for the youngsters and teachers to talk about the kinds of things they have been doing during the day. One way of getting the kids started is to ask each one in the circle to complete the following statement with a phrase based on that morning's experiences: *"The thing that I would most enjoy doing again is . . . "* After everyone in the circle has had a chance to respond (including the leader), try another completion statement which will take their ideas a bit further (e.g., *"I wish everyone could do it because . . . "*) or simply open up the circle for general discussion about everyone's choices.

Afterwards, the teachers may also want to start their classes thinking about the kinds of things they can do when they are back at school to share this sunship experience with other groups.

Concept Clarifiers
This is a time when the teachers can help the kids sort out and, if necessary, differentiate between the various concepts they have worked with during the morning. Asking the group to describe what took place at the stations will help the kids pin down their understandings and help the teachers watch for points which need clarification. This is particularly important for helping the kids make the connections between the concept components and the main concepts themselves. Reinforcing these connections can be accomplished by having the youngsters focus on the key concept statements. Later in the week, ask them to form teams and make up a rhyme about the three parts of Energy Flow, or a song with three verses for Interrelationships, or a riddle for the three parts of Cycles. Then each team can teach their composition to the whole group.

Values Building
All the teacher really needs to do with these simple values building methods is get the ball rolling by reading or giving the instructions.

Letters to the future—Each kid writes a letter which he or she will open five years from now. It is important to stress that this letter is for the writer's eyes only. No one will correct the spelling or even read it at all. It is private. Suggest that the writers record some of the things that they have done so far this week and their feelings about what they have been experiencing. When the kids are finished, have them put their names on the envelopes and the words: "To be opened on . . . ," with the date five years in the

future. Then have them pack the letters away so they don't get lost.

Natural things—Instruct the youngsters to make a list in their Logs of a dozen natural objects they like. Then, next to each one, they should write two words that describe something about how each object looks, smells, sounds, tastes, or feels. Encourage the youngsters to share their lists with someone else.

Encounters—Have the kids write about one of the following "meetings" for entries in their Logs, and then ask them to read their entries to the group.

+If you met a plant that could talk, would you talk or listen? If you talked, what would you say? If you listened, what would you hear?

+If you met someone that would grant three wishes and told you that one would be for you, one for your favorite animal, and one for your favorite wild place, what would your wishes be?

Sunship Monitor

At least twice a week during Quiet Time, all crew members receive the latest edition of the *Sunship Monitor*, to be read and then saved in the pouch with their Logs and Passports.

The classroom teachers put the *Monitor* together while the kids are with the other staff members on the Concept Paths. It is primarily a bulletin of discovery and a report on what has been happening so far during the week. Crew members can file ideas for stories at a special "suggestion stump" in the Outlook Inn. The teachers then compile and type up the stencils for the newsletters. Each *Monitor* is printed on both sides of half sheets of paper. Stories of the day include the discovery of other passengers and on-the-spot reports of interesting experiences. There are announcements of upcoming events, such as workshop choices, reports of rumors about the "Border Dispute" that is expected to erupt between the Elves and Trolls, a critic's review (all favorable, of course) of the artwork at "Earth Studios," contributions from the students' Logs, and entries from the Discovery Board. The *Monitor* plays several roles. It recognizes individuals, it provides an important role for teachers as active observers during the daily activities, and it heightens anticipation of future events. The *Monitor* also reinforces the sunship understandings by brief articles which differentiate between the seven concepts. Obituary notices include salutes to plants and animals that have become part of the soil cycle. A newly surfaced mushroom is applauded as the opening of a new waste treatment plant. Imagination and a bit of humor are keys to making the *Sunship Monitor* more than just a camp newspaper. It, too, helps realize the purpose of the whole program.

Chapter Twenty

CAMPFIRES

Campfires are a camp tradition, and for good reason. They are fun. There is just something about fire that makes people feel warm inside as well as outside. At the Sunship Study Station, we use a limited amount of fuel, emphasizing that we are using forms of stored energy that took years to produce. So our fire is a campfire, not a bonfire.

Themes are fun to plan. One evening, campfire entertainment can consist of skits and songs dedicated to "the plants and animals no one loves." A few cabin groups can make up skits in praise of one of these plants or animals, illustrating its virtues. Snakes and spiders are obvious selections, as are thistles and poison ivy. Or humorous skits can be put together to answer such challenging questions as "Why do bats hang upside down?", "Why do bees buzz?", or "How did the skunk get its stink?"

Songs can center on the sunship theme, too. Groups can try making up their own sunship song to a favorite tune. An old audience participation activity such as "Going on a Lion Hunt" can be converted to one that emphasizes plant succession.

It isn't necessary that all of the songs and skits have messages. After all, fun is important, too. But the theme woven through the campfire (American Indians, endangered species, etc.), as with the rest of the day's activities, should complement and reinforce the sunship theme.

And since this is a campfire, not a bonfire, it is still dark enough to see the world of night. As the kids return to their cabins, they can be encouraged to look at the stars and listen to the sounds of this dark side of the sunship. A final suggestion can be included about a constellation to look for, a sound to listen for, a smell to pick out.

231

Crew Campfires

An important cabin activity is a small sharing campfire Wednesday night. Since it is midweek, the crew of each cabin has already started to form the close ties of people who live and play together. The fire is small, about the size of a basketball, and all are huddled around it: about ten kids and their counselor share the magical, primeval sense of being drawn by the light and warmth of a fire in the night's darkness. The fire itself is a piece of the sun, the leader comments, because those flames are simply sunlight that took a detour through a tree. The light we see and heat we feel, even here at night, is a reminder of our dependence on the sun for all of our energy. Another reminder is the food we eat, seeds roasted in the fire that explode into popcorn. Each seed is a small package of energy that was stored as the sun shone on the plant that formed the seeds. As the counselor notes, "It gives us, in turn, the energy to sing our songs and tell our stories."

They will stay until the small fire burns down to ashes, telling stories and talking about experiences of the week and their feelings about what they have seen and done. The sharing is sometimes quiet and solemn, sometimes enthusiastic and energetic, but it is always spontaneous. The leader may have a story, or a quiet song to share, and so may the kids. But watching the last sparks fade away into darkness, they are reminded of the sun's energy used up. The fire is gone, and after their eyes adjust to the total darkness, the leader takes them back to the cabin in the dark.

"JOURNEY HOME"

(After the closing song of Thursday evening's campfire, the entire study station group is escorted silently along a torch-lit trail to a special ceremonial spot. They are seated before two small fires. An owl hoot sounds from the forest. A moment later, a station leader dressed as an old Indian emerges from the forest and slowly walks before the group of seated crew mates. His presence captures everyone's attention. They are spellbound. He begins softly . . .)

"Many seasons ago—as many seasons as there are grains in a handful of sand—there lived a people who called themselves Auroras, which in their language meant 'children of the sun.' One day a council of the elders was called because the people were in trouble. Where once waters ran cool and clear and swifter than the running deer, there were muddy pools where no living thing could drink. Where once bright-colored birds sang amid the trees, there were no birds nor trees, but haunting noises that were not birds. Where once the land had been rich, it was poor, and where the people had once seen beauty, all was wasteland. The elders, wise as they were, could find no answer to please them all. Finally, the wisest and eldest chief of the council asked to be heard. 'Bring to me the best, the noblest of our young people,' the Eldest said. 'We have forgotten the ancient secrets of life and the young ones will help us solve the problem of our people.'

"In time, the young people were brought to him, about as many as you now see seated here. The Eldest led the young people to one of the remaining green spots, where waters were still clear and birds still sang in the trees. There, from beneath a carefully placed layer of moss, he uncovered a large and very old canoe. He explained that it was a magic canoe that would take them on a journey down the river.

"A young Aurora then asked, *'Eldest, what is this journey of which you speak?'*

"'You must travel near and far to find the knowledge which was lost, to discover again how to restore the beauty and harmony of the earth. When you ride in the canoe, time will pass slowly, or quickly, to help you succeed in your quest. This canoe might take you back in time as well, so that on your journey you may see what once was, as well as what will be.

"'Take with you this one thing,' the Eldest added, drawing out a small pouch which, upon being opened, revealed six colored beads, seven white ones, and a piece of twisted cord.

(The storyteller takes a small pouch from his belt, opens it, and reveals the beads and cord. Continuing his story, he holds up the various colored beads and then strings them together with the white beads as he describes the meaning of the latter.)

"'These colored beads are older than the canoe, older even than the Auroras. As you see, one is a yellow bead, to represent the sun, father of our people. The light blue bead is for the sky and for the air we breathe. This dark blue bead is the water, where life is, and the brown bead is for mother earth, her rocks and rich soil.

"'The green bead, not as old as the rest, is still very old, older than the Auroras. It is the color and spirit of plants, the food of all animals. Out last round bead is red. It represents the animals of the world, the timid rabbit or daring eagle, the tiny ant or giant bear. These colored beads represent our needs of life: light, air, water, soil, plants, and animals.

"'Besides these six round beads I have seven long white beads which must accompany them. They represent the seven secrets of life, and they tell the story of how life works together for all living things. On your journey, you will have seven adventures, and will acquire one new understanding for each white bead. Pay close attention to the adventures, for they will help you understand how the light and air and water and soil and plants and animals work together to form one whole.

"'When you are prepared to learn one of the secrets of life, string a white bead and it will be revealed to you. Space the colored beads between the white ones, and when the necklace is complete, the white beads will link together the colored ones, just as the seven secrets link together all life. When the necklace is complete, you will have the knowledge you need to help solve the problems of our people.'

"The young Auroras launched the canoe and began paddling down the river. Soon the travelers decided they were ready for their first lesson, and they strung the first white bead. They came around a bend in the river and were blinded by a brilliant yellow glow shining from everything they saw. They had to shade their eyes from the light, but soon the glow softened and they could distinguish many different plants and animals. All the creatures around them seemed to have inside them their own sun, which was the source of their life. They watched as a rabbit eating grass became brighter and brighter, until suddenly an eagle swooped out of the sky upon the rabbit. As the eagle ate the rabbit, they saw the light of the rabbit join and strengthen that of the eagle. From this the Auroras learned that the warmth and light of the sun is in all living things, and that the sun's power and strength flows through all life. They saw that without the sun, there would be no food, and that many plants are needed to feed an animal, and many small animals to feed a larger one.

"The journey continued, and the Auroras pondered the meaning of the first secret they had seen. Not long afterward, they added the second white bead to the cord and prepared for their next adventure. Soon they met a woman sitting beneath a large tree.

They asked her what she was doing there. Holding up a seed in her hand, she replied that she was waiting for a new tree to grow. As they watched, time seemed to pass more swiftly—both the woman and the tree grew old together, died, and crumbled into the soil. Then a tiny thread of green appeared, and a new tree grew straight and tall where the first tree had been. From the Tree Woman, the Auroras learned the second secret of life—that the death of the old gives life to the new, that death and life are linked in a great circle, just as raindrops move in a circle from the sky to the rivers to the oceans and back to the sky. They learned that the things needed by living creatures are taken from the air and soil and water of the earth by each and returned, in time, by each.

"As the Auroras continued down the river and added the third white bead to the cord, they found themselves in a land which changed quickly from place to place. They saw hot places and cold places, wet places and dry places, and they saw that living things inhabited all of these areas. Life was everywhere, and though they saw many similar forms of life, they noticed that all were different. And so the Auroras learned the third secret of life—that many different conditions for life support the earth's wonderful variety of plants and animals.

"Before long the Auroras added the fourth bead to the cord, and as they did, the water of the river became crystal clear. They could see all the creatures that lived in the water—fish, clams, otters, beavers, and many strange and different insects and underwater plants. As they marveled at the sight of the creatures of the river, suddenly the surface of the water became like a mirror. Though they could no longer see into the river, the water reflected a clear image of all the trees, shrubs, animals, birds, and insects which lived on the dry land of the river shore. The Auroras quickly realized the meaning of what they had seen—on the water and the land are two separate groups of creatures, each group living together in the place where it can best survive.

"As the Auroras strung the fifth bead, the river widened into a large lake. As the travelers paddled out into the lake, they passed many small islands, and noticed that each island had only one living thing on it. Life was not good on the small islands—the plant or animal on each island was sick or dying. But in the center of the lake was a large island with many different kinds of creatures living on it, all sharing the island and interacting with each other. Here the life was good, and the Auroras saw that even though some creatures were helping each other and some were working against each other, each depended on everything around it for its survival. They realized that all things are connected.

"By this time, the Auroras were becoming tired and wanted to go home. They searched for a way out of the lake, but they could find no outlet where the river continued. So they returned to the place where they had entered the lake and began paddling upstream, back the way they had come. And as they did so they added the sixth bead to the cord. As the Auroras retraced their route up the river, they noticed that the river and the lands through which it flowed had changed, and it seemed as if a great deal of time had passed since their journey down the river. They saw that where there had been huge boulders in the river, there were now sandbars. Fields had grown into dense forest. The rabbit hid more easily from the eagle. And the river itself had changed its course. Before long they recognized the sixth secret of life—that all things are changing and nothing stays the same forever.

"The Auroras continued up the river and pondered the meaning of all the secrets they had learned. Then, as they approached their starting place, they saw the eldest chief waiting for them on the bank. And all around him, to their surprise, were several of the animals of the forests, fields, and streams, calmly watching them and waiting along with the chief. The Auroras paddled up and excitedly told the Eldest about the new knowledge they had gained. They had seen the sun's power in all living things. They had learned of the great circle of the materials of life and death. They understood that there was a wonderful variety of living things on the earth. They had seen that groups of plants and animals live together in the places where they can best survive. They had found that all things are connected. And they had seen that all things everywhere are changing. All of this they told to the Eldest, and he smiled and nodded his head. Finally they asked him, *'What of the seventh bead, Eldest? Is there another secret of life we have yet to learn?'*

"And the Eldest replied, 'Yes, this final lesson is left for me to teach you. String the seventh bead, and I will show you one of the most important secrets of all.'

"Then the Eldest challenged the Auroras to a series of contests with all of the animals around them. The swiftest of them tried to outrun the deer; the strongest wrestled with the bear; the best swimmer raced across the river with the otter; the best climber tried to catch a squirrel racing through the trees. And each time the Auroras were defeated in these contests. Finally one of the young people said to the Eldest, *'Honored One, these contests are not fair. We have no slender legs or sharp hooves like the deer, or strong muscles like the bear, or webbed feet like the otter, or sharp claws like the squirrel.'* And another added, *'Eldest, all of these animals have special gifts to help them in the way they live. We cannot possibly win any of these contests.'* The Eldest smiled and was silent for a short time. Then he said, 'You have spoken the truth, young one. This is, in fact, the seventh secret of life: all living things have their own special gifts, which make them perfectly built for their needs.

"'But you must realize that you have a gift, young ones, a gift that goes far beyond that of these animals. You have the awareness and understanding to recognize these seven secrets, and this wisdom is your most important gift.'

"Then the Eldest took the necklace from the young ones, knotted the string and replaced the necklace in its pouch. 'You young Auroras have gone on a great journey and learned seven secrets of life, which will help you to understand and live closer to the earth. But the most important part of your journey is yet ahead: the journey home. You must now return to our people, and tell them of these secrets, so that they may understand how to restore clean water, singing birds, and clear skies to the land. Go back to your village, young ones, and tell the Auroras that they must live in peace and harmony with the earth or they will not live at all.

(*At this point, the old man lays the pouch on the mat he sits on and silently walks away. Another station leader, not in costume, enters the circle and takes the pouch from the mat. As he begins speaking, he removes the necklace from the pouch and holds it up for all to see . . .*)

"You probably recognized the seven secrets of life which were shown to the young Auroras—you have learned those same seven secrets this week at the Sunship Study Station. When the Auroras saw the sun in each living creature, they learned about ENERGY FLOW. When they saw the great circle of life and death, they learned about CYCLES. When they saw the great variety of living things, they learned about DIVERSITY. When they saw the creatures of the river through the clear water and then the creatures of the land reflected on the surface, they learned about COMMUNITIES. When they came to the lake with the many islands, they learned about INTERRELATIONSHIPS. As they retraced their path traveling upstream, they witnessed CHANGE. And as they were defeated in the contests with all the animals, the Auroras learned about ADAPTATION.

"Energy flow, cycles, diversity, community, interrelationships, change, adaptation—which we remember by the formula EC-DC-IC-A—these are the seven secrets of life. Without them life would not exist on the earth. They tell the story of how the light, air, water, soil, plants, and animals are tied together in an unbroken circle.

"Like the Auroras, you now possess the knowledge which will help you to understand and respect the earth. And just as important are the feelings you have experienced here at the Sunship Study Station. We have all grown in closeness to the earth, just as we have become close to each other as friends. Tonight each of you will receive a set of beads from your crew counselor, just like those of the Auroras, to take home with you and to help remind you of how all life works together. They will also remind you to share your new understandings and appreciations about Sunship Earth with others.

"When you have finished stringing your beads back at your cabin and checking on your understanding of the story they tell, tie them closely around your neck like I am doing. In doing so, you are tying life together for yourself; you are completing a whole and you are part of it.

"Like the Auroras, you will be going home soon. It is the most important part of what you have been doing this week. Have a good journey."

THE ROUTINES—
GUIDELINES

Community Meeting

GENERAL NOTES:
1. Point out that the gasoline in the bus that brought the kids to the site was sunlight energy taking a several-hundred-thousand-year detour.
2. Include two or three of your most important general instructions for the camp (e.g., "Because we are sharing this place with a lot of other living things, like guests in their home, we should stay on the paths as much as possible").
3. You may want to use a master Sunship Log, where all the kids can sign in for their voyage.

Cabins and Crews

GENERAL NOTES:
1. Write thought-provoking quotations on cards for the corners of the washroom mirrors.
2. If cabin inspection is part of your routine, we suggest putting more emphasis on stopping sun and water leaks than in getting every last speck of soil off the floor.
3. Glue pictures of the appropriate decomposers to the inside of the lids on the toilets.

Meals and Snacks

GENERAL NOTES:
1. Place tear-out tickets to the dedication banquets in the Logs.
2. Use solar cookers to prepare the food received in the "Conversion Room."
3. Celebrate birthdays at the Sunship Study Station in terms of the number of completed revolutions around the sun.
4. Provide copies of *Diet for a Small Planet* and *Recipes for a Small Planet* for your cooks.
5. Place cards on your dining room tables with the following message: "The Sunship Study Station is proud to serve only the finest in packaged sunlight."
6. Ask the kids to bring cloth napkins as part of their gear. Provide hooks along the dining room wall for each napkin. (This just might start a new habit which will carry over when the kid gets back home.)
7. Select food for one of the snacks based on the distance away from the sun it is in a food chain. (Some kids get a small piece of beef jerky, others get a whole apple.)
8. Paint "Sun-to-food" murals on your dining hall tabletops. (Food is placed on the table where it fits in the flow of energy.)

Quiet Times

GENERAL NOTES:
1. Use an assistant station leader to help out with the Sharing Circles. Divide the group in half and conduct two sessions at the same time. (Include in one of your Sharing Circles an "I wonder . . . " sentence completion. It prompts lots of discussion.)
2. See "The Four 'R's' of Education" in *Trends*, Spring 1976, for additional Sharing Circle techniques.
3. See *Values and Teaching*, Louis Raths, et. al., for an overview of a valuing theory, but keep in mind that what we are trying to do is *build* environmental values. We select activities which we believe will help the participants strengthen their feelings about the natural world, thus heightening the chances that such feelings will be valued in the future. Also, see Cliff Knapp's article, "Outdoor Environmental Values Clarification," in *Communicator*, Fall 1975, for additional strategies.
4. Try to get each kid's name into at least one issue of the *Sunship Monitor*. (If you have an artist, also include humorous cartoons which clarify the differences and connections between the concepts.) Preprint paper with a *Sunship Monitor* masthead on it. With spirit masters, clipboards, and appropriate press visors and badges, the teachers can record their stories directly on the spirit masters while visiting the Concept Paths. The stories can easily be run off on the prepared masthead paper and distributed during Quiet Time.

Campfires

GENERAL NOTES:
1. Keep your fire relatively small, and when it burns down, the campfire should end. A good twenty-minute campfire is much better than a long, tedious one.
2. See "The Sharing Campfire" in the chapter, "Environmental Study Station," in *Acclimatizing* for help in planning your crew campfires.

THE BEGINNING

Interpretive Encounters:

"Model Planets"

Sunship Meeting

Passengers' Guide

Closing Ceremony:

"Beginnings and Ends"

Chapter Twenty-one

"MODEL PLANETS"

It is ten o'clock Friday morning. Eight groups of kids are busily working inside eight small circles of string spread throughout a stand of tall pine trees. The circles are about four feet in diameter, and a tremendous amount of activity is taking place in each one. The three kids working in each circle have been given the task of constructing a model planet.

Using only natural materials from the area near where they work, they are attempting to design a "life-support system," which incorporates examples of each of the concepts in the EC-DC-IC-A formula. Each group is equipped with seven flags, one for each of the seven concepts. As they figure out how a concept should be incorporated into the model planet and how it relates to the others, they place a flag next to that example.

"Hey, Bill, come over here. We've got a great flag for energy flow."

"See these blades of grass all in rows here?"

"Sure. It looks like you have a plowed field of something."

"Yeah, but it's not just any crop, it's a crop of soybeans. If there's a food shortage on our planet, we can eat the soybeans instead of feeding them to animals and then eating meat. We don't lose as much of the sun's energy that way."

"That's excellent. Were you winners or losers in the burger race on the Concept Paths?"

"We all lost."

"That's what I figured."

Bill suggests that since they have come up with a good way to show how energy will be used on their planet, they should send a courier over to where their teacher is working on a slightly larger circle, about seven feet across. (All nine circles just happen to be in a line that starts with a large yellow-painted weather balloon—the sun for these model planets.) The area the teacher is working on is the third planet from the Sun, the Earth, and that is where all the kids will eventually have to work since it is the only planet capable of sustaining life as we know it. Before the morning's construction began, all the groups knew that their individual planets were merely staging areas, and that they would be developing ideas which would ultimately be shared in order to construct a viable life-support system on the precious model of earth.

Bill is the "Planetary Commissioner," and upon finding a particularly good idea, such as the one developed by this group, he sounds a small horn to summon the "Ambassadors." After explaining the idea to the visiting Ambassadors from the other planets, the courier carries the concept flag which relates to this particular idea over to the third planet, where the teacher is using just these ideas relayed by the eight different groups to work on his or her project. Since each group's flags have different colors, the mother ship will have a truly interplanetary look.

The job of the Ambassadors is to share ideas from their own group, as well as to bring back good examples from other planets. The job and badge of Ambassador are traded off throughout the activity so that all members of each planet's crew get to disseminate information and see the progress of other planets, including the all-important third planet.

Another horn sounds, this time from the eighth planet. The system which these kids were working on and which caught the attention of the Commissioner was an example of the concept of cycles, specifically the water cycle.

"We're using the blue yarn to show where our water cycle flows. This mountain is covered with snow (the peak of their 'mountain' is covered with white rocks). *You can see that the yarn goes from there into this big glacier . . . "*

"Notice the giant crevasses."

" . . . Then down into this stream and into our trout pond here, then it gets a little hard to follow."

"See, it goes on up, hanging from this branch, and into the sky, and finally, back into the clouds, which we couldn't figure out how to make, and it snows back onto the mountain."

"Great job! Take it on over to the third planet. I'm going to have a look at planet one. It sounds like things are a bit hot over there."

Bill arrives just in time to take part in a heartfelt celebration. The group, after painstaking research, has finally figured out how they can have pizza on their model planet.

"We said we were gonna just import it at first, but we found out that wouldn't work 'cause everything we needed had to be right here. Anyway, Carrie sat down and thought about pizza ingredients while Dick and I started putting together some of the

other essentials, like an air cycle and stuff."

"Yeah, but I got stuck on the dough. Cheese and vegetables and those things were easy. We already had a garden and a cow and everything."

"Moooo."

"I see what you mean."

"Anyway, Dick went to a bunch of other planets, and finally somebody had a wheat field and a mill. We've got one now, too, and it's water-powered."

"And our pizza is cooked in a wood stove with spices from the garden!"

"Now we're trying to figure out how to string the energy flow yarn through all this stuff. It's hard because everything's all tied to everything else!"

Bill tells them they have about ten minutes to do that, and suggests they send an Ambassador to see what planet six came up with for handling that problem.

When all of the ideas have been relayed to the third planet, Bill starts at the sun and surveys the finished models. He has bad news for the first one.

"I'm sorry, but as Planetary Commissioner, it is my duty to inform you that temperatures here on your planet are much too high to support life as we know it. You have some excellent ideas, however. I suggest you take your best examples and as many supplies as you can over to that planet over there—the third planet from the sun. Conditions seem to be just perfect there for your kind of life."

And so it goes. The second planet is also too hot. The fourth, fifth, sixth, seventh, eighth, and ninth are much too cold, or have other shortcomings. They all start packing up their gear to go to the third planet.

As the groups migrate to this planet with all of their ideas, this larger circle quickly becomes crowded with imaginative examples—pizzas, cows made of pinecones, gardens, a well-adapted polar bear from planet four, a scale model of the "air cycle" painstakingly constructed of twigs, a large nightcrawler representing animals, a lichen-covered stone to represent change. Finally, planet nine arrives with a beautiful thatched-roof hut, one small component of what they had thought was a tropical world. They also bring a rusted tin can as an example of a "perished civilization."

The third planet is truly magnificent, a magical hodge-podge of interrelated examples of what every planet needs. But as the immigrants from the first two or three planets actually take their place on the third planet, it is apparent that the third planet is headed for big trouble. After all the groups are ushered into the seven-foot circle, even with constant reminders about the unique nature of the earth, no amount of careful footwork can avoid the inevitable. The destruction begins slowly but increases with new arrivals. Soon tempers are beginning to flare as personal works bite the dust. The carefully prepared water cycle of one group is tipped over; another's beautifully diverse community is crushed; still another group cries in alarm when someone inadvertently brushes against a food chain built with great care, knocking off several parts.

But the destruction gets worse. By the time all the crews are in, there are more than twenty-five people, including Bill and the classroom teacher, all trying to crowd into a circle. It is a tight squeeze, usually with some passengers just barely able to get a foot inside the string. The planet has, to say the least, become overpopulated. Its communities and complex energy flow patterns are wrecked, its air and water and soil cycles shattered.

Bill, still acting as Planetary Commissioner, suggests that they leave the third planet and go back to the circle of benches where their morning session began. Once they are seated where there is plenty of elbow room, Bill points out that they have failed in their mission to create a planet that would be able to operate indefinitely.

"If that had really been a planet and not just a model, we would have been in a lot of trouble. We could never have just left like that and come over here," he says grimly. "Something went wrong."

"Yeah, it got too crowded," says one youngster, stretching his legs.

"Too crowded is right!" Bill comments, "And people were having a little trouble communicating as well."

"*Yeah, and all the communities and cycles and stuff got squashed,*" adds another kid.

"Our air and water and other things we need sure wouldn't have lasted long," Bill agrees.

"Well, you know that model we were in was more than just a blueprint for a spaceship or a new planet," he points out. "That was Earth itself—the third planet from the sun. What's terrible is that just as the model of the third planet got overcrowded and its important systems abused, the earth is having a few troubles, too. Those trouble lights are blinking all over Sunship Earth. It's not as bad as on the model—not yet, at least. But it could happen.

"It seems like we didn't pay enough attention to one important item about our model of earth: everything is related to everything else. It's like when you pull on a loose thread sticking out of your sweater; if you aren't careful, the whole thing begins to come apart. Life on earth is like that. It's all tied together in so many ways that most of the time we don't have any idea what effect our actions might have. So when we all crowded onto the planet back there, we began breaking some of those threads, and our whole life-support system began to unravel."

Bill pulls out a passport. "What we are going to do right now is to make a very special last trip to our Magic Spots. People have always taken advantage of quiet places to look for solutions to large problems, or to look for ways out of seemingly impossible situations.

"Since each of us has an impact on everything else, what we need to do is think of something each of us does that is a bad habit in terms of the way the sunship operates. Even though it is a simple thing, it can affect many other things, as we have seen. Before we go, if everybody will pull out their passports and turn to the back, we can have a look at that page which says 'My Bad Habit.' We've put a few suggestions in there that may help you remember some of those things that we all often do without thinking about them. Now, look on the back of your bad habit page. You'll find that the heading on that side says 'What I Will Do About It.' After you have chosen which of your bad habits you will work on, you should write on this page what you will do to get rid of that habit. When we get back, we'll share what we have written in our passports."

The class is divided into groups of five kids and a crew counselor, and they all head off for a final visit to their Magic Spots. When they return, the groups share their statements about their own bad habits. These habits range from forgetting to turn off the radio to using too many paper towels to walking across plants which produce oxygen.

Each group selects the bad habit which they think should be singled out for action. They prepare a nominating speech about why this is a bad habit in terms of the welfare of the planet, and decide upon the constructive solutions they will include in their proposal. Finally, they select a speaker from the group to present their nominating speech, and everyone prepares to go to the Sunship Meeting.

Chapter Twenty-two

SUNSHIP MEETING

The dining hall this morning is arranged in a manner very different from its normal appearance. The tables have been removed, and the benches are organized into three distinct areas facing a central podium. Each section has a signpost bearing the name of one of the classroom teachers. A large photo of the earth is placed on a speaker's stand, which is flanked by two small tables. On one of these tables sit three globes. On the other, there is a pitcher of water with several glasses. Behind the podium and lectern, a banner welcomes the passengers to the sunship meeting. After everyone is seated, Jim welcomes the assembled passengers, and then introduces the group to the task at hand.

"All of you have just experienced the same catastrophe. All of you have spent the morning designing your model planets and transferring your best ideas to a model earth, only to have the rare opportunities offered by a unique site with conditions suited to life eliminated by problems which perhaps could have been avoided. We have come together now to share ideas to help us face these problems when we leave the Sunship Study Station."

The spokespeople from the first class go to the podium, taking their seats behind the small tables. They each give a short account of their group's nominee for a bad habit. They tell why they chose it above all others as a bad habit that no responsible sunship passenger would retain, and they explain what they will do instead. Jim keeps a tally of these bad habits as they are presented, writing each on a large chalkboard visible to all. If a bad habit is nominated more than once, it receives a large check mark next to it on the board.

Bobby is the fourth speaker to come to the podium. *"Well, my group had a bunch of good ideas, but we decided on one thing to share with everybody because it seemed like something which everybody would probably run into when they get home. When we all talked about it, it seemed like there wasn't really that much that kids could do to help not mess up the sunship. And it seemed like the hardest part was going to be to get people to listen. Like I know sometimes I've said things to my mom and dad about driving everywhere when lots of times we could be walking, and it would be better for us and everything, but they don't really listen. They say they do, but I know they don't because we keep doing it anyway. So Marie, Johnny, Dick, Rhonda, and I thought that the bad habit we should work on was something at home that we do, but which our parents and everybody could see. So when we get home, we're all going to start sorting out the garbage at our house for paper that can be taken to the recycling place—and glass and . . . uh, oh year, aluminum. And all our parents will have to do is the stuff over there on weekends.''*

Carrie, the seventh speaker, announces that her bad habit was chosen by their group as the worst. *"A lot of us do the same thing,"* she explains. *"When I break something, I usually just throw it away and get a new one. That's bad because it takes energy to make things, and it also uses up water and stuff like trees from the natural communities. So a bad habit is always buying something new instead of fixing what we have.''*

Leaving the water on when brushing their teeth, using lots of paper napkins instead of one cloth towel to wipe up a spill, asking their parents to drive them when they could walk or ride bicycles, buying things they could borrow from each other, asking for a whole list of things they don't need for their birthdays, taking too much food and throwing away the leftovers—these are the kinds of bad habits the kids usually come up with. Most of the ideas aren't new or revolutionary, but this time, the kids have thought of the ideas themselves. No one told them. They told themselves.

Chapter Twenty-three

PASSENGERS GUIDE

"I'm in the same boat—or sunship—that you are," the first teacher starts off. "We all share the responsibility as crew members of the sunship, and I don't want it to be wrecked any more than you do. I have an environmental bad habit of my own that I plan to do something about. Every day I drive the two miles to school and two miles home, rain or shine, cold or warm. Now, instead, I am going to dust off this old bicycle I have in the back of my garage and I'm going to see if I can still ride it."

The kids cheer. *"Yea, we can all ride bicycles."*

"I think we all have a few bad habits. We can work together on some of them, and encourage each other when we're trying to change our habits. I've seen crew members in my class come up with some really good habits this week, too; so that gets us off to a good start. We've put all of your ideas, and some other suggestions that we've been working on, into the Passengers' Guide. Next week we can begin pulling these ideas out of our globe and using them in our classroom activities. It will be fun to see how our new feelings and understandings about the sunship change our view of what we do back at school and at home."

After all three teachers have spoken, Jim takes over the podium again. On one of the tables, three globes now rest, filled by each group with slips of paper bearing their good intentions about changing bad habits and forming good ones. Jim reminds the assembly of a concept station which they all visited during the week, "Cradles to Coffins." He suggests that if they think back to the apparently crazy ceremony which took place there, they will see that it holds just as true for this final meeting as it did for the dead leaf. "Just as every end in the natural world is the beginning for another story, the end of our week together here at the Sunship

Study Station should be the beginning of a continuing story. In fact, the biggest problem with a week here is that we all tend to forget that the sunship isn't just here. It isn't something we leave when we drive out the main gate, just as we didn't enter it when we drove in. It was here all the time, and we just became aware of it. There's no way really to leave the sunship. It isn't a *model* planet; it's all we have.

"When you're sitting at home eating dinner tonight, you will still be screaming around the sun at the same sixty-five thousand miles per hour. You might mention that to whomever you're sitting with."

Then he says he hopes they will use the Passengers' Guide to good advantage. "Remember, when you begin drawing suggestions out of the globe, the same facts will hold true as when you were here." Turning to the teachers, he tosses a globe to each. It's in their hands now.

INTERPRETIVE ENCOUNTERS—
GUIDELINES

Model Planets

PROPS:
String—Cut pieces about fifteen feet long and wrap them around a stick—one per group. Use a twenty-five-foot piece for the earth circle.
Horn (conch shell or slide whistle)
Badges ("Ambassador"—one per group)
Yarn—Cut eight-foot lengths of blue, yellow, and white yarn—one set per group.
Flags—You will need sets of seven pennants in different colors

attached to ten-inch sticks; each pennant should be stamped with the name of one of the seven concepts—one set per group.
Sun—Use a yellow weather balloon.

GENERAL NOTES:
1. Designate a specific area where each group will set up its model planet. The areas should be close to one another in order to make sharing ideas between planets easier.
2. The station leader's role should be to visit the model planets, reinforcing what needs to be done and encouraging the Ambassadors to both share and seek out good ideas. (If they are having problems, suggest that they think back to the activities and examples at the concept stations, and, if necessary, check their passports.)
3. When the group crowds on to the "third planet," timing is important. As soon as the idea of overcrowding/noncommunication is apparent, the leader should move the group off to the nearby benches to reflect on what was happening.
4. After the activity, the crew counselors should return all natural objects that were used in the planets to the areas where they were found.

SUNSHIP MEETING—
GUIDELINES

PROPS:
Public Address System (set it up even if you don't turn it on)
Podium (including a speaker's stand, tables and chairs, water pitcher, and glasses)
"Earth from Space" Poster
"Welcome Sunship Delegates" Banner
Class Signposts (with the teachers' names)
Chalkboard
Globes (one for each class)

GENERAL NOTES:
1. Each group should elect a spokesperson to share the bad habit the group decides to nominate.
2. The crew counselor should help the spokesperson prepare for his or her presentation. The counselor can help by suggesting that a good presentation:
    +contains a personal example or story.
    +elaborates on the feelings of the group.
    +mentions the names of the kids in the group.
    +explains why the group chose the "bad habit" they are nominating.
    +offers an alternative to the habit.
3. Ushers should be on hand to seat kids in classroom groups as they enter the meeting hall.
4. A public address system can be used to help carry the kids' voices and add to the "convention" atmosphere.

PASSENGERS' GUIDE—
GUIDELINES

PROPS:

Passengers' Guides—These are papier-mache globes constructed by the teachers during the week. About the size of a basketball, each is painted to resemble the earth as seen from space, and each has a hole in the top large enough for a kid's hand to reach in and pull out a bad habit or a group task to work on.

GENERAL NOTES:

1. The speeches given by the teachers should:
   +include a personal environmental bad habit with a plan for correcting it.
   +note environmentally sound habits the kids have been forming.
   +point out that the teachers have been working on additions for the globes themselves.

2. One of the primary tasks of the teachers during the week is to prepare the classroom tasks which they will place in the Passengers' Guide for later use. These activities are things the kids can do themselves back at school or at home, things which will help them continue to apply their understandings of and appreciations for Sunship Earth. The exact nature of these tasks (time and numbers involved, location, etc.) will depend upon each teacher's personal lesson plans. (They should use a different color of paper so they can distinguish between the habits and tasks.)

Regardless of the length or the number of kids involved, the tasks should focus upon *applications and implications* of the sunship understandings the kids have been learning. The Passengers' Guide should be a source of ideas for helping individuals become more sensitive, understanding, and caring passengers on their journey in space. They should deal with fairly immediate problems that form part of the kids' experience. They should not involve a lot of research or discussion or reports. They should be active and interesting. They should be personal. (Not picking up paper on the school grounds, but figuring out how to use less paper in the classrooms; not writing letters to the utility company about its smokestack, but carrying out a plan for using less energy in their own school buildings.)

As individuals, we must begin to learn how to use less and reuse more. There's an old adage which should be posted in every classroom and home: "Use it up; wear it out; make it do or do without."

3. The Passengers' Guide can be used in several ways. Here are a few suggestions:
   +set aside a time each day when a kid reaches in and pulls out a "habit" or a "task" for the class to work on (or pulls out several for small groups to work on).
   +get the class to work on one habit each day and one task each week.

+share the Passengers' Guide with kids in other classes.

+let the kids decide when and how they want to use it.

+suggest at the end of the year that the kids pass the guide on to the teacher in the next grade.

+ask the team that nominated a particular habit to become the class monitors for that item.

4. The station leaders can add several items to the guide themselves:

+pages from the passports.

+personal quotations and messages (key phrases or sayings used during the week).

+fun facts (interesting ways of explaining things or ways of looking at things).

+values-building exercises.

+additional tasks which emphasize going outside, sharpening senses, and spending time alone (be sure to include each kid's bad habit, too, not just the one the group selected to present at the meeting).

Chapter Twenty-four

CLOSING CEREMONY

"Beginnings and Ends"

Four days have passed since this group arrived at the Sunship Study Station. Again the crew members are sitting in the Sunship Room, the darkened octagon built within another building.

(*The lights dim except for one ray that illuminates the globe hanging above their heads.*)

"Congratulations."

It is the same voice, apparently emanating from somewhere behind the center mural.

"You have completed a most difficult training course as crew members of Sunship Earth. You may have observed that older passengers here today are wearing their sunship buttons in honor of this special occasion. You will soon be wearing yours. These buttons signify that you understand the basic operation of the sunship.

"Of all the living things that share the earth, only some of its human passengers know that they are on a journey among the stars. You are now a part of this special crew. However, as crew members of the sunship, your role is limited. You must always remember that you can never completely understand everything here; there will always be more that you don't know. As a crew member your task is to speak out for all the plants and animals that live here. You must warn others that we cannot manage the support systems of the earth. They are too complicated. We must act with great caution.

"In fact, your training is not complete. It has just begun. You have learned that energy flows from the sun, the mother ship for the earth. You have investigated the systems of your ship and have seen how easily they can be disrupted. You have learned many things about your sunship but there is much, much more. The week you have just completed gives you the background you will need as you continue your training.

"You have seen that the fall's dead leaves are an end of summer, but at the same time the beginning of new spring plants as part of the cycle of soil. You saw the rain as both an end and a beginning of the water cycle. You learned of the constant exchange in the air between plant and animal, the cycle of oxygen and carbon dioxide.

"You are in a cycle, too. Like the autumn leaf, you are at the end of one experience. But like the small seed in the ground, you are beginning another. You have learned much, but you are just beginning your voyage as an enlightened crew member of Sunship Earth.

"As trained crew members, you also have another responsibility. No longer may you act recklessly yourself, ignoring the simple truths of how the sunship operates. You can never again say 'I didn't know.' You are now aware of the sunship's operating systems, so you are fully responsible for your actions. Remember that every breath you take is a gift from the plants. Recall that everything you do affects other passengers on the sunship. Take heed.

"You have also discovered some of the marvels of the sunship, its beautiful and fascinating array of rocks and waters, plants and animals. You have learned many ways to find joy in your travel through space. Walk lightly and take time to appreciate the wonderful design of this ship. Enjoy your journey.

"There is one other thing. Now that you have made these discoveries and gained these understandings, you are in a position to help others to be aware of Sunship Earth. This is your next task, to help your families and friends understand the beauty and fragility of life on this planet. Only a handful of the billion human families that live here understand how life works on this planet. We hope that you will help your families become a part of this special crew. Share your understanding.

"Take heed. Enjoy your journey. Share your understanding."

(*The tiny beam of light disappears, and again, the film, "Cosmic Zoom," flashes on in the space window. However, this time the sequence of pictures begins far out in space, beyond the solar system and galaxy and universe, then rapidly zooms in through countless stars and systems and ends with the earth filling the screen.*)

"Welcome aboard," the voice concludes.

(*The light fades again. The doors are thrown open and the crew members go out into the sun, where their Sunship Passenger buttons are pinned on.*)

The buses wait to carry them back to their schools and families. They have come full circle—and they are just beginning. They are traveling on a tiny piece of rock whirling through space, caught in the gravitational pull of a medium-sized star. But now, they are aware of their journey. So for them, it is just the beginning of a lifetime of joy in the miracles and delight in the discoveries of this small, fragile, wonderful place—Sunship Earth.

Welcome aboard.

EPILOGUE

In the preceding pages I have attempted to explain as completely as possible why we set out to put together a new Acclimatization program; what we decided to do, and how we went about doing it. If it appears that we have been somewhat dogmatic at times, even a bit arrogant, we hope you will overlook it. We put the program together with only the barest of funds—with no foundation grants nor government support. Whenever our commitment to the program and our pride in its development have shown through with a rather jarring note, it may be because we were trying too hard to explain our point of view.

There is no one way to do anything. The trick is to really know what you are pursuing and believe in it. Some people will use the activities recorded here to pursue other goals, while some will use other activities to pursue the goals we have set forth. We hope that every group will consider their choices as carefully as we did and trust that some of them will decide to set up a Sunship Study Station.

In environmental education, each program should be judged on the basis of what it is really trying to accomplish. It should not be sufficient to simply say that one has an environmental education program. The question that must be asked is what is the purpose of any given program, and does it appear to accomplish what it claims?

What is really important are the kids. Do they get excited about what they are learning? Is what they are learning really worthwhile? Can they do anything with what they learn? All of us must answer these questions for ourselves. And we should believe in our answers.

"Sunship Earth" is an Acclimatization program for helping upper elementary students build a sense of relationship with the natural world. Its development has represented a five-year journey for us—a journey marked by considerable struggle and punctuated by much laughter.

We enjoyed the journey.

We hope you will, too.

INDEX

INDEX